THE INTIMIDATION GAME

THE INTIMIDATION GAME

HOW THE LEFT IS SILENCING FREE SPEECH

KIMBERLEY STRASSEL

TWELVE

New York   Boston

Twelve
Hachette Book Group
1290 Avenue of the Americas
New York, NY 10104
twelvebooks.com
twitter.com/twelvebooks

First Edition: June 2016

Twelve is an imprint of Grand Central Publishing.
The Twelve name and logo are trademarks of Hachette Book Group, Inc.

The publisher is not responsible for websites (or their content) that are not owned by the publisher.

The Hachette Speakers Bureau provides a wide range of authors for speaking events. To find out more, go to www.hachettespeakersbureau.com or call (866) 376-6591.

PCN: 2016937405

ISBNs: 978-1-4555-9188-6 (hardcover), 978-1-4555-9190-9 (ebook)

Printed in the United States of America

RRD-C

10 9 8 7 6 5 4 3 2 1

To Oliver, Stella, and Frances—the loves of my life.
And to Alaska—for letting me dream again.

CONTENTS

INTRODUCTION

MOST PEOPLE wouldn't think of January 21, 2010, as an important date. It isn't Christmas. It isn't 9/11. It isn't a national holiday.

Yet that day marks a turning point in American politics.

January 21, 2010, is when the Supreme Court ruled on a case known as *Citizens United*. To listen to President Barack Obama, or Senator Harry Reid, or any number of self-proclaimed "good government" organizations, this decision mattered because it marked a new tidal wave of "dark" money and "shadowy" organizations into elections. It supposedly gave powerful special interests new control over democracy.

Citizens United didn't do any of that. But it did unleash a new era. It set off a new campaign of retribution and threats against conservatives. *Citizens United* launched the modern intimidation game.

Up to that day, Republicans and Democrats had played a different game, a familiar one. Both sides had spent a hundred years using speech laws, also known as campaign finance laws, to bar their respective opponents from taking part in elections. Democrats barred companies. Republicans barred unions. Democrats restricted right-leaning groups. Republicans restricted left-leaning groups. The laws kept piling up and up, until the Supreme Court could no longer justify the assault on the First

Amendment. *Citizens United* swept much of it away. Five justices restored the speech rights of millions of Americans.

The political right and libertarians mostly celebrated the decision as a triumph for democracy. The political left had the opposite reaction. Obama was on the ropes. He'd passed Obamacare, and Dodd-Frank, and a blowout stimulus spending bill—and America hadn't liked it. The party faced a wipeout in the 2010 elections. And now the high court had said Democrats could no longer legally shut up the companies and conservative nonprofits mobilizing against his party.

So the left moved to plan B. It moved to harass and scare and shame its opponents out of speaking.

Some in the liberal movement, including Obama and congressional Democrats, trained the federal government on opponents. They encouraged, explicitly and implicitly, the IRS to target and freeze conservative groups during election years. They called out conservative donors by name, making them the targets of a vast and threatening federal bureaucracy. They filed complaints with federal regulators and the Justice Department, calling on them to hassle or bar or prosecute their rivals. They came up with proposed executive orders and new IRS and SEC and FCC rules to order or frighten the other side out of the electoral process.

Powerful elected politicians used their positions to hold hearings into conservative political groups and to scare off donors to those operations. They sent letters to companies and think tanks and nonprofits, demanding to know who funded them, and whom they funded in turn. They launched investigations and leaked select details to the press. They flooded groups with document requests to drive up their costs and slow down their work. They made clear that those who donated "wrong" would end up on blacklists, or in front of Congress, or subject to boycotts.

Unions and liberal financial firms threatened to withdraw their money from companies that continued to speak. They pressured shareholders to force corporations to withdraw from the political scene. Activists camped outside CEOs' homes and staged rallies outside corporate headquarters.

Liberal prosecutors stepped up to threaten litigation against organizations that didn't hand over names of donors, so that those donors could be subject to the same treatment. Some prosecutors went much further: They sent armed police to march into houses in predawn raids, to let their opponents know that their exercise of free speech might land them in prison.

Liberal activists took to the streets—to urinate on houses, and block the entrances to stores, and stalk those who didn't agree with them on political issues. They left threatening telephone messages, and delivered ugly e-mails, and got people fired from their jobs for holding unpopular political views.

The intimidators embraced the tools that remained to them. They embraced disclosure laws, using the information they gleaned to create their lists of targets. They embraced arcane bits of campaign finance law, engineering new ways to persecute their opponents. They embraced the Internet and social media platforms, to launch protests, and badger free-market advocates, and even to create searchable, walkable maps that allowed them to harass people, one home at a time.

They also cleverly cloaked all this behind a claim of good government. *Citizens United*, they said, threatened to put powerful and nefarious forces in charge of democracy. And therefore all of their actions and tactics were justified in the name of the people. It was right to make Tea Party groups wait five years for permission to speak. It was right to send private investigators to dig into the divorce records of conservative donors. It was right to subject federal contractors to political litmus tests. It was right for prosecutors to issue gag orders. It was right to go to the Senate floor to vote to alter the First Amendment, and to put government in charge of speech. Getting rid of speech was for democracy's own good.

All these things happened. The stories are in this book. That they did happen, and are still happening, requires every American to rethink some conventional wisdom about the merits of speech and disclosure laws.

Nearly sixty years ago, the Supreme Court issued a ground-breaking decision, *NAACP v. Alabama*, that protected the rights of Americans to engage in politics with some degree of anonymity. This was the civil rights era, and blacks were being targeted, fire-bombed, and shot at for daring to speak out. The high court understood how corrosive this was to democracy, and declared that the Constitution provided some measure of refuge to citizens at risk of political retribution.

Yet the Court's brave stand slowly gave way to Nixon-era worries over electoral corruption. It rubber-stamped one campaign finance and disclosure law after another, eating away at its free-speech and anonymity legacy. Conservatives embraced the laws too, hoping to land on the right side of good-government history. In doing so, the conservative movement turbocharged its own muzzlers. Over time, the intimidators came to use the laws themselves—the ones supposedly designed to guard the electoral process—to intimidate.

Today, every American is at risk of retribution, because those who seek to control the debate do not make distinctions based on party affiliation. This book is largely about the new attempt by left-leaning organizations to shut down conservative speech. But the stories show that those who want absolute control over the debate are happy to silence anyone who proves a threat to their ideology.

They feel they must. Barack Obama ushered in a new era of liberal governance, yet one that has been rejected by significant numbers of Americans. The backlash brought the Democratic Party to new lows—to its smallest congressional and state majorities in nearly a century. Unable to win the debate in Washington, Obama has taken to imposing his will through executive orders. Unable to win the debate in the wider country, the liberal movement has decided to just shut it down.

This book chronicles the rise of those intimidation tactics—their genesis, their refinement, and the toll they've taken on free speech in America. The history is told through real stories, of real Americans, who faced silencing. The book as a result has almost accidentally become a record of the heroic attempts by those targeted to fight back, to make their voices heard, and to shore up the rights of their fellow citizens.

Those stories, though inspiring, ought to nonetheless be heard as a clarion call—particularly to the courts. In the 1950s, the high court recognized the stakes in the civil rights battle and felt compelled to secure the free-speech rights of black Americans. Today, Americans are again being targeted on the basis of their political views; they again risk losing their jobs and reputations for speaking out; they again face economic and community reprisal; they again face a government that is leading the charge to strip them of basic rights. Only this time, those who would shut them down are more powerful, and have more tools.

Indeed, today's environment is scarier. In the 1950s, the state and Jim Crow defenders had to work hard to conjure up a list of names of people to go after. They had to go to court. Today, all that information is available in a nanosecond, on any iPhone or computer, via any election disclosure site. Americans know this, and are increasingly scared to give to political causes, to join political groups. They have seen what happens. They know that if they take part, they will be called up, served up, beat up, and run out.

The intimidation game is working.

THE INTIMIDATION GAME

CHAPTER 1

An "Oh Shit" Moment

WASHINGTON SPENT two years denying Karen Kenney all the things she'd thought her basic rights: free speech, a fair hearing, equality under the law. Now it was denying her a bathroom break.

She'd got the call two days earlier. Come to Washington, said the House staffer, help us tell the world your story. She'd hustled—to cancel clients, to conjure up a dogsitter, to arrange the long flight from California. She'd rustled up a dress for the cameras. She'd touched down the night before the hearing, and only after a TSA agent confiscated the mousse she'd belatedly bought to bring order to her hair.

Kenney is hyperorganized, so she arrived that June 2013 day more than an hour before the big show. She sat in a little anteroom as Republican staffers prepped her and her fellow newbies in hearing basics: Sit here, not there; don't forget to turn on your mike; wait until you are called; do this if you are nervous; please hand in the requisite 150 copies of your remarks. Kenney observed that at least when it came to their own show, Washington really did care about rules. Twenty minutes in, the homily ended, and she decided on a quick trip to the ladies'.

The Longworth building is like every Washington federal building—an M. C. Escher drawing. No beginning, no end. She spent precious minutes hunting down the bathroom. Precious minutes later, she was back at the hearing room, only to discover she'd left her wallet in the stall. Another return trip, and she found spectators lined up, crowding into the gallery. House members were taking their seats. She rushed to the guard and anxiously explained that she was supposed to be in a witness chair. Really, truly, she needed to get in. He didn't believe her. He looked her up and down and judged her an eager bystander who was hoping to cut the line. Kenney politely explained that, while she may not look it, she really was supposed to testify. No dice.

At the last moment, a GOP staffer appeared at her arm and rushed her into the room. As they scurried in, Kenney contemplated just how fitting was this moment. She couldn't even get into her own hearing.

∿

The story Kenney tells that day is one that should never happen in America. Her tale involves the Internal Revenue Service. One mid-February day in 2012, she'd stood in the staff room of her group counseling practice in Encino, California, opening her mail. As she shuffled through the catalogs and bills, she noticed a large package from the IRS.

Kenney is a serious person and a careful speaker; most of her sentences are delivered with articulate precision. But she also has a habit of ending them with funny asides. (*My first thought on seeing that packet? The only two words any American thinks when they see a letter from the IRS: "Oh shit."*)

The tax agency wanted answers to more than eighty questions about her small nonprofit, the San Fernando Valley Patriots (SFVP). In 2010, Kenney used an Internet service to apply to the agency for tax-exempt status. It was a straightforward process, and she'd thought it would only take a few months. Instead, she'd sat in radio silence for two years. And now the IRS was telling her she had twenty days to answer its questions, and that if she got anything wrong she could go to federal prison for perjury. (*Like everything with the feds, they do it backwards. Most people, it is hurry up and wait. Them, it is wait and hurry up.*)

At the hearing, more than a year after that IRS letter day, Kenney impressed upon several dozen Ways and Means Committee members that these weren't your average factual inquiries. "Generally, the questions were a demand that read like the chilling words from the 1950s: 'Are you now, or have you ever been . . . ?'" The echo of McCarthy set members to shifting uneasily in their seats. The federal government was supposed to have learned something from those dark years. Or maybe not.

Kenney would find out only long after opening that packet that SFVP was one of 298 groups the IRS targeted—delaying their applications, freezing them out of elections. She'd learn that her own group had landed on the list for the simple reason that it had the word "patriot" in its name. She'd learn that top IRS officials, when questioned by Congress under oath, had for more than a year denied that this was happening. (*Now, remind me again, how many of* them *are in federal prison for perjury? Oh, that's right. None.*) She'd listen to IRS official Lois Lerner in 2013 finally use a planted question at a late-Friday tax conference to let slip the news that the agency had in fact been targeting and freezing conservative applications. She'd wait to get answers— from Congress, from the Justice Department, from the Obama administration—about how and why her right to speak had been put through a political wood chipper.

She's still waiting.

∿

George W. Bush, as one of his final acts, signed a $700 million bank bailout. Barack Obama had barely warmed his Oval Office chair before he signed his own blowout $831 billion stimulus into law. A day later, on February 18, 2009, the administration unveiled yet another spending bonanza, this one to subsidize underwater homeowners. A day after that, CNBC business editor Rick Santelli lost it on the Chicago trading floor, raging that Washington was on a bender. He proposed that his city host a modern Boston Tea Party, this time to dump derivatives securities into Lake Michigan. "President Obama, are you listening?" he shouted on prime-time television.

Obama wasn't. But plenty of pissed-off Americans were. Within hours of Santelli's cri de coeur, Tea Party websites started popping up across the country. Within a week, forty cities had coordinated to hold a Tea Party protest day. The reference was to 1773, but with a modern twist. The leaders declared themselves Taxed Enough Already. TEA. TEA Party.

Kenney was among those who'd watched with alarm as Bush bailed out the banks. The alarm grew to frustration as Obama pumped his stimulus and outlined plans for even bigger bailouts. In April 2009, she heard that local activists were staging an antispending rally on Tax Day, one of more than two thousand protests planned nationally. She'd jumped into her silver Honda Civic and motored to the Van Nuys Civic Center (*fifteen minutes with a tailwind; twenty when you hit the lights*) for the evening event. Eight hundred Americans lined the sidewalks, holding signs, waving flags. The microphone played host to a hit list of taxpayer advocates, talk-radio hosts, even a conservative comedian—all encouraging the attendees to be heard. Kenney left fired up.

These days, Kenney's a sixty-four-year-old psychotherapist working in a small practice in Encino, mostly with veterans with severe trauma. But it's a second career. She spent four years as a composing typist with the *Los Angeles Times*, then nine years as a reporter at the *Santa Monica Evening Outlook* and the *Los Angeles Daily News*—on the police blotter, doing medical writing, radio work. It was all exciting stuff, though it left her unfulfilled. Journalists shine lights on problems; they never *do* anything. So in

1987 she went back to school to become a counselor, and ultimately to grind out a doctorate in psychology. Her new mission is to change lives rather than document them. Her smallish waiting room at her practice is full of handouts and signs that celebrate learning, self-growth, and taking charge.

Which is all, too, very much Kenney. She's a Valley girl, with short brown hair, a wide-open face, and a frequent smile. (*I myself like the description short, pudgy, and cute.*) She's a history and government buff, able and willing to tell you the correct spelling of the fourth president's wife (*It's D-o-l-l-E-y!*), as well as the height of Dolley's diminutive husband (*four foot eleven*). Kenney married early, divorced early, and turned down six subsequent marriage proposals in penance for breaking her first vow. She lives in a tiny house with a big yard, along with a tiny dog with a big personality, in Lake Balboa. She's a thinker, knows her mind, has calm, happy energy, and looks fifteen years younger than her age. (*Turns out drinking formaldehyde really does work. Don't care what they say.*)

Kenney's long been a political activist, if never a partisan warrior. She and her two siblings were adopted, and raised in a rural part of the Valley. (*Did you know I have an identical twin sister? I weigh more than her now. Do I look pleased?*) Her father, who worked in construction, never had more than an elementary school education, and money was always tight. He nonetheless wanted more for his kids, and enrolled his daughters in Catholic school starting in second grade. Kenney credits the nuns for her moral base— for a work ethic, for a sense of duty, for a purpose. In her junior college, she was the first to organize an Earth Day. In her junior year, six chemistry majors drafted her to represent them on the student body senate, even though she was a history major. She did public speaking, volunteered for a local politician. She's missed voting in only one election in her life. (*Can't remember why. It was either because I was sick or had a flat tire. Every important thing I've ever missed is because I'm sick or have a flat tire.*)

Her parents were Kennedy Democrats, and she herself stuck

with the party for thirty-five years—until it moved so far left she couldn't see it anymore. She struggled mentally with changing her registration to read Republican (*The hard-ass party? Me?*), and to this day isn't overly comfortable with the label. Like so many Tea Party members, she calls herself a constitutional conservative; her first allegiance is to the Founders' vision of limited government. She'll dish against George W. Bush just as quickly as she will Nancy Pelosi. Her interest is in getting the country back on track, and she doesn't much care what party does it, so long as it happens.

Kenney spent the months following the Van Nuys rally wondering how to engage. Then she found herself having coffee with two friends, a young couple named Tad and Valerie Cronn. Tad had a simple answer: Just do *something*. A web designer and journalist, he offered to get Kenney an Internet presence, to start gathering people together. She got busy on her phone, ringing friends and neighbors. Would they like to meet up, talk about issues, figure out how to get involved? They would. Tell your friends and neighbors, said Kenney. They did.

In the early evening of August 1, 2009, forty patriots crammed into a meeting room in a little neighborhood restaurant called Coco's for the first official gathering of the San Fernando Valley Patriots. A lot had already happened. Kenney was now in regular e-mail contact with dozens of locals about political issues of interest—health care rallies, memorial events. She'd made ties with bigger grassroots groups—in particular the national group, the Tea Party Patriots—to keep informed, and gather ideas, and pass along information. Many in her core e-mail group (*my peeps!*) had jumped in, offering possible names for the group, potential meeting sites. Coco's got the nod, in part because it offered a cut rate on food and drinks. (*What's better than a little civics and affordable food?*)

The first few meetings were gripe sessions—about overspending, Obama, an out-of-touch Congress. Kenney reminded folks that they were there to *do*, not just talk, and then the gatherings took on a rhythm. Attendees—old, young, the extroverted, the shy—would take turns telling the group about a local or federal problem: water issues, property rights, tax proposals, classroom concerns. Kenney's rules: Each person had ten minutes to talk and was required to finish with a proposal for how the group might act—call this number; show up here; write this person. People started exchanging little cards with their names and numbers, making plans for rallies and e-mail campaigns. It reminded Kenney of those old colonial church halls—neighbors and strangers, brought briefly together to celebrate a shared calling.

The left and the mainstream media to this day tag Tea Party groups as Republican stooges—"astroturf" controlled by bigger political forces, as opposed to grassroots. That claim was central to their push for the IRS to investigate the activities of "partisan" nonprofits. Kenney's group is political, no question. It's made up of motivated, devoted Americans who want to see dramatic change in government. But it isn't partisan.

One of the great ironies of the IRS targeting scandal is that the tax agency barely brushed up against those powerful political pro-Republican nonprofits that Democrats so feared. It mostly stuck it to the little people, folks who had scant or no interest in party politics.

Groups like Kenney's for the most part see the problem as "Washington"—singular. That leviathan—from a Democratic president, to a Republican Congress, to the anonymous bureaucrat—has forgotten for whom it works, and for what purpose. Kenney would years later begin her Washington testimony by zinging Republicans and Democrats alike: "You and I speak different languages in this Republic. You speak the language of power: the pen, purse, or gavel. I speak grassroots American, the language of liberty through providence, property, and civic virtue."

That was the animating impulse of the San Fernando Valley Patriots: to learn, to educate others, to be heard. Kenney started inviting in speakers to teach on a wide range of subjects—net neutrality, health care, California's emissions regulations. Author Don Jans came in to talk about the threat of socialism in America. Egyptian-American human rights activist Nonie Darwish lectured on Islam and Sharia law. Larry Sand, who runs a labor watchdog group, regaled members with tales of union interference in the classroom. Kenney in a monthly flyer suggested things her members could read or watch in the lead-up to speakers, and reminded them of events they might attend or dates of elections and polling places.

Kenney's group started doing its own events, mostly on patriotic holidays or memorials, all with an eye to civic engagement and education. On the 2010 anniversary of 9/11 they staged a candlelit vigil at a local firehouse. Kenney spent eight hours in her garage with a friend, cutting and pasting onto a fifty-foot mural the names of the three thousand Americans who had perished. An electrician by the name of Greg created a scaffold out of PVC pipe and wires to hold banners. A retired soundman, Aspen, volunteered his audio equipment and skills. Kenney arranged for SFV Patriots to read the voices of passengers on the hijacked planes. She stumped up a few dollars for a Scottish bagpiper and drums. She stumped up a few more to hire a vocalist. Many attendees were moved to tears.

When the Kiwanis Club of Canoga Park didn't have enough people to hold portraits honoring dead veterans on Memorial Day, SFVP sent twenty-five members to do the job. They adopted a charity, the West Valley Food Pantry, run by a local church (*We do legitimate—nothing out of the back of a van*), and held flash-mob food drives, at which people spontaneously appeared with bags of donations. They joined Fourth of July rallies, holding "Warrior Flags" to honor the military. They held movie nights featuring documentaries about history or the Constitution. They stood on sidewalks handing out Constitutions. They sat at malls, signing up people (anyone, of any party) to vote.

SFVP attended some events that the media might cast as partisan, though members notably didn't see it that way. When the chief operating officer of Chick-fil-A in June 2012 made public comments opposing same-sex marriage, inspiring protests and counterprotests at Chick-fil-A franchises across the country, the press cast it as a showdown between gays and antigays. When Kenney's group showed up at a local Chick-fil-A, their interest was in backing the First Amendment, standing up for the right of corporate officers to have an opinion, and the right of chicken lovers to eat where they please.

Membership grew so much in the 2010 election year that Coco's became a tight squeeze. The group upped sticks to a local Denny's, with a meeting room large enough that Kenney had to invest in speakers and a microphone so all ninety regulars could hear. (*It was easier than watching half the audience try to turn up their hearing aids.*) The growing pains were almost humorous. One of Kenney's first stabs at an SFVP business card featured a glimpse of a flag. The banner was billowing, stirring—and also French. (*Definitely patriotic. Definitely the wrong country.*) They started advertising on a local radio station, running little thirty-second clips featuring tributes to important moments in history. Only after a time did it occur to the group that it might want to include its name and a contact number, so that people would know how to join or give support.

Kenney and Cronn spent hours designing a website, one with a patriotic and historical theme, and getting the group on social media. They started a regular newsletter—the *Patriots Almanac*. Every issue features prominently a statement that is a point of pride with the group: "No elephants. No donkeys. Just patriots." The publication always features little stories about history (Paul Revere's ride; American Indians in the Revolution), recipes for patriotic holidays (a presidential ice cream; an apple cake), celebrations of institutions and history (Christmas in the White House). Most issues contain at least one political feature, though these tend toward the broad: "Americans work longer to pay taxes," ran the title of one. "Big Government is enslaving us to debt," ran another. Kenney was so wary of getting dragged into the partisan minefield that she resisted calls from some members to get the words "Tea Party" into the group's official name. (*Didn't need that nail in that cross!*)

It was in fact civics, as it happens, not politics, that inspired Kenney to turn to the IRS. The Tea Party had popped up overnight, and networked just as quickly. Tens of thousands of grassroots activists plugged into each other's websites and joined weekly national conference calls. Kenney did, too, and in mid-2010 got word that an anonymous millionaire intended to dole out $1 million in grants to groups that worked to get out the vote.

Kenney loved the concept, and had an inspired idea for a grant. She designed a dramatic poster featuring at its center a big, rippling U.S. flag. (*Yeah, yeah, not French this time.*) Above it, in old-fashioned, Constitution-looking type, ran the words "We the People." Under the flag, in bold letters, was this simple plea: "Keep the promise. Vote." At the bottom was SFVP's name, its website, and its telephone number. The posters contained not a hint of party or partisan ideology, and Kenney's idea was to blow them up to ad size and pay to have them hung in twenty bus shelters along a main thoroughfare of her voting district. Cost: $17,000. It was far, far more than her little group could contemplate, but a grant might make it happen.

The hitch? Groups had to be "official" to apply. They needed to be incorporated and control a bank account. Kenney had up until this point operated SFVP as an informal club. Getting official meant getting into bed with the IRS.

Most Americans would be surprised to discover that even the smallest of groups, if they take in or spend even the smallest of dollars, are required to go to the IRS. To avoid paying taxes on those dollars—and to be in a position to really fund-raise, or apply for grants—a group needs special IRS recognition. An entire section of the tax code exists to confer precisely such "nonprofit" recognition on Americans who want to engage in civic life. Eye-glazingly known as Section 501(c) of the U.S. tax code, it contains twenty-nine different categories of organizations that qualify to avoid most federal taxes. Each category gets its own little number: 501(c)(3) groups are charities and religious and educational outfits; 501(c)(5) groups are labor unions; 501(c)(6) groups are industry associations; 501(c)(13) groups are cemetery companies.

SFVP fell under the catchall category of 501(c)(4)—a "social welfare" organization. By long-standing IRS language, the definition of such a group is any "that operates primarily to further the common good and general welfare of the people of the community." That's the catchall part. Since pretty much every Tom, Dick, or Harry has strong positions on what is "good" for a community, and since those ideas are entirely subjective, pretty much anybody can claim social-welfare recognition from the tax authority. If a group of ninety-year-old ladies claim that teaching four-year-olds to darn socks would benefit the country, the IRS would be hard pressed to deny them tax-exempt sock-darning status.

Kenney knew that going through the hoopla of IRS recognition was overkill. The group's fund-raising was skimpy. She thinks it insulting to ask an admission price to engage in democracy, so at each meeting she instead passes a hat, collecting $5 or $10 here or there. She holds a raffle at each event; six chances for $5. (*People do it because they just want a chance to win! I love it. It's just so American!*) To fulfill her promise that prizes will always be worth two to three times the raffle tickets, Kenney is a catalog queen, hunting for deals on cookbooks, kitchen equipment, pet supplies, home tools. On her best raffle night ever, she pulled in a whole $150.

She has a few high rollers. One retired couple gives $100 every three months. (*This was a big deal for them!*) Carmen, an elderly woman, regularly gives $20 to help pay for patriot movie nights. Most attendees just volunteer their time and skills, or supplies: Greg the electrician; Aspen the sound guy; Dee, a beauty consultant, who paid to print some posters for rallies; Karnig, an Eastern European immigrant, who made four pairs of handmade clogs for the raffle. (*He does it in European sizes, so it is very confusing. We are now figuring out they run small.*) A friend of Kenney's, Carol, serves as the group's treasurer and keeps track of the money. Todd does the social media. Some people show up to set up chairs. Some hand out literature.

Not much comes in, so not much money goes out. She's made a few "big" investments. The box amplifier and mikes for the meetings ran $900. Radio advertising cost about $1,000 for eight months of weekly ads. Their candlelit 9/11 memorial—their most expensive event ever—ran about $850. The rest is tiny, sporadic: $130 for a website domain; a one-day rental van to deliver the food donations; a table hire for an event. Some of the outgoing checks are token but grateful recognition of volunteer time. No one in SFVP draws a salary, though Kenney insists on paying Cronn a tiny stipend for serving as webmaster and to reimburse him for expenses. In response to a 2011 e-mail from Cronn about a few things he'd bought to create their first newsletter, Kenney replied, "I'll send you a check for $150 to cover your expenses and an enormously ridiculous 'bonus' of $50 to purchase aspirin, butt cushions and Pepto-Bismol."

She's (unsurprisingly) scrupulous about documenting every dollar in and out. (*Do I sound OCD? Really, I'm not OCD! Well . . . maybe I'm a little OCD.*) Kenney estimates that the group's annual income averages about $3,300. And she acknowledges that over its five years she's kicked in about $14,000 of her own money—money she doesn't have to spare. By comparison, the largest liberal 501(c)(4), the League of Conservation Voters, spent $9.6 million on the 2012 election alone.

SFVP was, in short, poorer than a Revolutionary-era church mouse. Asking the IRS to officially recognize that fact hardly seemed worth the effort. Then again, Kenney really wanted to inspire her neighbors to vote. And she figured on a further upside or two. Scoring IRS tax-exempt status would give SFVP some official ownership over its name. Owning a 501(c)(4) badge also tended to make people a little more comfortable about donating.

Kenney knew nothing about the IRS application process, so she fired up her computer. The process was no small thing. She needed official officers—a secretary, a treasurer—so she recruited some SFVP regulars. And she needed articles of incorporation, so she wrote them. They rang true: "The specific purpose of this corporation is to promote the values of a Constitutionally limited government, fiscal responsibility and free-market enterprise under the rule of law through non-partisan, political action (i.e. rallies, e-mail campaigns) and public education (i.e. legislative information, meetings, distribution of literature on the Founders and founding documents of the United States, and voter registration)."

Kenney didn't have money for a lawyer, so she did the IRS application the new-fashioned, DIY-Internet way: LegalZoom. It was straightforward—at least for a group like Kenney's. You give your basic data, names of officers, and your stated articles of incorporation. You describe past and planned activities, explain where you got your money, attach any literature you handed out. You fill out a little chart on your revenue and expenses. You ignore all the questions about capital stock, and classes of membership and assets, because you don't have a pot to piss in. You hit send, mail a check, and assume you get your IRS letter in fewer than three months. Especially because you write a $400 check for expedited service. And even more especially because the IRS's only real job in evaluating 501(c)(4) applications is to ensure that you've filled everything out the right way, and that you haven't mistakenly misfiled as a cemetery company.

Kenney hit send on October 23, 2010. She'd heard nothing by Christmas. Nothing by March. She dutifully filed her requisite tax forms with the federal and state authorities, and waited some more. She'd heard nothing by Easter. Nothing by the Fourth of July. Nothing by Halloween. Nothing a full year after filing.

She wasn't too worried. (*It's the government! It's always backed up. And with the feds, no news is good news, right?*) She'd been advised that she could operate as if SFVP were already a nonprofit, and that's what she did. She carried on with the grant competition, making it through two rounds before getting cut. (*I hate losing.*) She kept on with the rallies, events, meetings. Christmas 2011 came and went. And then that fateful day in February, and the "oh shit" moment.

The questionnaire Kenney opened that day was almost a perfect expression of Orwellian bureaucracy—a mix of boring officialdom and sinister intrusiveness. The entire first sheet contained a bewildering list of instructions and caveats. "Mail or fax your response to each of the items requested. . . . Fax to the name and fax number shown at the top of page 1 of this letter. If your response is greater than 20 pages do not fax. Do not fax and mail your response. . . . Each piece of correspondence submitted, whether fax or mail, must be processed, assigned and reviewed. . . . Do not fax your response multiple times."

What followed were six pages of close type, containing thirty-five broad questions and more than eighty subquestions. Some were redundant. Question 3 required Kenney to (re)submit her articles of incorporation. Some were straightforward: "How many members do you currently have? Provide details regarding all members' fees and benefits."

Most, however, were insanely invasive (*Ever had a proctology exam done through your nose? That's how this felt.*):

- Provide a printout of each of your website's pages, including any pages with restricted access.

- Provide details regarding all of your activity on Facebook and Twitter. Also provide hard copies of all advertising you have conducted using social media outlets.

- Indicate if any of your current and former officers, directors, and key employees are related to each other (include family and business relationships) and describe the nature of the relationship.

- Provide minutes of all board meetings since your creation.

- Regarding your current and planned volunteers:
    How many volunteers do you have?
    How many volunteers are/were devoted to each activity of the organization throughout the year?

- Provide a list of all issues that are important to your organization. Indicate your position regarding each issue.

- Are you associated with any other IRC 501(c)(3), 501(c)(4), or 527 organizations? If yes:
    Provide the name, federal employer identification number, and address of each organization.
    Describe in detail the nature of the relationship(s).
    Describe the nature of all contacts with the organizations.

- Has any person or organization provided educational services to you? If yes, provide the following:
    The name of the person or organization.
    A full description of the services provided.
    The political affiliation of the person or organization.

- You attempt to influence the outcome of specific legislation. Please answer the following:

    Provide copies of all communications, pamphlets, advertisements, and other materials distributed by you regarding the legislation.

    Do you directly or indirectly communicate with members of legislative bodies? If so, explain the amount and nature of the communication.

- Have you conducted any protests? If yes, please answer the following regarding your protest activities:

    What percentage of your time and funds are spent protesting?

    Has your organization ever conducted or promoted any illegal activity? If yes, explain.

    Have any of your members been arrested by the police during a demonstration? If yes, explain.

And on and on and on and on. From the first, Kenney knew there was something gravely wrong with these questions. The IRS had always been easy about bestowing tax-exempt status. Its bureaucrats perform basic due diligence—make sure the forms are filled out correctly, check that the organization isn't blatantly or erroneously applying. Assuming all is in order, the tax-exempt letter goes out. And correctly so. The IRS, after all, is a tax agency. Its job isn't to question the motives of an organization, but to examine its *later* spending—after it files its first tax reports—and make sure it followed the tax rules. That's why, between the years of 2001 and 2011, the IRS issued tax-exempt letters to more than fourteen thousand social-welfare organizations. It turned down only fifty-six.

There are rules, of course. Organizations like Kenney's are allowed to participate directly in politics (even going so far as to endorse and directly support candidates) so long as this doesn't constitute a "majority" of its efforts. The IRS looks at those first-

year tax forms with an eye to verifying that a group is devoting
at least 51 percent of its resources to its "primary" purpose. The
easiest way to test this is just to look at spending. If a 501(c)(4)
blows 60 percent of its money on ads calling for the reelection
of a senator, it likely loses its nonprofit status. And it's simple
to check. Any organization—a party, a trade association, a super
PAC, a nonprofit, an individual—that runs an ad expressly calling
for the election or defeat of a candidate is required by law to file
reports on that spending with the Federal Election Commission.

Kenney had barely started the process. She'd never filed tax information as a nonprofit. She'd never advertised in an election.
The IRS knew all this. Yet here was the agency asking about
her motives and views and associations, and suggesting that her
answers would guide whether she could get even initial status.
Kenney went from "oh shit" to "what the hell?" Why did the IRS
need a copy of every web page? Why all the board meeting minutes? Why did it need to know if SFVP attended protests? Why
did it need the names of every other nonprofit Kenney had ever
spoken to? What earthly value was there in explaining whether
current and past board members were related?

The interrogatory felt to Kenney to be both sweepingly
broad and terrifyingly specific. Lots of questions had little to do
with SFVP's particular circumstances, suggesting that the IRS
had unthinkingly mailed it a standardized form. Then again, it
contained detailed questions that made clear it had been monitoring SFVP. One demanded that Kenney provide details of
its "relationship" with the Tea Party Patriots—a nationally recognized Tea Party group. Kenney was particularly incensed by
question number 29, which read, "Provide details regarding the
townhall event planned on February 13, 2012, with Newt Gingrich." Mr. Gingrich, a presidential candidate at the time, was
indeed coming to California—to attend forums SFVP had absolutely nothing to do with. (*You know what, sports fans? That
wasn't even ours. Some other group, probably Republican, brought him*

out. I may be short, but I'm not stupid. That tells you right there how the IRS was operating.)

What most kept drawing Kenney's eyes was the second paragraph of the IRS cover letter. It read, "The information you submit should be accompanied by the following declaration: *Under penalties of perjury, I declare that I have examined this information, including accompanying documents, and, to the best of my knowledge and belief, the information contains all the relevant facts relating to the request for the information, and such facts are true, correct and complete.*"

It unnerved her. Did she have a complete record of everything the group had done? They were an informal club, just trying to be heard. More worrisome were the subjective questions. What did the IRS view as a "protest"? Were events at which participants spoke up for the Constitution—and so spoke against Obama policies—protests? What did it mean to "indirectly" communicate with members of legislative bodies? Did signing a petition count? If a member told the group about an issue of interest, was that educational?

Looking at the questions, Kenney was pretty sure the IRS had it in for her group. And she'd be on the hook if it decided her version of "true and correct" didn't match its own.

SFVP was no stranger to intimidation. Democrats had managed in a few short years to make "Tea Party" a dirty term and object of political scorn. Kenney and friends had in their early outings worn Revolutionary-era tricorne hats to pass out copies of the Constitution. They stopped wearing them after people spat on them. Kenney would post her upcoming events online, and left-wing groups started staging counter-rallies. At one Tax Day Rally, the local chapter of La Raza, a Latino advocacy group, showed up with speakers, drums, native dancers, and bullhorns to shout down those advocating lower taxes. Kenney had to issue instructions to her people about what to do in the face of threats. (*If you are shoved, don't shove back. If someone gets knocked down, everyone else circle that person and protect them. Such fun conversations.*)

She advocated that her group engage in silent rallies; these were more powerful than shouting back. One exception to this came in 2013, when Kenney's group showed up at a sidewalk event in support of Israel, with members carrying U.S. and Israeli flags. An opponent ran through the group, pushing people, calling Kenney a "fucking bitch." He came back a second time, shoving, this time addressing Kenney as a "dirty kike Jew." At this point some of Kenney's members (*weirdly, mostly the ones in their seventies—they have real spirit*) started agitating for a response, and Kenney had an idea. When the opponent came back around again, SFVP began shouting, over and over, "First Amendment!" He didn't run through again.

The IRS letter bore the date February 8, 2012, and it informed Kenney that she had until February 29—twenty-one days—to get her response in. Kenney doesn't always open her mail immediately—sometimes it stacks up—so when she had her "oh shit" moment, she realized that she had fewer than fourteen days to track down years of information and write answers to dozens of detailed questions. The form contained the name of an IRS official in Cincinnati she could contact with questions. She called and explained her concerns with the deadline. He kindly said she could have an additional week.

She holed up in the garage, where she keeps her SFVP boxes. It took dozens of hours, week after week, but she got the response done. Before she'd even mailed it, she received a second interrogatory from the IRS, with yet new questions. In June she'd get a third one, containing both follow-ups and new demands.

Included in that third questionnaire was an item that stopped Kenney cold. The IRS was demanding that she provide it with the names and Social Security numbers of every person who had ever donated their money or time to SFVP.

If there is one thing Kenney knows, it is the Constitution. While every American knows it guarantees freedom of speech, Kenney also knows that through that right flows others: the freedom of association, and of anonymity. She started making calls.

CHAPTER 2

Publius & Co.

ON A JANUARY DAY in 1958, Robert L. Carter entered the Supreme Court building. The steps leading up to the Great Hall were familiar to the civil rights lawyer. Carter had worked himself up from nothing to become the top dynamo at the NAACP, the center point of the group's legal campaign against segregation. Only a few years earlier he'd presented part of the oral argument in *Brown v. Board of Education*, in which the Supreme Court had finally declared separate schools for black children unconstitutional.

This January day he was back to do something equally notable: to win a case that would shore up the First Amendment and make him legendary in free-speech circles.

Born in Florida in 1917, Carter was the youngest of nine children. His father died when he was a year old, and his mother, now living with the family in New Jersey, paid the bills by taking in white people's laundry. Carter from a young age rebelled against discrimination. At his high school in East Orange, New Jersey, blacks were only allowed to use the pool on Fridays, and only after school. Carter had read that the state supreme court banned such segregation, and so one day he joined the white students at the pool. A teacher threatened to have him expelled; he didn't back down.

He was brainy, and skipped two grades to graduate high school at age sixteen. He worked his way through Lincoln University in Pennsylvania, and then through two law schools, Howard University and Columbia. He spent the war years in the Army Air Corps, where, as the only black officer at Harding Field in Baton Rouge, Louisiana, he again ruffled feathers by integrating the officers' club. He came back to join the NAACP's Legal Defense and Educational Fund, and quickly caught the eye of the legendary Thurgood Marshall, who was at that time the group's general counsel. Marshall brought Carter along, turning him within a few years into his chief legal assistant, and the duo spent a decade dismantling segregation in education. Carter took over from Marshall as general counsel in 1956, just in time to face a new legal threat. This one threatened to dismantle the NAACP itself.

On December 1, 1955, Rosa Parks, an NAACP member, refused to move to the back of a segregated bus in Montgomery, Alabama. She was arrested. E. D. Nixon, the president of the local NAACP chapter, recruited a young black minister by the name of Martin Luther King Jr. to serve as the public face of a bus boycott. The black community organized a series of carpools to supplant buses, and black taxi drivers offered discounted rides. Black churches across the country raised money to fund the movement and pay for new shoes for walkers. The boycott wreaked havoc on public transportation, and the city tried everything to break it. It fined taxi drivers; it pressured local insurance companies to stop covering carpool vehicles; it indicted King and eighty-nine other boycott leaders. But these actions only served to bring national attention and fortify the protestors. The NAACP had, for its part, helped file a lawsuit that would result in the U.S. Supreme Court on November 13, 1956, finding the state's bus segregation laws unconstitutional. The boycott ended a month later, after 381 days, a resounding victory for African Americans nationally.

Alabama's white political leadership was angry, and none more so than the state attorney general, John M. Patterson—a Democrat who would forge a career on his opposition to civil rights. After *Brown v. Board of Education*, Patterson kept throwing up state laws to stymie school desegregation. He went after the leaders of the Montgomery bus boycott, and fought the lawsuit right up to the Supreme Court.

A short time into the boycott, Patterson decided to take aim at what he viewed as his state's chief troublemaker: the NAACP. He set his legal team to examining the organization's activities, and they came back toting a state statute governing "corporations" in Alabama. According to the flimsy legal case Patterson would concoct, the NAACP, because it was based in New York, was a "foreign corporation" and therefore required to register with the state before it could function there. Since it had not, in 1956 he filed suit with the circuit court in Montgomery demanding an injunction against the NAACP's operating in his state.

The suit was filed with Judge Walter B. Jones, himself a segregationist, who immediately granted the injunction. But Patterson wanted to do more than just put a halt to NAACP activities. He wanted to expose the group, target it, send the message that any black who continued to support it—openly or otherwise—was at risk. So he also filed a request that the court require the NAACP to hand over all its records—including a list of its members, its donors, its property ownership, and its bank statements. Judge Jones happily complied, setting a deadline for document turnover.

Carter knew exactly what Patterson was looking to do. The boycott had already led to the violent targeting of its public leaders. King's home was firebombed; so was the home of his friend and fellow minister Ralph Abernathy. Four black Baptist churches were attacked and set on fire. Whites physically assaulted boycotters.

The Supreme Court victory would cause even more violence:

King's home came under shotgun fire; white men attacked a black teenager as she left a bus; snipers fired on buses, and in one incident shot a pregnant woman in both legs. Less than a month after the boycott ended, whites bombed five black churches. A few weeks after that, Klansmen lynched a black man, Willie Edwards. Rosa Parks would ultimately leave Montgomery, unable to find a job, the subject of death threats.

Carter knew an NAACP member and donor list would be, in the hands of segregationists, at best a blacklist, at worst a kill list. His organization could not and would not ever comply.

When the NAACP failed to provide the documents, Judge Jones held it in contempt and slapped it with a $10,000 fine. He warned that it would increase to $100,000 after five more days. The civil rights organization decided to legally fight the order, though in a show of goodwill it did provide a list of the names and addresses of the NAACP's officers in Alabama. That wasn't enough for Patterson, and the fine grew. The case worked up to the Alabama Supreme Court, which refused to modify or halt the fine or disclosure order. It landed with the Supremes.

And so Carter, almost sixty years to the day before Karen Kenney would receive her first IRS inquisition form, walked into the Court determined to broaden some basic rights.

The First Amendment doesn't contain a direct reference to "freedom of association." It does, however, guarantee the right to assembly and to petition government. And starting in about the 1930s, the Supreme Court began interpreting the Fourteenth Amendment's Due Process Clause to more widely guarantee the right of Americans to gather together in private or in public, and to collectively exercise free speech.

In 1945, for instance, the Court backed up Roland Jay Thomas, then the president of the United Automobile, Aircraft and Agricultural Implement Workers. Thomas flew into Houston in September 1943 to aid in organizing workers at the nearby Humble Oil and Refining Company. A few hours before he was due to speak at a public event, he was issued a restraining order by an antiunion state attorney general, told he'd be violating a law requiring union bosses to first obtain a special license to organize new members. Thomas spoke anyway, and was arrested. He pointed out to the Supreme Court that he did not personally sign up members, did not ask for or receive funds, and did not disturb or breach the peace. All he had done was speak—and Texas had no right to stop him. The Court agreed, tying together free speech and free association: The "exercise of the rights of free speech and free assembly" are "immune" to registration.

Shoring up freedom of assembly had meanwhile forced the Court to confront another question: anonymity in political speech. The twentieth century witnessed a startling and rapid rise in the size and power of both federal and state government. What good was freedom of speech, or freedom of assembly, if citizens were too frightened by a powerful state to exercise those rights?

In 1941, a political gadfly and publisher named Edward Rumely helped establish the Committee for Constitutional Government, an organization opposed to Franklin Roosevelt's government expansion and court-packing. Rumely distributed books and literature about the Constitution to a mass mailing list. House Democrats called him in front of Congress, demanding the names of those who had bought his books in bulk for further distribution. He refused to provide them and was convicted of obstructing a congressional inquiry. The Supreme Court struck down the conviction in a landmark decision, writing, "The Power to inquire into all efforts of private individuals to influence public opinion through books and periodicals raises doubts of constitutionality in view of the prohibition of the First Amendment."

These opinions mattered, yet the Court had mostly just flirted with the question of association and anonymity. Carter's goal on that 1958 day was to get the Court to commit, unequivocally, to both—and to tie them together. After a half hour of dry questioning from the justices about procedure, precedent, and the facts of the case, Carter was finally provided his opportunity to lay out in impassioned and precise terms the way in which anonymity was at the heart of free assembly, which in turn was at the heart of free speech. "It is our contention the entire proceeding in Alabama is void. They have no power, no authority, to oust us from the state. We have been deprived of the right to carry on our lawful activities," he said. The power of the NAACP came first and foremost from its collective voice, from the ability of many powerless and persecuted blacks to organize and speak as one (freedom of assembly). But it also came from that group being able to operate with protection (anonymity). Had Patterson obtained the list, Carter's members "would have been subject to harm and pressure and worse, and they would have fled the organization. They'd have lost their freedom to assemble, and with it lost their freedom of speech through the NAACP."

On June 30, 1958, the Court delivered its opinion by way of Justice John Marshall Harlan II—a fact not lost on Carter. Harlan's grandfather had sat on the Supreme Court generations earlier, where he became famous as the lone dissenter in *Plessy v. Ferguson*, the infamous decision upholding racial segregation. This Harlan, this time, led a unanimous Supreme Court in redefining free speech, and in support of an organization that had sprung into being partly to fight *Plessy* segregation.

"Effective advocacy of both public and private points of view, particularly controversial ones, is undeniably enhanced by group association," wrote Harlan, who pronounced it a fundamental aspect of "liberty." And yet such liberty could be wrecked by "compelled disclosure." The NAACP had shown that "revelation of the identity of its rank-and-file members has exposed these members to economic reprisal, loss of employment, threat of physical coercion and other manifestations of public hostility." Disclosure moreover "may induce members to withdraw from the Association and dissuade others from joining it because of fear of exposure of their beliefs."

Alabama never did get its names. The case dragged on for nine years and required Carter to make four more trips to the Supreme Court. But he would in the end overturn the contempt charge, and regain his group's right to operate freely in the state. Far more lasting, he convinced the U.S. Supreme Court—for the first time—to sanctify both freedom of assembly and anonymity, enshrining new and overdue guarantees of free speech.

These were guarantees that the high court would only strengthen in years to come. Patterson's strategy for ousting the NAACP from Alabama was quickly replicated by other segregationist states and cities. By the end of 1957, the NAACP was involved in at least twenty-five separate cases seeking its membership lists. Carter would win several more cases in front of the Supreme Court, each decision fortifying the new doctrines of association and anonymity. In *Bates v. Little Rock*, a unanimous high court overturned the conviction and fines of NAACP members who had refused to provide member names as required by newly crafted tax ordinances in Arkansas. The Court, even by then, was beginning to sound exasperated. "It is now beyond dispute that freedom of association for the purpose of advancing ideas and airing grievances is protected by the Due Process Clause of the 14th Amendment," wrote Potter Stewart in the unanimous ruling. The state has "not demonstrated so cogent an interest in obtaining and making public the membership lists of these organizations as to justify the substantial abridgement of associational freedom which such disclosure would effect."

The NAACP provided inspiration to others, as more and different groups of Americans sought to force the Court to look more closely at the risks of other forms of disclosure. In 1958, Manuel D. Talley, a black man and cofounder of the Los Angeles chapter of the Council for Racial Equality, began distributing handbills that urged consumers to stop shopping at businesses that contained products from "manufacturers who will not offer equal employment opportunities to Negroes, Mexicans and Orientals."

Talley's handbills contained the name of another group he'd founded, National Consumers Mobilization, and a post-office box address. Local officials arrested and fined Talley for violating a 1932 city ordinance that required any handbill in the city to include the "name and address of the person who printed, wrote, compiled or manufactured the same."

Cities and states had for some time been erecting such rules and bans on pamphlets, claiming it was a way of protecting citizens from fraud. That claim may have had some truth to it, but the politicians were also interested in keeping a grip on political information. The Supreme Court had already overturned ordinances that outright forbade the distribution of literature. Local jurisdictions had responded with new "disclosure" requirements. Talley's high-profile arrest, on flimsy charges, convinced many in the civil rights community that these new "transparency" rules were designed to intimidate activists out of political speech.

And once again, the Supreme Court agreed. In a 6–3 decision, Justice Hugo Black struck down L.A.'s ordinance, writing that "an identification requirement" restricted "freedom of expression." He cited the glorious history of "anonymous pamphlets, leaflets, brochures and even books" that had allowed "persecuted groups" to "criticize oppressive practices and laws."

Black's opinion marked an important shift for the Court, a much broader, more direct way of reinforcing anonymous political speech. In the NAACP case, the Court had cited anonymity as a form of protection—and thus a reason to stop the state from requiring lists of names. Here, Black was heralding anonymity as its own force for political good, a means of enriching political debate. "It is plain," he wrote, "that anonymity has sometimes been assumed for the most constructive purposes."

He was right. Western Europe boasted a riotous tradition of anonymous political writing, one that transferred to American colonial shores. A German-American printer in New York, John Peter Zenger, in 1733 published newspaper copies excoriating the new colonial governor, William Cosby. Zenger didn't write the articles; he published broadsides from political activists writing under pseudonyms. Cosby's council ordered Zenger's arrest for seditious libel and demanded that he reveal the names of the writers. He would not, and spent months in jail. His case became a sensation, encouraging one of the most famous lawyers of the day, Andrew Hamilton, to defend him at trial. Hamilton offered a ringing defense of the rights of the common man to speak and write freely, in any form. The jury took all of ten minutes to return a verdict of not guilty.

The most famous political words of the Revolutionary era, and of the Founding, were anonymous. Thomas Paine's *Common Sense*—his attack on the tyranny of George III—was an instant bestseller, with more than seventy-five thousand copies sold in just a few weeks in a nation that at that time contained just two and a half million residents. John Adams credited Paine with firing the Revolution, noting, "Without the pen of the author of 'Common Sense,' the sword of Washington would have been raised in vain." And yet the first edition of *Common Sense* bore no author, and the second only the inscription, "Written by an Englishman." Paine felt that what mattered was "the Doctrine, not the man."

In 1774, a wickedly bright college student, all of age seventeen, wrote his first essay—defending the Continental Congress—and published it anonymously. His name was Alexander Hamilton. John Adams wrote several anonymous essays in the *Boston Gazette* in 1765 in response to the newly imposed Stamp Act. Isaac Collins, who printed the first family Bible in America, famously refused an order by the upper house of the New Jersey state legislature to reveal the real name of "Cincinnatus," who'd written a scathing attack in his newspaper against Governor William Livingston. The very same governor would a few years later write under the name "Scipio" to criticize his legislature. Benjamin Rush, a Pennsylvania signer of the Declaration of

Independence, would anonymously (under the name "Leonidas") in the *Pennsylvania Packet* accuse members of Congress.

One of America's most famous political documents, the *Federalist Papers*, was written by Alexander Hamilton, James Madison, and John Jay under the collective name "Publius." These authors didn't fear for their lives, but still had good reason for choosing a collective pen name. Clinton Rossiter, a renowned historian of the *Federalist Papers*, explained that the men wanted their arguments debated on the merits, free of preconceptions readers might have about the authors themselves. And they didn't want controversial writings to undermine other work they were doing in government or their communities.

And the tradition continued. The chief justice of the U.S. Supreme Court, John Marshall, in 1819 wrote a series of pieces anonymously in a newspaper to elaborate on a landmark court ruling. And Abraham Lincoln was famous for writing anonymous attacks on his political opponents.

At the root of Justice Black's praise of anonymity was a heartfelt belief in the U.S. project. American democracy is premised on a belief in an educated, rational audience. The Founders didn't think government should be filtering speech. Americans could and must be trusted to hear the widest range of it—both disclosed and anonymous—and make their own judgments.

The Talley and NAACP cases would become the first in a growing pile of judicial decisions to protect the freedom of association and privacy, because the courts were getting hit with such cases right and left. Canny politicians had recognized the tool they had in disclosure laws. Segregationists like Patterson had got to the idea first, but it didn't take long for powerful state players, high and low, to realize that a little "transparency" could go a long way to shutting up an opposing politician or a meddlesome activist.

In 1967, a Democratic state attorney, Jeff Mobley, appears to have figured out a new way to do this: Go after donors. He issued subpoenas, calling on the chairman, secretary, and treasurer of the Arkansas Republican Party to hand over information about the party checking account. Arkansas had been essentially a one-party (Democratic) state since Reconstruction, but the GOP had started to gain a foothold—and Democrats didn't like it. Mobley claimed to be investigating whether Republicans had violated election laws during the 1966 election, when it paid supporters to knock on doors and get out the vote.

Republicans believed that what he really wanted was a list of the individuals contributing to his political rivals, and details on who the Republicans were paying to help it grow. GOP party officials sued in federal court, and in 1968 a panel of three judges expanded political anonymity to money and financing. The judges admitted that there are times when there is a legitimate state or public interest in seeing the financial records of political parties, and those records therefore should not be "completely immune from public disclosure." But they decreed that there was no reason here for Mobley to obtain the identities of contributors. The Court boldly plowed new ground, pointing out the connection between money and speech—noting that, apart from voting, "financial contributions" were the only other way "most people can participate effectively in politics." To the extent that the government "unreasonably inhibits or discourages" this, it violates the First Amendment. Moreover, forcing disclosure subjects some to "potential economic or political reprisals of greater or lesser severity."

Reprisals do happen. In 1998, Margaret McIntyre showed up at a public meeting at Blendon Middle School in Westerville, Ohio, and handed out flyers opposing a referendum on a new school tax levy. The flyers weren't misleading or false. A few referenced her, while a few said they represented "CONCERNED PARENTS AND TAX PAYERS." A local official didn't like that the school was being bucked in its campaign for more money, and filed a complaint with the Ohio Elections Commission claiming that she'd violated election law by not disclosing information required under Ohio laws. She was fined $100, and the Ohio Supreme Court upheld the fine. The U.S. Supreme Court did not. It instead broadened its privacy doctrine to encompass entirely anonymous political speech.

Liberal justice John Paul Stevens wrote for five other justices, finding that "the interest in having anonymous works enter the marketplace of ideas unquestionably outweighs any public interest in requiring disclosure as a condition of entry." Stevens reprised the arguments in favor of anonymity. He talked about the risk of economic reprisal or government retaliation; of a desire for privacy; of the fear of social ostracism. He noted that the practice "provides a way for a writer who may be personally unpopular to ensure that readers will not prejudge her message simply because they do not like its proponent." Justice Clarence Thomas, in a rousing concurrence, gave a powerful, chapter-and-verse rendition of the history and merits of anonymous speech in the United States.

The biggest disappointment of the *McIntyre* case was Justice Antonin Scalia, who normally supports freedom. Here instead, he filed a dissent (joined by William Rehnquist) in which he argued for more intrusive government power. His argument was weak: Because lots of states had disclosure rules, it was now a "tradition" that must be upheld.

The *McIntyre* decision was one of the last intelligent decisions the Supreme Court would issue on association and anonymity. In the nearly twenty years since, it has instead been in thrall to the growing public enthusiasm for more "transparency" in campaign speech and spending. The Court's failure to honor its past positions would play inexorably into the trammeling of Karen Kenney.

CHAPTER 3

Bare Knuckles

SENATOR BARACK OBAMA was frustrated. The presidential aspirant had pulled off a surprise victory in the Iowa caucuses, and only a few weeks later crushed Hillary Clinton in South Carolina. By the end of January he'd pushed every other credible Democrat but her from the race and surged in national polls. The press loved him, and quickly predicted that come Super Duper Tuesday—February 5, when twenty-four states held their contests—he'd have the nomination sewed up.

Instead, the Obama team ran into the grinding power of the Clinton machine. Hillary threw vast money and resources at targeted Super Tuesday states, and ended the day with nearly as many delegates as Obama. The race was once again in a standoff, and Obama was irritated. He wanted this done, and yet independent groups were gearing up to promote Clinton in the big upcoming primaries in Ohio and Texas. So a few weeks later, on February 21, 2008, the national presidential press corps was summoned to a conference call with Bob Bauer.

A bearded and bespectacled stereotype of a Washington lawyer, Bauer spent thirty years working political law on behalf of Democrats before becoming the Obama campaign's chief attorney. He is smart, aggressive, and steeped in politics. His wife, Anita Dunn, ran Obama's communications team. But the

skill that has come to define Bauer—and in consequence national politics—is his particular expertise in campaign finance
law. Bauer understands the power of money and speech in politics. More important, he understands the power of denying it
to others.

As the reporters tuned in, Bauer wasted no time identifying
his target: an outfit known as the American Leadership Project.
A pro-Clinton group, ALP was what's known in politics as a 527.
Under the election rules at the time, ALP could run pretty much
any kind of ad it wanted—so long as it didn't expressly endorse a
candidate. And it could accept money in unlimited amounts—so
long as it disclosed its donors to the IRS. ALP raised millions and
intended to put it all into spendy ads that either praised Clinton,
or hit Obama, on the issues. Obama was outmatching Clinton in
overall fund-raising, but ALP threatened to even the odds in key
primary states.

Bauer didn't like that, and he made his legal case to the reporters: ALP's clear support for Clinton was the functional
equivalent of expressly endorsing her, he insisted. He claimed
that ALP was, as a result, engaged in a "very clear runaway
case of lawbreaking" vis-à-vis campaign law. Bauer intended to
go to the Federal Election Commission to complain, though he
wasn't stopping there. Rather, he issued two threats, both near-
unprecedented in presidential politics.

First, he was calling on the Justice Department to undertake
a *criminal* investigation of the group. Second, he demanded that
federal law enforcement focus its probe not on ALP as an entity,
but on its individual leaders, its staff, and (most sinisterly) its
donors. "There's going to be a reckoning here," he warned. "It's
going to be rough—it's going to be rough on the officers, it's going to be rough on the employees, it's going to be rough on the
donors." In case any Hillary financial backers missed the point,
he repeated, "Whether it's at the FEC or in a broader criminal inquiry, those donors will be asked questions." He referred

reporters to a memo he'd authored the prior day, in which he'd laid out his legal case and had reiterated—twice—that "liability for violating the federal campaign finance laws is both civil and criminal," and "any investigation" will "involve the Project's officers, staff and donors."

The threat was jaw-dropping, given that independent groups were spending far more on behalf of Obama than they were on Clinton. Moreover, the FEC had issued a regulation a year earlier that spelled out how 527s could operate, and ALP was clearly following the rules. Bauer's charge of lawbreaking was bogus, and everyone—even the press corps—knew it. *Politico*'s Ben Smith was honest enough in his resulting story to cast the Bauer threat as a bare-knuckle effort to stop ALP "before it starts, and to scare off other, similar efforts."

A spokesman for ALP, Roger Salazar, was incredulous. "Is that guy for real?" he responded to the *New York Daily News*. "That [is] a blatant attempt to quell free-speech with unsupported legal attacks. It is the legal equivalent of schoolyard bullying." As Bauer in the coming months ratcheted up his threats, a furious Jason Kinney, head of ALP (and a fellow Democrat), would publicly accuse the Obama lawyer of having gone from "credible legal authority" to "political hatchet man."

The intimidation nonetheless worked. Bauer had made his threats clear, and ALP donors had no interest in an FBI knock on their door or in being named publicly by Mr. Bauer in his next national press conference. Contributions dried up. *Politico* would later report that Bauer's words had "the effect of scaring [Clinton] donors and consultants," even if his efforts hadn't "result[ed] in any prosecution."

Bauer had just laid the groundwork for an entire political movement to come.

Bauer understood the modern power of using government—even if only the threat of it—to silence political opponents. And his special insight was realizing that the tool for getting those government drones trained on the right targets was campaign finance law.

He was hardly the first person to figure it out—he was just a modern innovator. All throughout history and all across the planet, government officials have used state power to silence critics. It's what government officials do.

American politicians have always had a harder time of it, though. They've always faced a particular hurdle: the Constitution. The Framers understood the real threat to liberty, and so wrote freedom of speech into the opening lines of the Bill of Rights. Americans are passionate about those First Amendment freedoms. And the courts, too, have been highly reluctant to mess with pure speech expression. So what's a would-be censor to do?

Look to the money. (It's always about the money.)

The First Amendment guarantees a right to speech, but says nothing about a right to spend money on speech. Why would it? In colonial days, a frustrated citizen might stand in the town square to denounce government, and feel confident his friends and neighbors would hear. In today's modern campaign world, it takes money to do the equivalent. How else does a citizen or a group send a message about a useless U.S. president to a nation of three hundred million? How is that possible without spending a dime on a flyer or an Internet site or a radio ad or a homemade documentary?

And that is how U.S. politicians get their hands on the First Amendment. They do it by proxy. Regulate money and you regulate speech. And better yet for the pols, regulating by proxy has extra upsides.

For one, most Americans don't get the connection. Tell the average American that you intend to restrict his right to speak at a town hall meeting, and watch the pitchforks come out. Tell the average American that you intend to regulate money in politics, and watch the praise flow. The architects of money restrictions are very good at selling their campaign finance rules. They make the case that the laws stop corruption; Americans hate corruption. They make the case that the laws empower average citizens and hinder powerful players from buying elections; Americans love the idea of the little guy. They make the case that the laws provide honesty and openness in elections; Americans love to be honest and open.

What they never mention is that few politicians have ever passed a campaign finance law for those reasons. Washington has its share of fanciful good-government types, who honestly (if mistakenly) believe that campaign restrictions help elections. But the men and women who make the laws aren't that naïve; they pass these restrictions for their own benefit. Often, they pass them as a means of quieting their opposition. Just as often, they pass them to survive a scandal: Some official is caught misbehaving, and Washington's way of extracting itself from blame is to impose new speech and money regulations on everyone else.

Second, regulating speech by proxy provides politicians with useful information—information they wouldn't otherwise be able to obtain. As Justice Clarence Thomas wrote in that rousing 1995 concurrence, government has a long and inglorious history of harassment—one reason why the country has an equally long and glorious tradition of anonymous speech.

Government has plenty of tools for rooting out targets, but at least in the past it was hard work. New York colonial governor William Cosby had to arrest John Peter Zenger and hold a trial to try to force him to disclose the names of contributors to his newspaper. Republican senator Joseph McCarthy in his 1950s witch hunt had to hold hearings and issue subpoenas to rootle out suspected communists. Alabama attorney general John Patterson had to dig deep to find a law he could use to prosecute the NAACP to try to unearth the names of its members.

Campaign finance law, however, makes the job of identifying political opponents dead easy. You can't regulate money unless you know who is giving it, and so at the beating heart of every finance law are sweeping disclosure requirements. And in the age of the Internet, that means that a list of every person who has given to most every cause is sitting in the ether. Drafting an enemies list requires little more than a few mouse clicks. Bauer took care to include donors in his threats against ALP, because he knew they would prove sensitive to being outed and attacked.

Finally, regulating by proxy gives politicians new ways to intimidate. The First Amendment is a guarantee to the people and a restriction on government. "Congress shall make no law . . ." Campaign finance rules, by contrast, flip this. Finance laws are a restriction on the people; they empower government. As Bauer warned ALP, these modern finance laws have the force of both civil and criminal penalties behind them. The result is a bizarre situation. Stand on the street corner to complain about Barack Obama, and the First Amendment bars government from doing anything about it. Write a big check for a TV ad that complains about Barack Obama, and campaign finance rules may allow the government to arrest and jail you.

Around 2008, the left started to realize the potential of combining all these tools. They had disclosure rules that let them identify opponents. They had a (willing) government they could pressure to employ finance laws against those opponents. They had the extraordinary new power of the Internet and social media, which liberal activists could use to mobilize instant pressure campaigns against any target. And they had the "argument." They could tell a credulous public that all their actions were aimed at "cleaner" and "more open" elections.

This is the modern intimidation game. And it now defines American politics.

Bauer, as the author of several campaign finance books, knew better than most the real history of the laws and their potential for muzzling. Indeed, his call on that February day was only the most recent and most consequential of a series of moments that led to the intimidation game.

One came in 1907, courtesy of a deeply unpleasant man named Benjamin Tillman—a wealthy landowner, a Democrat, a South Carolina senator, and a white supremacist. For all those reasons, he hated Teddy Roosevelt and the corporations that disagreed with Jim Crow policies.

TR was a trust buster, but he was first and foremost a politician. He'd started attacking corporate giants not long after taking over for the assassinated William McKinley. But as the 1904 election approached, he knew he'd need business community support. He toned down his rhetoric and started courting every titan in the land. The E. H. Harrimans and J. P. Morgans were wary of Roosevelt, but they were far more wary of a populist and radical Democratic Party. And they saw in the reelection a chance to soften TR's stance toward them. They poured money into his campaign. Henry Clay Frick, the steel baron, gave him $100,000; J. P. Morgan, more than $150,000. (In today's dollars, each of those gifts would total well more than $2.5 million.) By some estimates, corporations floated nearly 75 percent of TR's reelection bid. He won easily, albeit against a highly flawed Democratic nominee.

Tillman, a committed Democrat, was incensed. The South Carolinian despised anyone and anything with a liberal attitude about race. That included Roosevelt, who had in Tillman's eyes committed the unforgivable sin of inviting Booker T. Washington to the White House. And it included corporations, many of which publicly opposed the South's segregationist policies, in part because they disliked having to spend money on separate-but-equal facilities.

Democrats had heaped abuse on TR for accepting all that

corporate cash, and by the end of the 1904 campaign had thoroughly soured the public on big money in politics. Tillman saw his opportunity to undercut both the GOP and its corporate benefactors, and so proposed one of the first sweeping federal finance laws: a total ban on corporate contributions to campaigns. He also had an unlikely and powerful backer for his campaign: Teddy Roosevelt. Eager to tamp down criticism of his donations and to relaunch his trust-busting campaign, the newly elected president used his first address to Congress to declare his new dedication to cleaning up the finance system he'd so skillfully used to get reelected. Roosevelt signed the Tillman Act into law in 1907.

And thus the pattern was set for nearly every finance law to come. The Tillman Act wasn't passed out of some thoughtful, benevolent congressional desire to clean up dirty politics. It *was* dirty politics. Democrats proposed and passed it to kneecap political rivals. A Republican signed it to mute criticism of his prior actions (a decision made monumentally easier by the fact that TR had already pledged not to run for office again, so he wouldn't need any cash in the future). And the joke was that subsequent events proved that corporate money wasn't in fact corrupting. TR would go on to tear down most of the industrialists who'd backed him in 1904. Frick would later famously moan to fellow millionaires, "We bought the son of a bitch, and then he didn't stay bought." The Tillman Act was government silencing a sweeping category of critics. All under the guise of good government.

Thirty years after the Tillman Act, a different Roosevelt was sitting in the White House, and congressional Republicans suspected him of using his ever-growing New Deal program to construct a permanent power base for the Democratic Party. Those suspicions turned to outrage in 1938, following accusations that employees at the Works Progress Administration had influenced congressional elections. Republicans, working with conservative Democrats, in 1939 used the scandal as an excuse to pass the Hatch Act, which limited the political activity of federal employees. In 1940, Republicans expanded the law, putting a dollar limit on federal employee contributions to candidates and extending other political restrictions to certain employees of state agencies that received federal funds.

Three years later, Roosevelt's allies gave Republicans an excuse to shut down the speech of an even bigger prize. FDR had done more to grow the union movement than any other president, and Big Labor returned the favor by throwing vast sums of money at Democratic candidates. But in 1943 the United Mine Workers made the monumental error of going on strike over wages—in the middle of a global war. Republicans played off the resulting public anger and fear to whip through the Smith-Connally Act. In theory, the law was about giving the federal government power to seize and operate wartime industries threatened by strike. But Republicans made sure to throw in a provision prohibiting labor unions from federal campaign contributions for the duration of the war. In 1947 they made that ban permanent, and upped the ante. Up to then, Congress had concentrated its fire on restricting direct contributions to candidates. The 1947 Taft-Hartley Act banned both unions and corporations from spending money on pretty much any federal political activity. No giving dollars to candidates, but also no spending money independently to endorse or disapprove of politicians. In the space of forty short years, Democrats and Republicans had teamed up to make themselves immune from criticism from two of the biggest political constituencies in the country—businesses and workers (both private and public).

Next up were private citizens, and the moment this time was provided by Richard Nixon. Despite the Tillman Act, the Hatch Act, the Smith-Connally Act, and the Taft-Hartley Act, campaign spending just kept going up. Congress wanted a better handle on where all the money was coming from, and in 1971 it passed the Federal Election Campaign Act (FECA), instituting the nation's first formalized disclosure laws. And what that disclosure found was that a lot of individual Americans, including wealthy ones, were giving a lot of money to campaigns. Including to Richard Nixon.

Watergate has come to stand in many Americans' minds as the ultimate reason why the country needs campaign finance laws. Yet Nixon's campaign-finance infractions were almost incidental to his broader crimes. Nixon's real offense was his abuse of power—his decision to use all the levers of the federal government to "screw" his political enemies. His administration ultimately stood accused of bugging the offices of political opponents, of using the CIA, the FBI, and the IRS to harass his adversaries, of hiring thugs to break into the Democratic National Committee headquarters, and of digging up dirt on adversaries.

The wrongdoing flowed from the skewed morals of a corrupt chief executive, and Nixon's resignation—and the subsequent incarceration of forty-eight of his officials—might have ended the story. Yet Congress felt it must do more to reassure the public and get credit for action. And because some of Nixon's activities had been funded via an outside campaign organization, and because some of that money had been donated illegally and secretly, Congress settled on passing yet another campaign finance law.

Washington in 1974 amended the 1971 FECA law to include sweeping new disclosure laws, restrictions on how much money private individuals and independent outfits might contribute to campaigns, and restrictions on how much politicians and parties could spend in elections. It also set up a new body to referee all these disputes—the Federal Election Commission. Campaign finance expert (and onetime FEC commissioner) Brad Smith, in his book *Unfree Speech*, calls FECA "one of the most radical laws ever passed in the United States; for the first time in history, Congress had passed a law requiring citizens to register with the government in order to criticize its office holders."

The Supreme Court wasn't impressed. FECA required the high court to meditate for the first time on the question of money

and speech. Unfortunately, the Court fell for the same political sell-job as most of the nation. In its 1976 *Buckley v. Valeo*
decision—one of the nation's most far-reaching cases—it did
strike down a few important chunks of FECA, including limits on
spending. But it would at the same time give its blessing to one of
the more radical parts of the law—forced disclosure.

In doing so, the Supreme Court undermined the impressive
body of law it had been building protecting political anonymity.
The Court of course referenced its recent prior decisions—
NAACP v. Alabama, *Bates v. Little Rock*. It had to—those decisions
were less than twenty years old. Yet it cleverly wrote around
them, pretending it wasn't undoing anything. The government,
the Court found, had a compelling "interest" in disclosure, on the
grounds that it prevented corruption and that this was necessary
for the "free functioning of our national institutions." Yes, yes,
said the Court, "compelled disclosure" can seriously infringe "on
privacy of association and belief guaranteed by the First Amendment." And yes, yes, it conceded that there could well be a
situation in the future in which that threat is so "serious" that the
new disclosure rules "cannot be constitutionally applied." When
might that moment come? Like pornography, the Court would
know it when it saw it. Supposed victims need only come back
to the judiciary, which would decide the issue on the merits, on a
case-by-case basis.

Even critics of disclosure will point out that the Burger Court
sanctioned only "limited" disclosure in *Buckley v. Valeo*. But it was a
sanctioning nonetheless, and it licensed the political class to think
of yet new ways to track and make public the political activity of
private citizens. It was a big moment.

CHAPTER 4

Fascist Monstrosity

***BUCKLEY* WAS HUGE.** It was overshadowed only by the most modern moment—the one that would create the rules that Bauer would help mold into a new culture of intimidation.

The author of that moment was the son and grandson of four-star admirals. He followed his kin into the U.S. Navy, and in 1967, while on a bombing mission over Hanoi, was shot down and captured by the North Vietnamese. He spent more than five years as a prisoner of war, subjected to brutal torture, yet refused Hanoi's offer to return him home early. He wouldn't step back on U.S. soil until 1973.

John McCain came back to the United States a war hero, a reputation that meant everything to him. When he finally retired from the Navy in 1981, he chose a run for Congress. He spent four years as an Arizona representative in the House, then jumped to the U.S. Senate. And that's when the trouble began.

McCain, starting in his time in the House, had benefited from campaign contributions from a man named Charles Keating Jr., the head of Lincoln Savings and Loan Association. A few months after McCain took his Senate seat, Keating contacted him and four other senators to ask for help in preventing the federal government from seizing his company, which was teetering at the edge of bankruptcy in the savings and loan crisis. McCain met twice with federal regulators to discuss the situation.

The episode blew up into the "Keating Five" scandal, with the accusation that the senators had been bought and had corruptly intervened in federal business on Keating's behalf. The Senate Ethics Committee held embarrassing public hearings and ultimately found that three of the senators had acted improperly. McCain and Senator John Glenn were cleared of wrongdoing but criticized for exercising "poor judgment."

McCain had not been in the Senate for long when the scandal erupted, and it scarred him. The war hero had never been anything but that—a hero—in the public's eye, and here he was enmeshed in what he'd later describe as one long "public humiliation." He'd write that those two meetings were "the worst mistake" of his life.

McCain chose to atone by devoting his Senate career to erecting new finance rules that would make it harder for people to engage in politics. He resented that Keating's donations had put him in a questionable position. It never seemed to occur to the Arizona senator that his problem wasn't the money, but his own actions. Later chronicles of the Keating episode would reveal that McCain had been nervous and troubled all along about attending the meetings or intervening on Keating's behalf. He knew that what he was doing was a problem. He did it anyway. It was, as he admitted, his mistake.

But that didn't stop him from blaming money. Within a few years of his humiliation, McCain had teamed up with Wisconsin Democrat Russ Feingold to introduce in the Senate in 1995 the most sweeping change in political money laws since Nixon and the FECA. McCain had the backing of most Democrats. He'd made the centerpiece of his bill regulations to bar the business community from any meaningful interaction in elections whatsoever. Democrats knew that business mostly supported Republicans, so they adored his approach.

McCain meanwhile also had flanking cover from an array of left-wing foundations and "good government" groups—Common Cause, Democracy 21, the Center for Responsive Politics, the Pew Memorial Trusts. And with the mainstream media running daily stories about the virtues of finance law and "clean" government, the population got behind the cause as well. McCain and Feingold pushed their rock up their hill for seven long years, adding provision after provision with each new version of their bill. By the time the Bipartisan Campaign Reform Act came to the floor in 2002, it contained more ornamental restrictions than a government Christmas tree: new rules on donations; on the definition of ads; on the types of ads groups could run; on the time frame in which they could run them; and on the types of organizations that could participate in elections. It moreover contained breathtaking new disclosure rules—expanding the scope of who was required to report to the federal government, and narrowing the time limit in which this needed to happen. You know the annoying phrase that now comes at the end of every political advertisement: "I'm Joe Blow, and I approve this message"? You can thank John McCain for that.

The bill was hardly a sure thing. McCain aside, most Republicans had grown wary of the finance "reform" craze. Democrats had glommed onto it for all the usual reasons—to handicap Republicans and to improve the party's reputation after the Clinton money scandals. The corporate financial scandals of the late 1990s (Tyco, Enron, Global Crossing) had also put the public in a mood for financial reform of any kind. Republicans, however, were re-remembering their roots as the constitutional party and defenders of free speech, and the McCain bill was over the top. They opposed nearly every element.

Save this: disclosure. Political memories are short, and Watergate had helped politicians to forget the way government had abused disclosure during the McCarthy and civil rights eras. They bought into the idea that more information about political involvement would yield cleaner government. (They had yet to be introduced to the Obama presidency.) This public view played a big role in the Burger Court's decision to sanction disclosure in its *Buckley* decision. Disclosure was already so in vogue that even those who brought the lawsuit against FECA didn't really challenge its disclosure provisions.

Republicans also saw political refuge in disclosure. They knew the public wanted more money regulations (which they opposed), and they didn't want to stand for nothing. So they adopted a new cause: transparency. By the mid-1990s, the stated conservative position was as follows: We should get rid of all government rules on money and speech and replace them with a system of full and instantaneous disclosure. That position allowed the GOP to be in favor of more speech, in favor of "clean" government, and in favor of leaving it to the public (rather than the government) to decide what influence money was having on elections. It sounded good. And in fairness, the left hadn't yet zeroed in on disclosure as an intimidation weapon.

This idea was such a craze that at the height of the reform craze, House whip Tom DeLay and California Republican John Doolittle put forward their own alternative to McCain-Feingold. It proposed lifting existing regulations on political money and replacing the whole shebang with a system of immediate and complete disclosure on the Internet. DeLay was at least honest about the political realities of finance reform, and his own motivations. Democrats, and even some Republicans, continued to pretend they were pushing reform in the name of cleaner elections. The Texas Republican leader called them out, noting that McCain-Feingold was all about silencing certain classes of political participants—namely the business community, which tended to support Republicans "I am for full disclosure. I am for instant disclosure," said DeLay. "But I am not for unilateral disarmament."

Democrats sensed the public tide on their side and slammed

the proposal. The *New Republic* wrote about the DeLay-Doolittle legislation under the headline "Cynics United." The left nicknamed the bill "do little and delay." DeLay-Doolittle never did get a vote. And it would come under retrospective ridicule when DeLay a few years later was indicted in a finance probe. But the bill mattered. It staked out for years the conservative position on campaign finance: disclosure, disclosure, disclosure. That position would last right up to the point at which the right's grassroots supporters became IRS quarry.

Not every conservative fell for it, though, even in the early days. In 1996, a little-known faculty member at Capital University Law School in Columbus, Ohio, by the name of Brad Smith published an article in the *Yale Law Journal* under the title "Faulty Assumptions." Smith laid out a precise and damning critique of campaign finance laws. They were based on incorrect beliefs about the effect of money in politics, and they inspired perverse consequences, he wrote. The article, and his follow-up book, *Unfree Speech*, turned him into a nationally recognized free-speech expert. He became a fixture at congressional hearings; his voluminous writings worked their way into judicial decisions.

Mostly, Smith became a guiding influence on the conservative turn against political-speech laws. Senate Republican leader Mitch McConnell, one of Congress's most ardent free-speech defenders, would ultimately send Smith's name to the Clinton White House as a GOP choice for the FEC. The academic was by then so controversial that the left staged near-riotous objections to the nomination, and the confirmation process dragged on and on. When he finally got a vote, in May 2000, thirty-four Democrats (and John McCain) voted no in protest. The *New York Times* would begrudgingly title him the "intellectual powerhouse" behind the conservative movement's new effort to deregulate finance laws. His opponents—including Democrats and so-called good-government groups—immediately despised him, deriding him as a "flat-earth society poohbah." One editorial

page would liken him to David Duke, the Unabomber, and Slo-
bodan Milošević—all in the same article.

That's amusing, because Smith is the furthest thing from a Ser-
bian dictator. He's from Michigan, and he has that understated
midwestern thing going on. He's a law professor, and he looks the
part. He has a wry sense of humor. (Underappreciated fact: Some
of the quirkiest people in America are campaign finance lawyers.)
Smith's particular gift, however—and what makes Democrats
dislike him so—is his ability to use uncomfortable realities in
crafting his arguments, and to then make those arguments in ways
that average people can understand.

Smith's early criticisms of campaign finance laws are now the
standard case against "reform": The laws protect incumbents;
they lock out new entrants to the political scene; they force candidates to spend all hours of the day and night fund-raising (rather
than governing); they reduce political accountability; they kill
free speech. They are inherently unfair; they give vast rights to
the press, but deny them to average Americans. They are ineffec-
tual; money always finds a way, and the laws drive it to darker
places. What particularly drove the left doolally about Smith
was his ability to blow up their most basic arguments. The "re-
formers": Money in politics is corrupting. Smith: How can it be
corrupting to spend money to try to convince someone to vote a
certain way? Isn't that just democracy?

What was most notable about Smith's work—even his earliest
tracts—was his skepticism of disclosure laws. Most Republicans
didn't buy into his cautionary note; disclosure was their political
cover, and they were sticking with it. Even other conservative
scholars didn't agree; disclosure simply sounded too good. His
wariness would nonetheless prove justified, and in the wake of the
IRS and other targeting, he's only grown in his belief that, as he
tells me, "there should be a very heavy burden on anybody who
wants to invade your political privacy."

When Smith talks about disclosure, he likes to reference that

McIntyre decision of 1995. "You've got to think about this in context, not legal speak," he says. Here is an average mom just trying to raise the alarm about a school tax. "Which means she is a person whose kids could easily face retaliation from teachers who don't appreciate a parent opposed to more school funding," he says. Smith is himself the child of two teachers, and grew up understanding how vindictive the profession can be. "Those kids might have trouble getting references for college; they might be punished in band, or chess club, or in their athletics. There's a whole bunch of reasons, in a public school, that you don't want to be known as the kid whose parent is leading the charge against the tax increase."

And the *McIntyre* case, Smith adds, was about vindictiveness. School officials knew exactly who had distributed the flyer; it is how they were able to file a complaint against McIntyre with the Ohio Elections Commission in the first place. There was no "disclosure" problem. "The complaint was instead filed to send a message to others to not do the same thing," says Smith. "Is that what we want disclosure laws used for?"

As an FEC commissioner, Smith saw up close and in person the ways that disclosure discouraged political speech. He also saw how the burdens always fell disproportionately on the little guys—folks like Karen Kenney. Corporate America and powerful political groups hire teams of lawyers to walk the right side of the law. But the average American has no such legal adviser, and their hardest area of compliance is disclosure. "Even small, grassroots groups, they generally understand the big rules. There is an easy cheat sheet for them to follow," says Smith. "But the disclosure forms are insanely complex. Nobody can get them right."

Conservatives are fortunate to have had a string of distinguished free-speech advocates at the FEC, including one who immediately followed Smith, Hans von Spakovsky. Von Spakovsky worked years in the Justice Department before serving at the FEC as a commissioner in 2006 and 2007. He remembers his own first realization that conservatives had made a mistake in embracing disclosure. The FEC was contacted by a woman who had given a contribution to a political candidate whom animal rights groups detested. Those groups tracked down her name with disclosure forms and started harassing her. "She wanted her name off these public lists, so they'd leave her alone," he recalls. "We evaluated it, but there was nothing we could do under the law. And that was one of the first times I saw the really bad purposes to which disclosure laws could be put. They sound innocuous, but there are all kinds of things that are innocuous until they are used in a bad way. Say, box cutters."

The problem is that disclosure and finance laws have become an article of faith for much of America, particularly liberals. Smith remembers getting in an elevator at the 2000 Republican convention and discovering himself in the company of the liberal Al Hunt, then a *Wall Street Journal* columnist. Hunt had written critically of Smith during his nomination to the FEC. Smith recalls that after a few seconds of polite chitchat, Hunt proclaimed that it didn't matter that Smith had recently been confirmed, because the FEC never did anything useful anyway. Smith disagreed; the FEC played an enormous (often terrible) role. He attempted to explain to Hunt that he'd met many average Americans who were "scared to death" of the FEC and of running afoul of its scary laws, and that this discouraged them from taking part in politics. By the end of the elevator ride, Smith remembers, Hunt was screaming at him—and the conservative law professor had learned something about the depths of liberal love for finance regulation.

(I felt obliged in our interview to break it to Smith that his elevator ride wasn't all that special. When I was a young editor for the *Wall Street Journal* editorial page, one of my first jobs was editing Hunt's weekly column. Hunt is a jolly, warm, and smart man, and I always enjoyed our weekly talks. He's also known for a short fuse, and another of my jobs was to submit to the occasional Hunt scream-fest. It was my first lesson in hanging up on someone. To Al's credit, he'd often follow these up with a wine-and-cheese basket, sent by way of apology. As a young and poorly paid staffer at that time, I occasionally joked whether, in moments of low funds, it might be worth provoking Al into a temper.)

Smith points out that you also don't have to be the average unknown citizen to feel intimidated. He himself is a respected academic, operating in a world of higher education that rarely practices the tolerance it preaches to its students. He ticks off the long list of ways that a university can make life difficult for a professor who practices the "wrong" politics. Want tenure? You may not get it. Want that deanship? Not likely. Want to teach a particular class? They may say no. Want more money in your department? Not possible. And the insidious part is that schools and faculties can access that disclosure information on the sly and make those judgments without ever admitting to them. "How do you even know when you are getting harassed?" notes Smith. "How do you know what jobs you didn't get because of your political views?" Smith admits that even he at times has limited his political contributions to $199, just short of the enforced disclosure limit. "I'm a pretty tough guy. I like to think I meet Scalia's standard for 'courage.' I've made a career of saying what I think, and standing by it. But there are times when I know a donation might disturb a social relationship I have, or a case that I'm working on, or a situation with an organization I'm connected to. Some people want to preserve family harmony; or they don't want their neighbors to know what they are worth; or they don't want their kids passed over for the varsity team. And that's the point: There are all kinds of reasons why people, in different circumstances, might not want to broadcast their politics. What right has the government to force them to do so?" A lot of the intimidation is subtle, but Smith muses that it is only a matter of time before disclosure leads to deadly retribution—say the bombing or shooting of a pro–abortion rights or anti–gay marriage financial contributor.

Smith's other insight at the FEC: the degree to which disclosure is the hook for yet more speech laws. "It's standard operating procedure for the pro-regulation crowd," he explains. "They will say, 'Well, we just need to know what this group or that group is doing.' But once they have that information they will say, 'Look, how bad it is what this group and that group are doing! We need more rules and regulations to stop it.' And that's how you end up with the insane system we have today."

∿

Smith became one of Washington's loudest opponents of McCain-Feingold, an archnemesis to John McCain, and a big reason why the legislation barely passed the Senate. Among his predictions was that the law—the most massive and complex juggernaut of regulations yet—would set off an unprecedented round of political jockeying, as the dueling parties tried to game the new system to their electoral benefit. In this, too, he was right. Washington had done the Tillman Act, Smith-Connally, Taft-Hartley, FECA. But it was McCain-Feingold that laid the groundwork for a new era of political brutality, one that led directly to the left's new tactics and the modern intimidation game.

President Bush signed the law on March 27, 2002. Bush had publicly said that he thought parts of the law were unconstitutional, yet he feared a public hammering if he vetoed it. So he signed—a sin for which many free-speech advocates have never forgiven him. The new rules weren't set to kick in until 2003, but well before that Democrats and Republicans geared up to manipulate the law.

Democrats pushed the bill because they hoped it would resonate with the public and help against opponents. But savvier party members were outright terrified that it would all go wrong.

This was the clear-eyed crowd that knew, for all its complaints about big, shadowy money in politics, that the left had long been far more dependent on it than the right. McCain-Feingold essentially outlawed it, and therefore potentially gave Republicans—who thrived on small donations—a big advantage in the upcoming 2004 presidential race.

In a 2003 piece by Seth Gitell in the *Atlantic* entitled "The Democratic Party Suicide Bill," Joseph Sandler, counsel to the Democratic National Committee, said what few other Democrats were willing to say. The law was "a fascist monstrosity." He continued, "It is grossly offensive . . . and on a fundamental level it's horrible public policy. . . . And it's a disaster for the Democrats. Other than that, it's great." Bauer, at that time a counsel to the Democratic Senatorial and Congressional Campaign Committees (which exist to elect and reelect Democrats to Congress), also made the rounds, warning party leaders that they needed a plan.

They had one pretty quickly. For decades, the IRS code had allowed Americans to create tax-exempt political groups known as 527s. These groups could accept unlimited donations, so long as they didn't coordinate with campaigns and focused solely on issues. The political parties and their operatives had never been much interested in them, since the parties had always been able to raise plenty of money in their own right. But McCain-Feingold severely cracked down on party fund-raising. It hadn't, however, imposed nearly as many restrictions on 527s. Suddenly, every Democrat and their dog was setting one up. And all that big money the party had traditionally relied on flowed into them. George Soros, the billionaire liberal financier, in the space of three months had dumped more than $15 million into three 527 groups—the Media Fund, Americans Coming Together (ACT), and MoveOn.org. He'd ultimately give more than $23 million in the cycle to 527s. Peter Lewis, the owner of the Progressive insurance company, threw that much again at groups set up by Big Labor and trial lawyers.

President Bush's financial advantage rapidly began to shrink. The GOP might have tried matching the Democrats with 527 money. Instead, Republicans became the first in the McCain-Feingold era to (unforgivably) call in the forces of government to silence their opponents. They went running to the FEC, demanding that the campaign finance umpire devise a new rule that would explicitly extend the big-money ban to 527s. Eighty percent of congressional Republicans had voted against McCain-Feingold on free-speech principles, yet in the face of an electoral shellacking those principles went out the Capitol window.

Sitting as chairman of the FEC at that time was none other than Smith. The professor and his two Republican colleagues on the commission knew that Republicans, and the White House in particular, desperately wanted restrictions placed on the 527s. But to the GOP's absolute fury, Smith refused to abandon his free-speech principles and essentially declined to silence the groups. He was publicly scathing about the Republicans' hypocrisy and their attempts to use a law they supposedly hated to cripple their opponents. "If Republicans think they can win by silencing their opposition, they are wrong and they are going to deserve to lose," he said. Democrats crowed over the victory, with Jim Jordan, the spokesman for both the Media Fund and ACT, telling the *Washington Post* that the FEC's decision meant his groups would charge into the election operating "robustly and effectively." The media, unsurprisingly, largely failed to point out that it was Democrats who'd wanted all these new rules, and yet were celebrating the continued use of "big money." Smith earned himself short-term enmity from the right. And he earned no credit from the left, which still viewed him as the enemy.

The operating words here are "short-term." For it happens that even as the FEC and Republicans were duking it out, a retired rear admiral by the name of Roy Hoffmann had himself discovered the merits of a 527. Hoffmann patrolled the Mekong Delta on Swift Boats during the Vietnam War. In early 2004, historian Douglas Brinkley published *Tour of Duty*, an account of Senator John Kerry's "heroic" Vietnam service. Hoffmann read it. He didn't like it. He remembered Kerry criticizing his fellow servicemen in the 1970s when he was spokesman for Vietnam Veterans Against the War.

Mr. Hoffmann started calling fellow Vietnam veterans. The result was Swift Boat Veterans for Truth (SBVT), a 527 group that would receive generous conservative funding. SBVT launched a campaign against Kerry's presidential bid, with hundreds of Swift Boat sailors signing a statement accusing the nominee of both distorting the conduct of his fellow servicemen and overstating his own contribution to the war. The group would continue to go after Kerry, publishing a book and running extensive advertising hitting him in swing presidential states during the campaign. The allegations caused a firestorm for the Democrat, who spent no small amount of time attempting to rebut the claims. And this time it was Democrats who went running to the FEC; liberal groups like Democracy 21 filed complaints with the FEC, as did the Kerry campaign itself. (The Bush campaign, for the record, also filed complaints about left-wing 527s. Tit for tat.)

John Kerry lost the 2004 election, for a myriad of reasons, of which the Swift Boat allegations were but one. Democrats knew Kerry's many flaws, but they needed someone or something to blame for his defeat, and they latched on to SBVT. Conveniently forgetting that Kerry had benefited immensely from their own well-funded 527 groups, the liberal left decried SBVT as a return of big and ugly money in politics, a skirt-around of all their carefully crafted finance rules.

It's worth noting the depths to which Democrats internalized SBVT as their downfall in 2004. They turned the organization into a verb, referring to any political attack that they viewed as unfair as "swiftboating." They particularly resented the nature of the attack. Democrats had banked that Kerry, as a veteran, would prove a shield against the public perception that Democrats were weak on national security, especially after 9/11. And they were furious that Republicans had outmatched them in the 527 game, which they'd carefully nurtured as their path to the White House. Years later, the bitterness lingered. When Bush in 2007 nominated naval veteran and businessman Sam Fox as ambassador to Belgium, Kerry led Democrats in a filibuster. Connecticut senator Chris Dodd would spit that he could never give approval to Fox because of his "unwillingness to express regret for providing $50,000 to bankroll" SBVT. In Dodd's view, Fox's willingness to participate in an election made him unfit to represent the world's greatest democracy.

SBVT received financial contributions from well over fifty thousand Americans, mostly in small amounts. Democrats nonetheless obsessed on the contributions from a handful of wealthy Republican donors, including Houston builder Bob Perry, oil baron T. Boone Pickens, and businessman Harold Simmons. Soros had single-handedly given more to Democratic 527 groups than all three of those conservatives combined had given to SBVT. But there's no accounting for a political party scorned.

So they determined it wouldn't happen again. Democrats had a good 2006 midterm election; they took control of the House (the first time since 1994), the Senate, and a majority of governorships. The GOP flailed against an unpopular war, congressional scandals, and the perception that it had lost its ability to effectively govern.

~~~

The country slid into the 2008 elections. The Democratic Party, and especially its newest force, Barack Obama, wasn't taking any chances.

Enter Bauer—who wasn't taking any chances with Republicans or Democrats. His attack on the Clinton group during the primary caught a lot of headlines, but it wasn't the first time the

Obama maestro pulled this trick. Very early in the primaries, when North Carolina senator John Edwards looked to be a potent force, Bauer took his first steps toward using finance intimidation against an opponent.

It was late December 2007, and Edwards was riding an unexpected surge in the Iowa polls. He was helped by a lot of positive airtime from 527 groups, one (the Alliance for a New America) run by a former Edwards campaign manager and another funded by the big carpenters' union. In a memo released five days before the primary, Obama campaign manager David Plouffe took aim at both. Under the title "Flood of Washington Money in Iowa," Plouffe slammed the "underhanded" financial support. He berated Edwards for exploiting loopholes and hinted that the groups were breaking finance laws. The goal of Plouffe's memo was twofold: to send a warning shot to the 527s, and to make Obama look pure by comparison (no 527s were supporting him in Iowa). Obama had already joined in the attack, criticizing what he called "huge, unregulated contributions from special interests" and accusing Edwards of trying to get around finance laws. Obama ended up winning the caucuses decisively. Edwards collapsed, and dropped out of the race a few weeks later.

With Edwards out, Bauer trained his fire on Clinton and her own 527 support. The whole campaign joined in. "News broke yesterday that a few wealthy Clinton supporters are gearing up for a massive spending campaign to boost her chances in the big upcoming contests in Texas and Ohio on March 4th," Plouffe wrote in a February fund-raising e-mail. Knowing how scarred many Democratic voters still were over the Kerry experience, Plouffe took care to blow the dog whistle. "The so-called 'American Leadership Project' will take unlimited contributions from individuals and is organized the same way as the infamous Swift Boat Veterans for Truth." Bauer would repeat the accusation, calling ALP a "Swift-boat wannabee." And he issued his threats to haul the group in front of Justice and the FEC.

All of this was designed to scare off ALP's donors, and the initial attack nearly worked. The ads that ALP planned for Texas and Ohio didn't appear for days, and then only after some funding from a large union came through. The threat was particularly rich given that Obama was in these states benefiting from significant independent help himself. The Service Employees International Union (SEIU) had moved to his camp, and was spending some $1.4 million to support his candidacy in Ohio and Texas. A separate 527, the Fund for America, bankrolled (yet again) by George Soros, was pouring money into ads attacking John McCain on his behalf.

Bauer's threats against ALP nonetheless did scare donors, and he'd continue to play the finance card to Obama's advantage, lambasting "special interest" money even as his boss gained from it. Obama would go so far as to use 527s as an excuse to break his own promise to abide by the presidential public financing system; he was the first presidential candidate of a major party ever to opt out. "The public financing of presidential elections as it exists today is broken, and we face opponents who've become masters at gaming this broken system," Obama would declare in June 2008. "John McCain's campaign and the Republican National Committee are fueled by contributions from Washington lobbyists and special-interest PACs. And we've already seen that he's not going to stop the smears and attacks from his allies running so-called 527 groups, who will spend millions and millions of dollars in unlimited donations." Democrats would also benefit from "millions and millions of dollars in unlimited donations," though the press largely failed to note it. And McCain himself stayed in the presidential financing system.

Hillary Clinton's supporters railed against the Bauer attacks. They were floored, and somewhat disgusted, that Bauer would stoop to a Swift Boat characterization of her groups, or that he'd go so far as to threaten her donors with prosecution. But as the primary ended and the party healed, the entire left realized the power of Bauer-like threats and the potential they held to handi-cap Republicans.

One guy paying attention was Tom Matzzie, a committed lib-eral political activist. Matzzie's background gave him insight into the power of money and ways to stop it. From 2000 to 2004 he worked as the online mobilization director for the giant AFL-CIO union, building an Internet army of labor activists. He shifted to director of online organization for the Kerry/Edwards campaign in 2004, where he saw up close the Swift Boat attacks. He then moved to Washington director for MoveOn.org, the liberal on-line mobilization group. He also ran a group called Americans Against Escalation in Iraq, and is credited with raising more than $150 million for various causes.

In August 2008 he founded a new group called Accountable America. As the *New York Times* reported, the organization had but one purpose: to put Republican donors on notice. Matzzie explained that his group intended to send a "warning" letter to ten thousand GOP donors, alerting them, as the *Times* put it, to "a variety of potential dangers, including legal trouble, public ex-posure, and watchdog groups digging into their lives." The *Times* noted that the goal was to "create a chilling effect that will dry up contributions" for the GOP side. Matzzie told the liberal publica-tion *Mother Jones* (in a quote eerily reminiscent of Bauer's), "We're going to put them at risk." He also offered a $100,000 reward to anyone who could gin up a credible civil or criminal case against a conservative independent group.

Matzzie was able to come up with his list of ten thousand GOP donors because of disclosure laws. In the age of the Internet, Matzzie could have his list in a few hours.

And his threats were an escalation of even Bauer's. Like the Obama counsel, he suggested that donors might face prosecu-tion. But he took the warning to a new level, explaining that the left intended to make Republican donors the targets of public smear campaigns—poking into their lives, elevating their pro-

files, making the world difficult for them. In the gradual escalation of the intimidation campaign, this was a moment.

Meanwhile, Bauer himself was only getting started. He'd tried
out his tactics on Edwards and Clinton, and they'd largely been
successful. As the Obama campaign moved into the general election, he honed that strategy against John McCain.

Around the time Matzzie announced his intent to harass GOP
donors, a conservative group, a 501(c)(4) organization called the
American Issues Project (AIP), went on the air against Barack
Obama. The organization highlighted the Chicago politician's ties
with Bill Ayers, the former Weather Underground member who
went to jail for helping bomb the New York City Police Department, the Pentagon, and the Capitol. AIP was partly funded by
Harold Simmons, one of the same men who'd given money to
Swift Boat Veterans for Truth.

The Obama campaign was livid, and demanded, as is common
practice in campaigns, that TV stations pull the ad. Bauer announced that Team Obama would in fact organize supporters to
target every station that ran the ads, as well as their advertisers.
The campaign mobilized its supporters in particular to go after
Sinclair Broadcasting Group, which had dared to run a documentary in 2004 critical of Kerry. Obama spokesman Tommy Vietor
bragged that Obama supporters had slammed Sinclair stations
with ninety-three thousand e-mails calling for the ad to come
down. Some outlets, like CNN, succumbed to the pressure.

Bauer went much further. He sent a letter to the criminal division of the Justice Department demanding an investigation into
AIP, "its officers and directors," and its "anonymous donors." He
claimed the AIP project was a "knowing and willful attempt to violate the strictures of federal election law," and wanted "action to
enforce against criminal violations."

AIP patiently explained to Justice why it was not in violation,
noting that it operated exactly in the same fashion as dozens of
liberal groups such as NARAL Pro-Choice America. It pointed

out that it had willingly disclosed its donor, Harold Simmons. Bauer's response was a second letter calling for the direct prosecution of the Texas businessman. He sent a third letter on September 8, again calling for action, again slamming AIP's "illegal electoral purpose."

On the same day, he went to the FEC, demanding that the regulator do something about AIP and Simmons. He also went to the IRS seeking tax documents (to which he had a public right). And he sent a letter directly to AIP hounding it for confidential information (to which he had no legal right). Outside liberal groups piled on, with Democracy 21 filing its own FEC complaint against AIP.

AIP didn't take down its ads. It had the counsel of one of Washington's most hard-charging and effective free-speech lawyers, Cleta Mitchell. But Bauer's effort nonetheless had an effect. A long-ranging one, as it happens.

The Justice Department never did prosecute AIP. Mr. Simmons never backed away from his donations. But the FEC did take note of Bauer's complaint.

Months after the election was over, after Barack Obama was already sitting in the White House, activist FEC attorneys sent an e-mail to an IRS official requesting that she share "any information" she had about the conservative organization the American Issues Project. A mere nine minutes after receiving the inquiry, that IRS official directed her staff to fulfill the request.

Her name was Lois Lerner.

CHAPTER 5

The Big Banana

LARRY TRIBE is a very smart man. So when the liberal Harvard law professor pronounces, a lot of folk on his side pay attention. Quite a few were reading raptly what Tribe had to say on January 24, 2010.

The left had just suffered an enormous political blow. Three days earlier, the Supreme Court had issued its opinion in *Citizens United*, knocking down a central plank of McCain-Feingold. That finance law had restricted corporations from endorsing candidates in broadcast ads in the run-up to elections. Five justices found this a clear abuse of the First Amendment and struck down those rules.

The president and his party went bonkers. For more than a decade they'd worked to shut up their corporate nemeses, and John McCain had finally got them over the finish line. They'd privately credited the law with aiding in their stunning election victories in 2008. Barack Obama had crushed McCain in fundraising, and the Democratic congressional election committees had stomped all over their Republican counterparts. The best measure of the law's success, from the Democrats' perspective, was the final tallies of spending from independent groups. Liberal organizations had vastly outspent conservative ones. Shutting up business had been worth the legislative struggle.

And now here was the Supreme Court, undoing all that hard work. Within hours of the ruling, Obama was scolding the justices: "The Supreme Court has given a green light to a new stampede of special interest money in our politics," the president said. "It is a major victory for big oil, Wall Street banks, health insurance companies and the other powerful interests that marshal their power every day in Washington to drown out the voices of everyday Americans." Obama would a few weeks later, at a nationally televised State of the Union address, again publicly rebuke the Supreme Court justices sitting in the audience.

Democratic representative Chris Van Hollen joined Obama to complain that the decision would "allow the biggest corporations in the United States to engage in the buying and selling of elections." The press largely failed to note that Van Hollen ran the Democratic Congressional Campaign Committee, the group charged with electing and reelecting Democrats to the House. Van Hollen knew all about the "buying and selling" of elections, and was frustrated that the price of his buying had gone up.

His outrage was matched only by that of New York senator Charles Schumer, who had only just left the top job of electing and reelecting Senate Democrats. The decision was "poisonous to our democracy," he complained. The Schumers and Van Hollens were given covering fire from a phalanx of left-leaning groups. Fred Wertheimer of the campaign finance reform organization Democracy 21 pronounced the decision to be nothing less than "a disaster for the American people."

It didn't matter to Democrats that the Court had in its ruling also freed up their union allies to reengage in elections. Democrats knew that (at least at this time in history) labor unions mattered more in terms of people than in money. They were the boots on the ground, the folks who knocked on doors. Nor did it matter to Democrats that the Court had left in place the long-standing ban on corporations contributing money directly to candidates. (All the *Citizens* ruling did was allow companies to run their own endorsements of candidates in the run-up to an election.)

At least some liberal commentators were honest about why they were so annoyed—and it had nothing to do with clean elections. Jeffrey Toobin, the legal affairs writer for the *New Yorker* magazine, gave his immediate reaction to the ruling: "Two thoughts. First, Republicans will benefit, of course. Corporations have vastly more money than unions and corporations by and large prefer to support the G.O.P." Toobin consoled himself that perhaps companies might face consumer boycotts if they spent too much money in support of "Barack Obama's opponent in 2012."

But what most worried the left about the ruling was the political climate. In August of the prior year, Democrats had gone home for summer break to face a tsunami of outrage over Obamacare. Public anger hit breaking point in the late fall, as both the House and Senate passed versions of the bill. And then in January, Republican Scott Brown won a special election to the Senate in deep-blue Massachusetts. Democrats saw in that GOP victory in Massachusetts the makings of an electoral revolt that might sweep them back out of Congress, and perhaps out of the White House. Two days later, the high court issued *Citizens United*, turning Democratic worry into panic.

The question, though: What to do? The parties had dueled over campaign finance law for generations, each side using "reforms" to lard more restrictions on their political opponents. The courts had largely gone along with the exercise, unwilling to buck public sentiment. Yet now the Supremes had found a constitutional right for companies and unions and independent political groups to speak freely in elections. It was an expansive decision. And that meant the tool that professional politicians had relied on for so long—the outright silencing of political speech via government regulation—was no longer at their disposal.

"The left found itself at a high-water mark in 2010; it had

knocked completely out of public discourse most of the free-market voices out there. It hadn't needed intimidation or retaliation, because it had simply censored the other side," says Lee Goodman, one of the current Republicans on the Federal Election Commission. "Then came *Citizens United*, and it couldn't censor outright anymore." Goodman continues, "Of course, the left didn't give up on the idea; it just realized it had to be far more creative about suppressing speech. And so it moved to plan B, which was to find other levers of government power to eliminate unwanted viewpoints."

Tribe, in his article that appeared just a few days after the ruling on the popular *SCOTUSblog*, partly laid out that plan B. The law professor offered some fairly dry legal analysis of the decision, before moving on to the meat of his proposal. Companies that engage in elections, explained Tribe, were doing so with "other people's money"—that of shareholders. That justified the federal government's passing legislation to help shareholders "ensure that his or her investment is not deployed to advance or obstruct the election of particular candidates to federal (or indeed, state) office contrary both to that shareholder's own wishes and, more importantly in this context, to the corporation's business interests." At the very minimum, said Tribe, Congress should dramatically beef up "disclosure and disclaimer requirements" forcing CEOs to have to publicly explain in each ad how much money was being used, and how it supposedly helped the company. And that, explained Tribe, would be as good as a ban: The process of requiring companies to go public would embarrass them out of participating.

Cut out the legal jargon, and Tribe was advocating something extremely simple: humiliation. Force companies to have to justify their speech, and bet that this would intimidate them out of doing so. The Tribe prescription was an amplification of Toobin's thought on boycotts. Companies live in fear of shareholder or customer backlash. So the left needed to pass enhanced disclosure laws that would make companies fear that backlash. And those disclosure laws would, as a bonus, give Democrats more information, allowing them to go after specific businesses and damage their reputation if they came out for the wrong side.

Tribe's essay wasn't novel. It was more the public announcement of a strategy that had been in the works for months. Democrats had always understood that the Court might rule against them in *Citizens*, and they'd been preparing a response. That's why President Obama, just hours after the decision, announced that he was telling his administration "to get to work immediately with Congress on this issue. We are going to talk with bipartisan congressional leaders to develop a forceful response to this decision. The public interest requires nothing less." Obama already knew what that response would be.

∿

When Ted Olson looks back, he wishes he'd focused a bit more on the disclosure question. But hindsight is always 20/20 and—at least at the time—what he was understandably focused on is what he calls "the big banana." That "big banana" was the limits on corporate participation in elections. Olson argued the case on behalf of the free-speech contingent, and is one of a handful of brave souls who can take credit for the Court's striking down those limitations.

One of Washington's more high-profile lawyers, Olson was an interesting choice for the assignment. George W. Bush tapped him at the beginning of his first term as solicitor general. Bush's signature on McCain-Feingold set off a series of court fights, and Olson successfully and dutifully defended parts of the law on the president's behalf in 2003. Only six months later he returned to private practice at the respected firm of Gibson, Dunn & Crutcher, where he rejoined the ranks of free-speech warriors.

Americans think most Supreme Court cases are happenstance.

Some random citizen—a Margaret McIntyre—suffers an injustice, and her case slowly wends its way to the highest court in the land, where precedent is set. That does happen. But just as often, cases are engineered. Dedicated lawyers and activists look at laws and identify potential challenges. They pick through scenarios and attempt to create a situation—a set of circumstances—that forces courts to act. That was the history of *Citizens United*.

David Bossie came of political age in the Clinton scandal years, joining a conservative nonprofit called Citizens United. He spent a number of years doggedly researching the shady financial practices of the Clintons, and became the group's president in 2000.

Bossie ultimately turned Citizens United into a movie studio, devoted to conservative documentaries that might aid in elections. He wasn't the first to come up with the idea. Liberal filmmaker Michael Moore had created *Fahrenheit 9/11*, his hit job on George W. Bush's war on terror, with the aim of influencing the 2004 presidential race. He debuted it five months before election day, and publicly admitted that his goal was to energize anti-Bush forces and increase turnout for John Kerry. Moore's documentary was technically a movie—covered completely by the First Amendment—yet every time a thirty-second promotion for it ran on TV, it was the functional equivalent of a campaign ad.

Bossie noticed. He reached out to James Bopp Jr., a lawyer who'd made a reputation forcing the Supreme Court to confront the free-speech hypocrisies of campaign finance law. He'd already helped strike down part of McCain-Feingold. Bopp ended up working with Bossie on *Hillary: The Movie*, an exposé of the former First Lady's business dealings and checkered political past. Under Bopp's guidance, the documentary team took special care to craft the script in a way that would challenge several provisions of McCain-Feingold, including its ban (by companies, unions, and outside groups) on issue ads in the run-up to an election, as well as its disclosure regime. And then Citizens United prepared to roll it out in 2007, to tie it to the presidential election and force the constitutional question.

"The movie was designed to highlight the absurdity of this law," says Bopp, who works out of Indiana. "We started out with a big advantage in this case—we had the law on our side. 'Congress shall make no law'—that's a command, not a suggestion. How can a movie about Hillary be legal, but an ad about the movie not be?"

Citizens United went straight to the FEC to get a ruling, and, unsurprisingly, the FEC ruled that it was in essence an election ad, barred by McCain-Feingold. The group appealed it up, and a federal court upheld the bar on running any TV ads or video-on-demand. When it came time to argue it to the Supreme Court, Bossie enlisted Olson, who he knew held a stellar track record in front of the high court.

Olson felt that the best way to win the case was to keep it focused on that "big banana"—the basic question of free speech. So he narrowed the scope. "We were thinking about disclosure, because it was also an issue in this situation. There was an important point about just how much disclosure this little group ought to be forced to do under McCain-Feingold, and would they be harassed or intimidated," he recalls. "But we really wanted to win on the unconstitutionality of restricting the use of money and speech per se, and we were worried if we took too much time in the [Supreme Court] briefing on the disclosure point, we'd weaken our ability to get that big banana."

Olson also (wisely) bet that the Court would want a "fallback"—a way to soften the blow of the decision. And he bet that that fallback might be the Court's full embrace of the law's disclosure regime. He couldn't have been more correct. The decision, written by Justice Anthony Kennedy, was bold on the free-speech point. The Court had spent years coddling the finance-restriction crowd, but the Citizens case highlighted too many inconsistencies. So five justices took a strong stance on the

First Amendment, restoring the rights of many groups to take part in elections. At the same time, *all* the justices knew that the decision would be met with a firestorm, and most wanted political cover. Their "fallback"—to use Olson's word—was to hail McCain-Feingold's disclosure rules. Kennedy even argued that those disclosure provisions were what had allowed the Court to more fully embrace free speech. "The First Amendment protects political speech; and disclosure permits citizens and shareholders to react to the speech of corporate entities in a proper way. This transparency enables the electorate to make informed decisions and give proper weight to different speakers and messages." Eight of the justices would ultimately join in the part of the decision upholding disclosure.

Olson still thinks it was the correct call at the time, and he's right. "It was a tactical thing; we didn't put a lot of energy or enthusiasm into the disclosure question," he says. "And remember, this was a moment at which a lot of people on the conservative side of the spectrum embraced that view. Their argument to the left was, 'Why are you complaining about more free speech? If we just have disclosure, everything will be open, and that is the remedy.'"

But subsequent events changed most conservatives' view on disclosure, including his own. "It is something that maybe we'd do differently today, given all that has come since. It wasn't too important at the time to the folks at Citizens United, although we all have become a lot more focused on it over time. We are all now realizing that this can be a very potent weapon to intimidate people or discourage them from participating in democracy. It's a huge threat."

The one brave soul on the Court to dissent would be—once again—Clarence Thomas. His scathing takedown of the law's disclosure regime, and his worries over its ramifications, today read like an eerie road map of what ultimately would come.

"The disclosure, disclaimer, and reporting requirements in

[McCain-Feingold] are also unconstitutional," Thomas bluntly began, pointing out that the Court had backed the idea of anonymous speech as recently as the *McIntyre* case. He chided his colleagues for ignoring briefs filed as part of *Citizens United* that illustrated how disclosure was already causing donors to be "blacklisted, threatened, or otherwise targeted for retaliation." Political operatives weren't just using disclosure to punish citizens for their donations, but were wielding it to close off speech before it even happened. As Thomas wrote, the "success of such intimidation tactics has apparently spawned a cottage industry that uses forcibly disclosed donor information to *pre-empt* citizens' exercise of their First Amendment rights." He made special note of the Matzzie letter warning off donors in the 2008 election.

Thomas then predicted another problem. It was bad enough, he noted, that citizens were using disclosure to threaten and retaliate against each other. But his colleagues needed to consider that transparency might ultimately prove a weapon in the hands of a more menacing power—government. In what is surely the first and last time I will ever be mentioned in a Supreme Court decision, Thomas referenced a column I'd written about West Virginia attorney general Darrell McGraw. McGraw had terrorized his state's business community, filing questionable lawsuits against them. The AG doled out the work for these cases to his trial bar buddies, who in return funneled huge amounts of their state-provided contingency fees to McGraw's reelection. An upstart Republican lawyer named Dan Greear in 2008 boldly chose to challenge the fourteen-year incumbent Democrat for his seat, but quickly ran up against a fund-raising problem. Businesses feared donating to Greear, because McGraw would know about it. As I quoted Greear at the time, "I go to so many people and hear the same thing: 'I sure hope you beat him, but I can't afford to have my name on your records. He might come after me next.'" Thomas summed up, "Disclaimer and disclosure requirements enable private citizens and elected officials to implement political strategies *specifically calculated* to curtail campaign-related activity and prevent the lawful, peaceful exercise of First Amendment rights."

Thomas meanwhile disagreed with the majority's claim that the Court could guard against any free-speech abuses that arose from more disclosure. The eight justices in favor of the transparency provisions again argued in their *Citizens* decision that any American subject to harassment need only come to the Court, which could—on a case-by-case basis—suspend disclosure. This was the majority's way of claiming it hadn't overruled its prior decisions on anonymity. It was still in favor of political anonymity, it said, so long as there was a good reason for it.

But as Thomas pointed out, the majority had wrapped itself in a pretzel. It had hailed the Internet and immediate disclosure as a good thing for democracy, and a reason to allow companies and unions to again participate. Yet that "prompt disclosure," said Thomas, meant political opponents had the ability to immediately intimidate and retaliate against their foes. The "improper" use of the information would happen "long before" a plaintiff could get a court to intervene. The harm would already be done. As Thomas rang out in closing, "I cannot endorse a view of the First Amendment that subjects citizens of this Nation to death threats, ruined careers, damaged or defaced property, or preemptive and threatening warning letters as the price for engaging in 'core political speech, the primary object of First Amendment protection.'"

∿

Democrats could endorse that view, and they did. Two years earlier, they'd witnessed the power of Bauer's threats against supporters of any political rivals to Obama. It had worked swimmingly at the time, even if had received little note outside the political world. Now the *Citizens United* decision had given them a new way to elevate their campaign. Few people outside of Clarence Thomas remembered the ugly history of the NAACP, or *McIntyre*, or the risk of exposing Americans to retribution. *Citizens* had instead refocused Americans on the threat of "dark money" (undisclosed money)—and Democrats intended to use that to their favor.

Two months prior to the *Citizens United* decision, Bauer had been appointed White House counsel—the top legal adviser to Obama. He was a perfect fit for a White House that, in a few short months in office, had brought Chicago-style politics to Washington—going after Chrysler bondholders; against insurers that balked at Obamacare; against Fox News for its coverage; against the Chamber of Commerce for opposing its plans on climate change. This theme—of shutting down and shutting up the other side—was the administration's approach from the start.

Bauer's handiwork looked to be all over the legislative response that followed the *Citizens* ruling. Within one day of the decision, congressional Democrats, out of Van Hollen's and Schumer's offices, were telling the press that their response would involve (as the *Washington Post* reported) "strengthened disclosure requirements for companies that directly sponsor ad campaigns" in elections. Democrats also believed that the public would be "outraged by the possibility of foreign influence in U.S. election campaigns," and so would consider legislation to restrict activity by companies that were subsidiaries of overseas corporations. "Do we really want the Chinese or any other country to spend money on our elections?" asked Van Hollen, who had himself raised plenty of money from executives who worked for exactly such subsidiaries.

Congress usually moves slowly. Not here. The quick response was testament that Democrats had a strategy. And that strategy was modeled on what Bauer had done in 2008—find out who was doing what via disclosure laws, then embarrass, intimidate, humiliate, and threaten. On April 29, three months after the *Citizens* ruling, Van Hollen introduced the amusingly named Democracy Is Strengthened by Casting Light on Spending in Elections Act, backwardly constructed to spell out DISCLOSE. Schumer would debut his own Senate version a few months later, in July. The duo, focused on protecting their own incumbents and electing new Democrats, at least get credit for producing an artful bill. They managed to conjure legislation that would crack down on—and enforce disclosure from—companies that might support Republicans, while retaining all the freedoms the Court had given to unions and independent groups that supported liberals. Some conservatives would later joke that the bill should be known as the "Democratic Incumbents Seeking to Contain Losses by Outlawing Speech in Elections Act."

The DISCLOSE Act required CEOs (much as Tribe had advocated) to appear in ads to "approve" their messages. It technically required companies, business groups (like the Chamber of Commerce), unions, and third-party organizations (like 501(c)(4)s and 527s) to "out" their donors. And the bill was designed to whip up some good old-fashioned xenophobia, by including provisions restricting political participation by companies with foreign ownership.

Unions, which support Democrats, were nonetheless cleverly carved out of most provisions. The bill, for instance, required both corporations and unions to report donors of more than $600 a year. But since the average (forced) dues of the nation's fifteen largest unions was $377 in 2004, nearly every union member would prove exempt. And while the bill also restricted political participation by government contractors, it had no such constraints on unions that received federal money or had collective bargaining agreements with the government. The AFL-CIO and the SEIU would be able to continue speaking loudly and freely.

Van Hollen nonetheless took care to present his bill as an exercise in clean government, claiming it was all about the public's "right to know." He stoked worries about what would come of the status quo: Companies, he said, could alter elections by pouring money into "sham organizations" and "dummy corporations." It would protect the public from "organizations who hide behind nice-sounding names like Americans for Clean Oceans funded by BP." (The *Deepwater Horizon* blowout had happened only a week before he introduced his bill.)

It was far more revelatory (and amusing) to listen to Schumer, who is somewhat infamous in Washington for letting the political cat out of the bag. Schumer didn't pretend the bill was about educating voters or cutting through political front groups. The legislation, he crowed, was about shutting his political opponents out of the democratic process. The DISCLOSE Act, declared Schumer, would make companies "think twice" before spending any political money. "The deterrent effect," he pronounced smugly, "should not be underestimated."

Republicans didn't underestimate it, and in the space of a few months were forced to reevaluate their longtime (if unthinking) love affair with disclosure laws. Few if any had envisioned Democrats using transparency as a weapon, and fewer yet had fully contemplated the implications of that for free speech, or for their prospects in the 2010 midterm elections. Senate Republican leader Mitch McConnell—himself one of the party's early clear-eyed free-speech stalwarts—began briefing his colleagues on the bill's First Amendment implications, as well as the public on the left's blatant attempt to censor its opponents for political advantage. DISCLOSE, declared McConnell, wasn't about clean government; it was "a transparent attempt to rig the fall election."

Still, most of the GOP was on record supporting the type of disclosure Van Hollen and Schumer now demanded, and when Republicans en masse revolted against the bill, Democrats had a field day accusing them of hypocrisy. Moreover, the *Citizens* decision was unpopular, transparency resonated with the public, and Democrats ran both the House and the Senate. The DISCLOSE bill looked inevitable, and Van Hollen and Schumer were in a rush to get it passed over the summer, so that it would start working to Democrats' advantage in the heat of the fall election season.

The group that ultimately saved the country from DISCLOSE was, strangely, the National Rifle Association (though that was hardly the NRA's intent). The gun-rights lobby voiced screeching opposition to DISCLOSE, on the grounds that the bill would require it—along with other 501(c)(4) groups—to disclose its donors. The NRA has always had amazing pull in Washington with both Republicans and moderate Democrats, and its opposition left the bill short of the necessary votes. Had the NRA stayed strong, it likely would have killed the bill outright. Instead, the group's leadership decided on a more cynical approach, and began working with Democrats to gain a special carve-out to the legislation. The NRA was happy to saddle the country with First Amendment restrictions and turbo-arm the unions in the upcoming election, so long as it got a pass.

The carve-out, however, ended up being the bill's undoing. Other outside political groups cried foul, and the exemption was extended to yet more of them. These favored exclusions gave the entire bill a backroom stench. Olson testified in front of the House in May, pointing out that the bill's problems weren't limited to disclosure. Democrats had snuck back in many of the same types of speech restrictions that the Court had only just invalidated. It contained, for instance, a bar on government contractors from spending money on political ads in an election, which Olson termed a "thinly veiled and utterly unwarranted attempt to resurrect the unconstitutional regime of speech suppression that *Citizens United* emphatically struck down." Between the shady dealings and the constitutional argument, even moderate Republicans—those with long pro-disclosure records—had plenty of cover to join the rest of their party to oppose it.

The House passed DISCLOSE in late June, with only two Republicans crossing over. Democratic leader Harry Reid nonetheless failed to get a single Republican vote in the Senate, and thus couldn't move the legislation past a filibuster. Obama predictably blasted the GOP, accusing it of "using every tactic and maneuver they can to prevent the DISCLOSE Act from even coming up for a vote." Schumer vowed that he'd just keep bringing up the bill "again and again and again until we pass it." He declared it "vital" to "people's faith in the functioning of this government." In truth, the bill was vital in only one regard: to Democrats' ballot tallies.

Despite Schumer's public bravado, Democrats privately admitted they were unlikely to get DISCLOSE. They'd been too obvious in their political maneuvering, and Republicans had come to view the bill in the same way as their opponents: as a matter of political survival. They'd stick with a filibuster. And so as the summer of 2010 wore on, the left began turning its attention to a different part of its new post-*Citizens* disclosure drive. The IRS.

CHAPTER 6

Call Out the Dogs

DISCLOSE WAS PRIMARILY AIMED at shutting down the business community. But Democrats were also stressed by the flood of Tea Party and conservative organizations signing up as 501(c)(4) social-welfare groups. These groups had sprung to life at a local level, and most, like Kenney's, were doing their civic work entirely within their own neighborhoods. But their status as social-welfare organizations gave them the right to take part in national elections—the *Citizens* decision had guaranteed that. Their status also meant they were not required to publicly disclose their donors.

Social-welfare 501(c)(4) groups have been around forever, and are largely apolitical—Rotary Clubs, the Miss America Foundation, volunteer fire departments, veterans' organizations. Of those that do take part in politics, many of the biggest work on behalf of Democrats. The AARP, the Sierra Club, the ACLU, the League of Women Voters—they've all been claiming tax-free status for years, and using it to elect the left. Democrats loved 501(c)(4)s—right up until conservatives looked to have more of them. And Democrats had never before complained about the rights accorded to them—namely their ability to maintain some level of anonymity in their funding.

But that all changed as conservatives started to pour into the

501(c)(4) field, and with some big names. Former Bush adviser Karl Rove helped set up a political group called American Cross-roads, which had a 501(c)(4) arm. The Koch brothers arranged their own influential group, Americans for Prosperity. Former Minnesota senator Norm Coleman and businessman Fred Malek in 2010 set up another heavyweight 501(c)(4), the American Action Network. And some of the new grassroots conservative organizations, like the Tea Party Patriots, had beefed up, building a national presence. Democrats feared that the combination of all this 501(c)(4) political firepower would swamp their side.

Even as Democrats were pushing forward with DISCLOSE, they were casting about for other levers of government they might pull to grind to a halt the conservative 501(c)(4) move-ment. They settled on the IRS. Top officials—folks like Lois Lerner—had already expressed public concern about the growth in 501(c)(4) political groups, and the groups' involvement in pol-itics. Democrats saw an easily influenced target.

As is usually the case, the tone was set at the top—from the White House—where Bauer was still serving as general counsel. Obama ultimately crammed in more than twenty-five campaign trips on behalf of Democratic candidates. By August, he was blowing a dog whistle for the IRS at every stop.

The debut of this new attack came August 9, as President Obama appeared at a Democratic National Committee campaign event in Austin, Texas. Obama spent twenty minutes slamming Republicans—on taxes, education, energy—and then launched into what would become a standard warning in pretty much every speech he'd give up through November. "Right now all around this country there are groups with harmless-sounding names like Americans for Prosperity, who are running millions of dollars of ads against Democratic candidates all across the country. And they don't have to say who exactly the Americans for Prosper-ity are. You don't know if it's a foreign-controlled corporation. You don't know if it's a big oil company, or a big bank. You don't know if it's an insurance company that wants to see some of the provisions in health reform repealed because it's good for their bottom line, even if it's not good for the American people.

"A Supreme Court decision allowed this to happen. And we tried to fix it, just by saying disclose what's going on, and making sure that foreign companies can't influence our elections. Seemed pretty straightforward. The other side said no.

"They don't want you to know who the Americans for Prosperity are, because they're thinking about the next election. But we've got to think about future generations. We've got to make sure that we're fighting for reform. We've got to make sure that we don't have a corporate takeover of our democracy."

This Obama monologue was both absurd and pointed. Absurd, because it monumentally overstated the situation. Democrats have made an obsession of talking about "dark money," even as they know that it is a bare blip on the election radar. The Federal Election Commission keeps tallies of all spending—every disbursement, by every political actor. Pretty much any organization in this country that spends money expressly calling for the election or a defeat of a candidate must quickly report that spending to the FEC. That rule is the same for everyone—super PACs, 501(c) groups, 527s, political parties. And most of those groups also must disclose their donors. One exception is 501(c) organizations, which are generally allowed to keep their donors anonymous. The left now calls this "dark" money.

In the 2012 election year, U.S. political actors spent about $7 billion attempting to get their favored candidates elected. It sounds like a lot, but then again, Americans spend roughly $7 billion every year on Halloween. National elections happen only every two years, which means that the U.S population spends twice as much every cycle buying Supergirl costumes and Milk Duds than they do electing the people who will govern their country.

Of that $7 billion spent in 2012 to form a government, about

$320 million of it was "dark money." Do the math, and 96 percent of the money spent in elections is disclosed. Only 3 to 4 percent (it varies by cycle) is done anonymously, and even then, most of it is hardly anonymous. The media is obsessed with 501(c)(4) groups, and have done a very good job of "outing" a lot of their donors. It isn't very difficult to guess what types of groups or people are funding the Sierra Club, or the League of Women Voters, or the Chamber of Commerce, or the NRA.

Democrats were long happy for these organizations to get their dollars from liberal benefactors and not to have to disclose them. That's why these liberal groups, in part, obtained their 501(c)(4) designations in the first place. Obama's own community-organizing group, Organizing for America, filed as a 501(c)(4).

Obama's comments were absurd, too, because they were misleading. Foreign nationals, foreign governments, foreign political parties, foreign corporations or associations—all are completely banned from giving money in U.S. elections. The Chinese, as Obama and Chris Van Hollen well know, aren't allowed to directly contribute to Americans for Prosperity. That's why Obama deliberately and carefully continued to use the phrase "foreign-controlled" entities. It sounds menacing—it was designed to sound menacing. But parse Obama's words, and what he was talking about was, say, a U.S. dealership for Toyota, or a U.S. citizen who works for Toyota, giving money to campaigns. It is perfectly legal for them to do so, since the courts have held that it is wrong to bar American entities and citizens from participating in the democratic process by virtue of the fact that they are connected to a foreign corporation. "Think about it," says Olson. "Where does that point end? How many corporations have foreign stockholders? Look at the major book publishers—several are owned by foreign corporations. Or then there's the *New York Times*—its largest shareholder is [Mexican investor] Carlos Slim. Should none of these organizations be able to speak during an election?"

Perhaps the bigger point is that nobody truly believes that the union guy who assembles cars at a Toyota plant in South Carolina, and who donates to a Senate race, is acting as an agent for the Japanese government. The carefully phrased "foreign-controlled" entity line was designed to stoke an imaginary public fear.

Obama figured most Americans wouldn't see the absurdity. And in any event, he wasn't speaking to the public; he was pointing his comments at the IRS. Social-welfare organizations were already at the center of a debate in Washington. Thousands of applications were pouring into the IRS, and the *Citizens* decision— and the DISCLOSE fight—had set off a discussion among the media and political types and tax lawyers about whether those groups deserved closer scrutiny.

Democrats and campaign finance organizations had also grown bitter over the Federal Election Commission, which is legally charged with policing election activity, and is the rightful entity to look at the political activity of nonprofits. But the FEC was deliberately set up to be nonpartisan; it contains three Republicans and three Democrats. Since it requires a majority of commissioners to institute a finding against a political actor, many complaints don't result in penalties or fines. It's a smart safeguard, given the political motivations behind many FEC complaints. But it didn't suit the purposes of Democrats, who wanted a crackdown on conservative groups. So part of the Democrats' new strategy was (as the *Washington Post* explained in an October 2010 article) "increasing pressure on the IRS to broker such disputes amid gridlock at the Federal Election Commission."

The president would weave versions of his "shady" nonprofits line into nearly every election speech going forward—in Connecticut, Pennsylvania, Wisconsin. In a clear sign of coordination, the rest of the Democratic apparatus joined him. Only two days after the president's speech in Austin, the Democratic Congressional Campaign Committee (which Van Hollen ran) sent out a fund-raising e-mail warning about "Karl Rove–inspired shadow groups." His administration staff went on national television to warn about "front groups for foreign-controlled companies."

Obama devoted weekly radio addresses to the threat of "deceptive attack ads sponsored by special interests using front groups with misleading names. We don't know who's behind these ads or who's paying for them. Even foreign-controlled corporations seeking to influence our democracy are able to spend freely in order to swing an election toward a candidate they prefer."

He kept mentioning Americans for Prosperity, a habit that surprised nobody more than AFP president Tim Phillips. "In 2010, we were small, and new to the national stage, and it was shocking to hear the president of the United States go on an extended riff about us," he says. And it turns out getting singled out by the president isn't a lot of fun. Phillips remembers that bigger donors in particular voiced concern to him. "In some ways, the attention helped us with those $10 online donors. But the bigger donors, they were like, 'The president of the United States is attacking you, and he does control a rather large federal bureaucracy. What is that going to mean for me?' There was a chilling effect."

And that was the least of it. AFP started getting bomb threats at the office. It had to put in a security system with swipe keys and stronger doors. There was regular harassment over the telephone and in the mail. Opponents would take AFP's prepaid donation envelopes and send back bricks, to run up the cost of postage. Sometimes they'd send back far more disgusting things in the envelopes. Hackers associated with the group Anonymous shut down the AFP website. Phillips notes that all this explains why it is so important that donors retain anonymity. "A lot of our donors are in privately held companies. And they are often more vulnerable because they are smaller, and intimidation and harassment, by outside groups or by the government, has the potential to really throw a monkey wrench in their operation."

The White House also enlisted the liberal media to help with the cause. The ground had already been broken. In August, the

New Yorker's Jane Mayer authored a hit piece on the Koch brothers, entitled (what else?) "Covert Operations." Mayer, hewing closely to Obama talking points, accused the brothers of funding "political front groups" and creating "slippery organizations with generic-sounding names" that have "made it difficult to ascertain the extent of their influence in Washington." She called this funding the "subsidization of a pro-corporate movement," which she variously described as "obscure," "evasive," and a "front operation." Mayer managed to write more than ten thousand words on the Kochs, including details that ranged from apartments they'd bought, to the businesses they ran, to donations they'd made, to the amounts they'd spent on lobbying, to a list of all the political organizations they'd funded, to events AFP held (including speeches from the lectern). And she spoke to and included an exhaustive list of people who'd worked for or with the Kochs. She'd go on to write an entire book on them, published in 2015. Which was remarkable, given the supposedly "covert" nature of the Koch operation.

The Mayer model set, the White House encouraged others in the media to follow suit. In a September 21 *Huffington Post* article headlined "Obama, Dems Try to Make Shadowy Conservative Groups a Problem for Conservatives," writer Sam Stein explained that the day before that second presidential address, a "senior administration official urged a small gathering of reporters to start writing on what he deemed 'the most insidious power grab that we have seen in a very long time.'" The senior official, wrote Stein, specifically pointed out the Mayer piece, telling the assembled journalists that the Kochs were "feeding Tea Party rallies" and "[pushing] information" to "try to reverse the gains we have made here on behalf of everyday people and the country as a whole." The liberal media needed to expose all this, he said, because "I think a lot of Tea Party people would be shocked to know that the candidates they favored are now being largely propelled by the dollars of the special interests that they revile." Soon, the press was pumping out stories about "shadowy" conservative groups, claiming many were abusing the IRS and the tax code.

Had Obama ordered the IRS to look into conservative groups, during an election year, he'd have been reviled as a new Nixon. So he limited himself to using his public megaphone to send a message. But the Democratic Party's elected members in Congress and outside liberal groups were under no such restriction. By the end of the summer they were jointly working to turn Obama's suggestion into a command.

The Democratic Congressional Campaign Committee kicked it off in August, filing a complaint with the IRS claiming that the Americans for Prosperity Foundation was violating its tax-exempt status. An outfit called U.S. Chamber Watch, set up by labor unions, in September followed suit, filing its own complaint with the IRS alleging that the Chamber of Commerce was breaking its nonprofit bounds. Two liberal campaign finance outfits, Democracy 21 and the Campaign Legal Center, in October requested that the IRS specifically investigate Crossroads GPS.

This was a one-eighty. Back in 2005, the George W. Bush IRS took the very stupid step of investigating a large and liberal California church, All Saints Episcopal in Pasadena, where the rector had delivered a sermon critical of Bush's war policies just a few days before the 2004 election. Churches are 501(c)(3) organizations—true charities—and are prohibited from supporting or opposing candidates. Then again, the rector wasn't urging his congregation to vote one way or another. And religious entities certainly have an interest in questions of war and peace.

In any event, the left (rightly) attacked the IRS action. Liberal groups complained that the Bush administration was attacking liberal churches. California Democratic representative Adam Schiff called for a Government Accountability Office investigation into the IRS action. "An overzealous IRS must not be permitted to chill the speech of the nation's clergy on matters of such great importance as war and peace," he railed. Robert Edgar, general secretary of the National Council of Churches, and a former Democratic congressman from Pennsylvania, called the probe "a political witch hunt on [the reverend] and progressive ideology. It's got to stop." Marcus Owens, who once ran the tax-exempt division at the IRS (the position Lois Lerner would take) and went on to represent All Saints as a private attorney, complained that recent IRS changes had given agents more freedom to look into groups. "This is exactly the sort of 1st Amendment briar patch the Congress wanted to keep the IRS out of," he told the *Los Angeles Times*.

But Democrats had clearly forgotten that outrage. So much so that in September 2010, Montana Democrat Max Baucus, head of the powerful Senate Finance Committee, sent a letter to IRS commissioner Doug Shulman demanding an investigation into nonprofits. The letter referenced recent news stories on 501(c)(4)s—stories that the White House had pushed—as evidence of the need for a probe. The finance chairman laid out clearly what he wanted to see happen: a "survey" of "[nonprofits] involved in political campaign activity to examine whether they are operated for the organization's intended tax-exempt purpose and to ensure that political campaign activity is not the organization's primary activity." Baucus even named at least one 501(c)(6)—a conservative trade organization called Americans for Job Security—as a possible subject for the investigation. And he cited a *Time* magazine article that named several 501(c)(4) groups that Democrats hated, including Crossroads GPS and American Action Network. Baucus phrased his letter as a "request" but made clear that he viewed it as an immediate order: "Please report back to the Finance Committee as soon as possible with your findings and recommended actions regarding this matter." Three years later, when the IRS scandal came out, Baucus would express great outrage that the IRS had done exactly what he ordered it to do.

The Baucus letter was only the first of a number of demands

from Senate Democrats that the IRS go after nonprofits. The letters didn't go unnoticed. Republicans immediately accused Democrats of misusing the agency to go after conservative groups. They pointed out that the IRS, even forty years later, still labored under its Nixon-era reputation as a political hit agency, and that it needed to take great care to avoid anything that would smack of a repeat. Within a few days of the Baucus letter, Republican senators Orrin Hatch and Jon Kyl had sent their own letter to the IRS, warning the agency that such an investigation threatened to "chill the legitimate exercise of First Amendment rights," and reminding it that "I.R.S. audits and investigations are specifically intended to be separated from the political process. We expect the I.R.S. will adhere to those standards despite requests to the contrary from high-level political officials."

In short, the IRS had been warned. It knew its own history. It knew the law. But it also had its boss, the president of the United States, sending it very clear signals every day about "shadowy" conservative "front" groups "posing" as tax-exempt entities and illegally controlled by "foreign" players, engaged in "unsupervised" spending that was a "threat" to democracy. It had formal complaints. It had some of the nation's most influential Democratic senators demanding an investigation. It heard the call. And it acted.

CHAPTER 7

True the Targeting

IT HAPPENED at an American Bar Association conference at the Grand Hyatt in Washington, D.C. Many Americans have never heard of the ABA, and fewer still know that it holds conferences. That changed on May 10, 2013, when an otherwise obscure government official named Lois Lerner took to the stage at the ABA event to announce that she had been front and center in one of the more notorious episodes of government abuse in U.S. history.

Lerner didn't put it that way, of course. She instead slipped into a question-and-answer period the news that her agency had separated out and applied special scrutiny to conservative political groups asking for tax-exempt status. She also acknowledged that in doing so the IRS had acted in a manner that was "incorrect, insensitive, and inappropriate."

She went on to explain that all this had happened at some outpost of "line people" in Cincinnati, and that Washington hadn't known about it until later. So "the IRS should apologize for that, it was not intentional, and as soon as we [D.C.] found out what was going on, we took steps to make it better."

What Lois Lerner said that day was a lie. The country would only later discover that she'd gone to great lengths to plant a question in the audience that would allow her to give a formulaic answer that attempted to brush the IRS actions under the carpet.

It didn't work.

ᕫᕬ

Cleta Mitchell was sitting in front of her computer in Pinehurst, North Carolina. Mitchell is one of Washington's most high-powered (and hardworking) conservative lawyers, so she spirits off to her home there any chance she gets, for a change of scenery. It was a Friday, May 10, 2013, and she was clearing off the last to-do items, looking forward to a quiet weekend.

Instead, her laptop started pinging like mad, notes flooding in from Republican and Democratic colleagues alike. "They all said the same thing: 'Cleta, did you see? Did you? Lerner admitted it! She admitted the targeting. She apologized. You weren't nuts after all!'" recalls the lawyer in an amused voice.

The e-mails came within minutes of Lois Lerner's confession. And that was much to the IRS's chagrin. The agency had carefully strategized the moment, choosing an obscure tax meeting as the place where Lerner would let slip the news that her IRS unit had spent three years harassing and silencing conservative groups. Lerner had hoped the little-noticed forum, and the Friday timing, would help skate the moment past the press.

Instead, Washington exploded. "I don't go to those ABA events—they are all communists," says Mitchell (only half kidding). "But a lot of my Washington colleagues and lawyers were present, and they'd been following this, and they knew exactly what a bomb this was. The IRS was idiotic to think this wouldn't blow up."

Mitchell certainly wasn't surprised. She'd been ferrying—or rather attempting to ferry—several of her clients through the IRS's tax-exempt program for three years. She'd known there was something rotten on Constitution Avenue since at least 2010, as her applications sat on hold.

What did surprise her was Lerner's description of events. The head of the IRS's Exempt Organizations unit assured the ABA audience that this was just a little low-level slipup. Some "line people in Cincinnati" had "centralized" and delayed tax-exempt applications in a way that was "wrong." They also sent out some letters that "were far too broad," asking questions that "weren't really necessary." Luckily, crowed Lerner, the Washington IRS office was on hand to make it better. All better.

Mitchell couldn't believe what she was reading. "When I heard her blaming this all on Cincinnati—when I'd been dealing with the Washington office from day one—well . . . I was ripshit."

∿

A ripshit Mitchell is not something most people would like to see. A partner at the respected Foley & Lardner law firm, the sixty-five-year-old is a fixture at Washington events, and a charming one. She's tall, blonde, always well dressed. Born in Oklahoma, she still has a lilting southern accent, which gives voice to a stockpile of down-home aphorisms. Whenever I call Mitchell, desperately confused over some legal point, she usually begins her response with, "Awww. Bless your heart." She's quick with a smile and can chat your ear off.

Get in Mitchell's face, however, and she turns from posy to piranha in a nanosecond. Her eyes narrow, her voice drops an octave, and that southern accent suddenly goes to steel on flint. She has a vast mastery of facts, a deep knowledge of the law, and the ability to instantly blow a hole in a flawed argument. And she has no fear.

Mitchell's one of those conservatives who started as a Democrat, which gives her the zeal of a convert. She served a stint in the Oklahoma legislature as a Democrat, and then a time in Oklahoma City private practice, where she completed her political conversion. In 1991, she moved to sin city, D.C., to run a legal institute. She soon became a go-to political law attorney for the entire Republican ecosphere, counseling everyone from the National Rifle Association, to political campaigns, to state and national party committees. She has a specialty in election and finance law.

One of Mitchell's areas of expertise is navigating conservative groups through the minefields of IRS and FEC tax and election law. (When Bauer in 2008 went after the American Issues Project, calling in Justice, the IRS, and the FEC, it was Mitchell running defense for the group.) She's shepherded dozens of conservative organizations through the IRS tax-exempt process, and when in 2009 she went to file for her latest client, a social-welfare group, she at first didn't think anything of it. "I sent in the application in October, and they cashed our check—because, of course, it's the IRS and you have to pay up front," she recalls. "And then nothing. And that started to get weird, the nothing."

Mitchell was used to dusting an entire tax-exempt process for a client in about three weeks. It's supposed to be a quick process. That's because, as Mitchell likes to stress again and again, the IRS's only job at the application stage is to make sure the paperwork is in order. "This isn't about asking permission—this isn't about a group saying, 'Please, can I be an LLC, or a C-corporation, or a social-welfare group?'" she explains. "No. You go to the IRS and *tell* them what you are. They then make sure your basic articles of incorporation are in order, and that you have enough board members and whatnot, and then you get your letter saying you are tax-exempt. This is something so easy you should be able to do it from home.

"It isn't until much later, until you've existed for a time and filed your first tax forms, that the IRS gets to start looking at how you spent your money and asking the questions. In all my years of doing this, I never got a call from the IRS about the purpose of an organization. Never, never, never. And appropriately so."

She got a call that time—though not until many months later.

The IRS rang in June 2010 with an odd request: It wanted her to send copies of all her client's advertisements. Mitchell remembers it vividly, because she'd never been asked to do anything like that before, and she struggled to figure out how to format and send the ads. Mostly, she thought it strange. The group she represented was spending 100 percent of the money it raised on ads about Obamacare. Lobbying falls entirely within the definition of social welfare, and the group had zero involvement in any election activity. So there wasn't even any question that her client met that 51 percent "primary" purpose test. It was 100 percent legit. (Not to mention—as she stresses again and again—that the IRS has no business looking at spending in the application phase.)

Mitchell ended up calling the IRS. She got routed to an exempt-office agent in D.C., who marked the request for ads down to confusion among his colleagues about different types of tax-exempt groups.

Yet as 2010 wore on, Mitchell began realizing that none of the applications she submitted were moving. "It was complete radio silence, pretty much that whole year," she says. Then in February 2011, she got a call from Catherine Engelbrecht.

∿

Engelbrecht is Texan. She used to run a small manufacturing plant outside Houston. In 2009, she volunteered as a poll watcher in the Texas elections, where she (as she puts it) "saw some weird stuff" that made her worry about potential election fraud. So she formed a social-welfare organization, King Street Patriots (KSP), a pro-liberty community group, which aimed to support and defend constitutional governance and civic duty. She filed an application with the IRS for 501(c)(4) status in the spring of 2010.

In July, she filed an application for an offshoot group, True the Vote, a 501(c)(3) charity designed to restore integrity to the electoral system by training poll volunteers and researching and reporting on the polling process. "When I think about how little I knew or understood of politics back then, it almost makes me laugh," she says. "I had no knowledge of anything other than this thought that it might be good to have average citizens volunteering and helping out at the polls." For the rest of 2010, she heard nothing from the IRS about those applications.

She did, however, hear from the government in different regards. In late 2010, the FBI showed up, saying it was looking for an individual who it thought was affiliated with KSP, and asking to see a list of "members." Engelbrecht didn't keep lists—her events were open to all, and people came and went. She offered to let the FBI know if she saw him. The bureau came back for a follow-up in January. In that same month, the IRS also appeared, to conduct an on-site audit of two previous years of business tax returns. Engelbrecht thought these events "strange, but I didn't connect the dots." She was, however, concerned about the status of her applications, and was increasingly being attacked by Democrats. She realized she needed some professional help, so on a trip in early 2011 to Washington's annual conservative CPAC conference, she reached out to Mitchell. The Washington lawyer had no idea what she was about to sign up for.

Mitchell and Engelbrecht had barely met when True the Vote received a questionnaire from the IRS—five long months after filing. It was a request for more information regarding the application.

Engelbrecht worked through the questions and returned the info to the IRS. Mitchell had told Engelbrecht when they met in February to get back in touch if she hadn't heard anything from the agency in a few months.

Summer came and went, and still no word from the IRS. Mitchell stewed, and then suggested to Engelbrecht that they supplement the application and note for the IRS other groups like True the Vote that had already been granted charitable status. In October 2011, Mitchell reached out to the agent in Cincinnati listed at the top of the case, advising him that she'd been retained and telling him she was preparing additional information. She was surprised during that conversation to be told by the agent that a "task force" in Washington was "handling" this application.

When she sent in the supplement in November, Mitchell memorialized that conversation by heading her cover letter with a request that Cincinnati forward the package to its "task force" in Washington. That letter would end up providing the explosive first proof that pretty much nothing Lerner said at that ABA meeting about how all this had happened in Cincinnati was true.

Another month passed. No word. A now fully agitated Mitchell put in another call to the Cincinnati agent just before Christmas 2011. She remembers his words exactly. "We haven't heard anything. Everything is in Washington. Take it up with them."

∿∿∿

Lerner's confession at that conference did contain one small truth. The IRS targeting scandal did indeed start in "Cincy"—as D.C. headquarters refers to that outpost. On a cold late February day in 2010, a Cincinnati screener named Jack Koester found himself focused on an application from a local Tea Party group.

The IRS is a vast organization, employing ninety-five thousand people, who enforce a code 3.7 million words long that oversees taxes on everything from income to corporations to employment to estates to gifts to excises. It's home to agents and auditors and specialists and examiners and investigators and lots and lots and lots of lawyers. It also oversees organizations that are "exempt" from paying taxes. The Exempt Organizations unit at the IRS is in fact a big operation; on any given day it oversees a universe of 1.5 million recognized tax-exempt organizations.

Precisely because the IRS handles so many nonprofit groups, it maintains a dedicated unit in Cincinnati—known as the Determinations unit—that processes initial tax-exempt applications.

The Cincy Determinations unit in turn is divided into thirteen groups, one of which handles the initial "screens" of applications. The typical screener spends fifteen to thirty minutes on an application, and completes twenty to thirty a day.

Koester's eye nonetheless settled for more than a few beats on the Tea Party application in front of him. He forwarded the application to his supervisor, noting, "Recent media attention to this type of organization indicates to me that this is a 'high profile' case." His alert worked its way up the chain, all the way to Cincinnati's boss of exempt operations, Cindy Thomas. She in turn forwarded it to one of Washington's senior officials, Holly Paz, asking "whether [Washington] wants this case because of recent media attention." Paz took less than a day to respond: "I think sending it up here is a good idea given the potential for media interest."

So Lerner, the IRS, Obama—they were all correct that the targeting fiasco started with a "line agent" in Cincinnati. They just neglected to mention that within twenty-four hours of that agent's alert—and every minute thereafter—it was political types in Washington running the show.

When Koester talked about "media interest," he was undoubtedly referring to the wall-to-wall coverage that had just followed the *Citizens United* decision. He'd likely seen the White House's furious reaction to the Court's decision to free up speech rights, and Obama's dressing-down of the Supremes. He'd likely seen the Democratic Party and its media allies bang on daily about the evils of conservative "nonprofits." He'd likely taken in the nonstop stories about the Tea Party gearing up in opposition to Obama, and how they were rushing into the (c)(4) realm. And he likely knew those groups were having an effect. Only a month earlier, Scott Brown had won that Senate race, against all odds. Koester was a prime example of how an executive branch—and a political party—can drive a story and make the bureaucracy take notice.

We know that one person in particular took notice: an ambitious partisan by the name of Lois Lerner.

∿

Lerner shocked Washington with her May 2013 admission that her agency had harassed Americans. The shocking thing was that anyone was shocked.

Lerner to this day won't cooperate with any real investigation; the nation has been denied the opportunity to hear her story. But e-mail is a wondrous thing. Between her records and the recollections of her colleagues, we have a vivid portrait of the former head of the IRS's Exempt Organizations unit. She was a brassy, self-assured bureaucrat with Democratic leanings and a near-messianic belief in the need for more speech regulations. And she had a long history.

Before landing at the IRS, Lerner spent twenty years at the FEC, rising to become its acting general counsel. Never in all that time did she hide her views that money was a problem in politics and needed more restrictions. She was seen even then as a highly biased FEC enforcer—one who harassed conservative groups that wanted more freedoms in politics.

While head of FEC enforcement, Lerner played a role in the 1990s in going after former Mississippi governor Haley Barbour over a nonprofit group he established called the National Policy Forum, which had been accused of taking illegal foreign contributions. (The Justice Department would later find no evidence of a crime.) She was part of an effort to take down a dozen Republican state party chairmen and the Republican National Committee, over accusations that they had broken finance laws during George H. W. Bush's 1988 presidential bid. That case stayed open for seven years. She'd most famously help wage a small war against the Christian Coalition, in one of the largest enforcement actions in FEC history. The coalition was accused (with no proof) of illegally coordinating its advocacy with Republican candidates. Mark Hemingway of the *Weekly Standard* documented that the harassment cost the conservative group "hundreds of thousands of dollars, and countless hours of lost work." James Bopp (of later *Citizens United* fame) handled that case, and he revealed in testimony that the FEC team deposed 48 different people, conducted 81 depositions, put in 127 separate document requests, and sent the group 32 different interrogatories containing hundreds upon hundreds of questions. The agency demanded donor lists, and even inquired into whether people in the group were "praying" for each other. Each of the coalition's 49 affiliates got document demands; it would ultimately hand over 100,000 pages of information.

So Lerner had a lot of practice in harassment even before she geared up at the IRS. Her e-mails show that she was at home in Democratic politics, with biases against conservatives. There's a 2004 e-mail with a former colleague in which she's hopeful she'll be able to get together to "celebrate" a John Kerry presidential victory. In 2012, a friend would muse to her about the "scary" Romney/Ryan ticket and ask how a "creep like Romney" was ever elected in Massachusetts. She'd later that year decline an invitation to a party to celebrate Obama's expected victory, noting that she was nonetheless keeping her "fingers crossed. And, I did vote!" When told that Democrats had kept control of the Senate in 2012, she responded, "WooHoo! [I]t was important to keep the Senate. If it had switched, it would be the same as a Rep president."

Her husband, Michael Miles, comes off as a passionate liberal who egged his wife on. On election day in 2012, he told his wife that he hadn't been able to find the "socialist-labor candidates on the ballot, so I wrote them in." Three days after the 2012 election, he complained to her about the losers, "Well, you should hear the whacko wing of the GOP. The US is through; too many foreigners sucking the teat; time to hunker down, buy ammo and food, and prepare for the end. The right wing radio shows are scary to listen to." Lerner replied, "Great. Maybe we are through if there are that many assholes." Conservatives, she explained, were "crazy" and worse than "alien terrorists." In March 2014, a friend wrote to complain about Texas Republicans. Lerner responded, "Look my view is that Lincoln was our worst president not our best. He should'[v]e let the south go. We really do seem to have 2 totally different mindsets." Around the height of Congress's probe into her actions, she'd write to a friend that Republican congressional investigators were "evil and dishonest" and interested only in "hate-mongering."

Lerner's e-mails also reveal that she held a self-righteous view on finance laws. She spent a career trying to shut down free speech. And since Republicans were generally opposed to that concept, they were in her eyes a threat. The inestimable George Will after the scandal broke would report on how Lerner had in 1996, from her perch at the FEC, told one Republican candidate, "Promise me you will never run for office again, and we'll drop this case [against you]." Lerner's e-mails all begin from the premise that the nation needs more finance laws and express great excitement over the possibility of Supreme Court restrictions or a new DISCLOSE Act, or tougher rules. She was tight with the senior leadership of pro–campaign finance groups. She railed against the *Citizens United* decision, telling a friend it was "by far the worst thing that has ever happened to this country." She continued, "We are witnessing the end of 'America.' . . . Religion has usually tempered the selfishness of capitalism, but the rabid, hellfire piece of religion has hijacked the game and in the end, we will all lose out. [I]t's all tied together—money can buy the Congress and the Presidency, so in turn, money packs [the Supreme Court]. And the court usually backs the money— the 'old boys' still win." Such was the view of the woman charged with "fairly" enforcing tax exemption laws.

And she didn't lack confidence. Lerner had little time for other people's views, above or below her. She rarely took issues up the chain of command. And she treated those below her with contempt. Colleagues noted that she liked to "scream" and "yell"; one explained that she wasn't "ideal" to talk to Congress because she was "unpredictable" and "emotional." Cindy Thomas, the manager of the Cincinnati Determinations unit, explained to Congress, "I don't think that she valued what employees were doing . . . she didn't really listen to what others had to say. She would cut you off and didn't allow people to express what was going on. . . . [I]t was like it didn't matter if other people had questions, so to speak."

∿

When Thomas got the order to send along that Tea Party application to Washington, she didn't worry about it. It was, after all, just another application.

To this day, Democrats perpetuate the myth that the IRS targeting was partly a result of the agency's becoming overwhelmed by a flood of (c)(4) applications. It's a laughable argument. Cincinnati is and has been an assembly line for tax-exempt processing for years. It's what it does. In 2012 alone, the height of the Tea Party scandal, the IRS approved fifty-two thousand nonprofits. Yet somehow we are to believe that the agency was flummoxed by three hundred Tea Party applications.

Cincinnati is able to process applications like the wind because, as Mitchell likes to repeat, its initial job is mostly to make sure the paperwork is in order. In about 35 percent of cases, the screener immediately recommends approval. In another 50 percent, the screener refers the application to one of Cincinnati's revenue agents to resolve a minor technical issue. About 13 percent of cases contain bigger concerns, and also get sent to an agent, though even these are usually solved in-house. All told, Cincinnati resolves 85 percent of applications all on its own, and quickly.

In very rare circumstances, the outpost will send a troublesome application to Washington, which headquarters the Exempt Organizations unit and includes a "Technical" office that brims with exempt-law specialists. Applications that land at the big house usually have some glaring problem—a question over whether someone might be profiting off the venture; a group that seems clearly to be operating outside exempt guidelines. They don't get sent for "media interest"—or at least they shouldn't.

Still, it didn't matter why Washington wanted the case; what mattered is that it did. Bureaucracies like to please, and when Cincy got the news that the Washington big boys approved of its Tea Party case, it went to further work. John Shafer, who ran the screening unit, immediately told his group to identify similar applications. By mid-March, Thomas was able to report that Cincy had at least ten more "tea party cases," and asked if Paz, who ran Washington's Technical unit, wanted those too. Paz sent out the order to send Washington "a few more" and to "hold the rest" until headquarters had figured out the situation. Cincinnati sent along a charitable (501(c)(3)) application filed by Arizona's Prescott Tea Party, and a social-welfare (501(c)(4)) application from the Albuquerque Tea Party.

Shafer clearly read "hold the rest" as an order to begin identifying any application that might count as Tea Party–like. He tasked a screener with coming up with a process, and that screener took to the Internet to investigate the Tea Party movement. He went back to Shafer, alarmed: "I said, 'John, there's hundreds of these things, maybe thousands.'" The screener ended up compiling a list of code words: "Tea Party," "Patriots," and "9/12" (a reference to the day after the September 11 attacks, when, as movement founder Glenn Beck described it, "we were united as Americans"). Other screeners came up with additional criteria, and the group was soon segregating out any applications that dealt with "government spending, government debt and taxes," or that contained statements that were critical of how Obama was running the country. By early April, Cincinnati had its first Tea Party targeting list—all at the request of Washington.

Washington was making its own list. The day after Paz asked

for several more applications, a manager in the Washington office sent an e-mail to his D.C.-based "technical" agents. "Be on the lookout for a tea party case. If you have received or do receive a case in the future involving an exemption for an organization having to do with [the] tea party let me know."

Paz that spring went on maternity leave, and her temporary replacement, Steve Grodnitzky, took up her cudgel. He wanted more information on the two Tea Party cases Washington was now working, and he wanted the issue elevated to senior leadership. He ordered an underling to create a "sensitive case report" on the Tea Party issue, to be included on a list that is every month sent up through the ranks of the IRS to alert top officials to key issues. This sensitive report, sent to Lerner in April 2010, showed the extent to which Washington was already in charge. It informed Lerner that D.C. was working two cases, that Cincy was holding another thirteen, and that Washington was "coordinating" with that outpost to "provide direction as to how to develop those cases based on our development of the ones in D.C."

So we know that as early as April 28, 2010, Lerner knew about the Tea Party issue. A few weeks later, she asked Grodnitzky on what "basis" the "Tea Party" was asking for 501(c)(3) charitable status. Grodnitzky's reply was dripping with institutional bias: They "are arguing education, but the big issue for us is whether they are engaged in political campaign activity." The comment reveals how the IRS was already veering off the prescribed rails. Charities, it is true, are barred from endorsing candidates. But they are absolutely free to engage in education, including political education—whether it be the importance of voting, of the Constitution, or of the environment. They can even legally lobby for causes. The Center for American Progress? Defenders of Wildlife? The NAACP? Media Matters for America? Those are all wildly political groups, and all charities. And not a one was ever harassed by the IRS. It's telling that the IRS immediately doubted the conservative claim of education.

In any event, only a small number of Tea Party groups even asked for charitable status. Most were asking for (c)(4) status—as social-welfare organizations—a category that allows entirely for direct political activity.

Lerner would admit this only a few months later in an October 2010 talk at Duke University. That talk later became famous, because in it Lerner acknowledged that the IRS was acutely aware of outside demands for it to act against conservative groups. Talking about the Democratic and media uproar over (c)(4) groups, she said, "So everybody is screaming at us right now, 'Fix it now before the election. Can't you see how much these people are spending?'" Lerner nonetheless acknowledged that there was no formal way for the IRS to stop the activity, because "(c)(4)s can do straight political activity. They can go out and pay for an ad that says, 'Vote for Joe Blow.'"

In any event, Grodnitzky assured Lerner that nothing would happen until she gave "clearance." And it was already becoming clear that nobody intended to approve any Tea Party groups before the 2010 midterms.

Ronald Shoemaker, a senior employee in the D.C. Exempt unit, tasked tax specialist Carter Hull to work the two "test cases," with the idea that these would guide the IRS on how to handle the rest of the Tea Party stash. Hull was a fifty-year veteran of the federal government and a respected authority on (c)(4) applications. The specialist got busy, and already by mid-April he'd sent letters requesting additional information or clarification to the Prescott and Albuquerque Tea Party groups. A slight delay cropped up when the Prescott group never responded, forcing Washington to go back to Cincy to get a replacement "test" case for Hull to work. Still, Hull's notes show that he had finished his review of the Albuquerque (c)(4) application by July 8. His conclusion: It should receive tax-exempt status. This all transpired over the summer of 2010.

Back in Cincinnati, another veteran of the service, Elizabeth

Hofacre, was charged with working through that office's Tea Party backlog, which by April numbered twenty applications. Hofacre created the first version of what would become the infamous Be On the Lookout (BOLO) list, a document designed to help other agents identify "local organizations in the Tea Party movement [that] are applying for exemption." Hofacre's BOLO spreadsheet continued to be updated and refined over the next three years, ultimately encompassing dozens of terms designed to ensnare hundreds of conservative groups. For now, she zipped the first version to some agents in Cincinnati and in Washington, and set out to work through the queue of stranded Tea Party applications.

She got nowhere. Hull told Hofacre that all letters she wrote to a group requesting information must be sent to him first, so that he could review and edit them. She was similarly told to send to Washington every response letter from any group. In all her years at the IRS, Hofacre had never had her daily work reviewed by Washington Technical. She'd also had broad discretion to recommend the outcome of applications. But now she was blocked from making those decisions.

At first, Hull got back to her quickly. But as the months went on, the feedback tapered off. She'd bitterly complain that she had been "micromanaged to death, and it was just really frustrating." Hull later testified that he couldn't provide any guidance to Cincinnati "until I knew which way the service was going." And the service—meaning Lerner and other higher-ups—wasn't saying.

What they were doing was absorbing the thundering daily drumbeat of liberal and media criticism about the IRS and (c)(4) groups in politics. Obama and his surrogates delivered regular broadsides about "shady" conservative groups. Congressional Democrats were still hot in the middle of their DISCLOSE Act fight, flooding the airwaves with diatribes about "anonymous" donors and "dark money." Arms of the Democratic Party, with assists from independent liberal organizations, filed direct complaints with the IRS about their conservative (c)(4) counterparts. And every senior leader of the IRS was fully aware of the debate and pressure and the political stakes.

In early August, a member of the IRS media team zapped an e-mail straight up the agency chain, clear to the top. The recipients included Lerner; her boss, Sarah Hall Ingram (the commissioner of the Tax Exempt and Government Entities Division); Ingram's boss, Deputy Commissioner Steven Miller; and the chief of staff to IRS commissioner Doug Shulman. The subject was an upcoming *Washington Post* article about—as the reporter put it—the need for "IRS regulations covering campaign/election related activity for section 501c4...in light of [*Citizens United*]." She explained that the premise of the story was that the IRS was underequipped to "regulat[e] money in politics."

A few weeks later, Lerner sent an SOS to Ingram, noting that the Democratic Congressional Campaign Committee had lodged a complaint with the agency about Obama's favorite bogeyman—Americans for Prosperity. "We won't be able to stay out of this—we need a plan!" explained Lerner. A few weeks later she announced that she did have a plan, to do a "c4 project," though she warned that "we need to be cautious so it isn't a per se political project."

In September, Lerner launched herself in the public debate, agreeing to an interview for a front-page story by the *New York Times* that the IRS knew would be focused on the "large upswing in the money donated to 501(c)(4)s [and] that the IRS has too few resources to monitor and deal with compliance and enforcement issues in this area." Ingram sent an e-mail the day the story appeared, praising it and the agency's media team, and noting that the " 'secret donor' theme will continue—see Obama salvo and today's Diane Reehm [*sic*]." Diane Rehm, a liberal radio host, had that day aired an interview with Representative Chris Van Hollen, who was again banging on about the problems of *Citizens United*.

An adviser to Ingram, Joseph Urban, also kept the leadership team straight on congressional Democrats' wishes. A September alert let everyone know about the Democratic Congressional Campaign Committee complaint about Americans for Prosperity. In October he passed around a press release from Illinois senator Dick Durbin demanding that the agency take aim at the conservative organization American Crossroads. Every senior IRS official later admitted to Congress that they were well aware of the raging (c)(4) debate. As were senior Treasury officials, who circulated e-mails at the time in which they worried to each other about "aggressive c4s" that can act with "impunity," all fueled by "anonymous donors." All this was happening as Hull's and Hofacre's cases sat in limbo.

⌁

No one in America has ever bought the fiction that the IRS is a politically immune agency. Most might nonetheless be surprised to hear that it isn't even an "independent" agency, as the press likes to suggest. It is officially a bureau of the Treasury Department, which reports directly to the president. That bureau is tasked by law with carrying out "the responsibilities of the secretary of the Treasury" to enforce the tax code. The government itself doesn't list it as an independent agency, and the law allows the president to remove IRS commissioners "at will"—something he can't do at truly independent agencies like the Federal Reserve Board. Even the chief of the Federal Maritime Commission has more political insulation than the IRS head.

Plenty of presidents have co-opted the IRS for partisan aims, but Obama took this to new heights, tasking the agency with enforcing big parts of his partisan agenda, such as his health care law. That's one reason why his first-term IRS commissioner, Doug Shulman, made so many visits to the White House in the first three years of the Obama administration. E-mails show an IRS top brass that increasingly worked as an arm of the administration, collaborating with congressional Democrats and the White House to thwart Republicans——on health care, and the contraception mandate, and sequestration.

This co-optation is an important part of the targeting scandal. An IRS that views itself as a neutral enforcer of tax law would have blocked out the (c)(4) noise. An IRS that viewed itself as an extension of the Obama team would have felt compelled to do something. As Cindy Thomas would later say about Lerner, when asked what she thought motivated the Exempt Organizations head, "I believe that she cares about power and that it's important to her maybe to be more involved with what's going on politically." Thomas noted that Washington had started complaining that Cincinnati was not as "politically sensitive as they would like us to be."

Back in Cincy, Elizabeth Hofacre became so disgusted by the micromanagement and Washington's refusal to deal with the Tea Party cases on the merits that in July she requested a transfer. She got it in October. Her replacement, Ron Bell, inherited her lockdown, and was told to simply wait for "guidance" from D.C. As the days ticked down to the 2010 election, Cindy Thomas grew alarmed. In late October, she sent a blunt e-mail to Paz, who was now back from maternity leave: "I have a concern with the approach being used to develop the tea party cases we have here in Cincinnati. . . . Personally, I don't know why [Carter Hull] needs to look at each and every additional information letter." Her office, she wrote, was now sitting on at least forty-five applications. She wanted to schedule time to "come up with a process so we can get these moving." Washington kept promising it would send instructions; instead, it kept pushing off the timeline.

∿

Lerner wasn't processing applications, but that doesn't mean she wasn't busy. In September, yet another federal agency noticed

Obama's anger with conservative operations. Jack Smith, the head of the Justice Department's Public Integrity Unit, read the *New York Times* article that Lerner had assisted with and tipped off his bosses: "Check out [the *Times* article] regarding misuse of non-profits for indirectly funding campaigns. This seems egregious to me—could we ever charge a [conspiracy] to violate laws of the USA for misuse of such non profits to get around existing campaign finance laws + limits? I know 501s are legal but if they are knowingly using them beyond what they are allowed to use them for (and we could prove that factually)? IRS Commissioner sarah ingram oversees these groups. . . . [M]aybe we should try to set up a meeting this week."

Smith's idea was breathtaking. He was proposing that the most powerful law enforcement agency in the land begin prosecuting and jailing average Americans for exercising free speech in opposition to Obama. Yet he got the green light. Smith directed the head of his Election Crimes Branch, Richard Pilger, to meet with Lerner about being "more vigilant to the opportunities from more crime" from (c)(4)s.

Lerner knew Pilger from her days at the FEC, and happily arranged to meet him in early October. A memo summarizing the meeting showed that all the participants had taken to using President Obama's favorite rhetoric about groups "posing" as nonprofits. The participants proposed a "three-way partnership" between the DOJ, the FEC, and the IRS. Lerner in the meantime also arranged for the IRS to transmit 1.1 million pages of non-profit tax-return data to the FBI, so that G-men could start trolling through the database for potential crimes. This was a few days before the 2010 elections. The database contained confidential taxpayer information that is protected by federal law and that Justice should never have possessed.

The election came and went. The end of the year came and went. Lerner's underlings increasingly started badgering her for answers, and in February 2011 she finally fully engaged in the stalled application process. In an e-mail to Michael Seto, who in January had replaced Paz as the head of Washington's Technical unit, she declared, "Tea Party Matter, very dangerous." She fretted that the cases could be a vehicle for nonprofits to go back to the Supreme Court and demand even more freedoms. Hull had early in 2011 made his recommendations for how the two test cases should be handled, but Lerner dismissed those findings and instead directed that the two groups be subject to an unprecedented multilayer review. They would first get a vetting by one of her own senior advisers, Judith Kindell, and then go through the wringer at the IRS chief counsel's office. She finished, "Cincy should probably NOT have these cases." Paz, who was still involved in the discussion, reassured her that Hull was nitpicking everything, and that nothing would move "out of Cincy" until Washington got through "its process." Hull would testify later that he'd never in his fifty years seen anything like this approach.

Lerner's review meant another ten months of torturous inaction, in which IRS attorneys strung out the process and Cincinnati continued to sit on hold. Lerner grew more and more enmeshed in the (c)(4) debate, taking actions that all looked aimed at shutting down the Tea Party movement. She and Kindell worked on ways that the agency might plausibly deny the groups both (c)(3) and (c)(4) status. She tightened Washington's control—warning that Cincinnati must not "make a move" without D.C.'s say-so—explaining that "these could blow up like crazy if [Cincy] let[s] one out incorrectly." She demanded more investigation and details into the test cases. In July, she requested and received a briefing on the status of the Tea Party cache, and was told there were now more than a hundred cases in the Cincy backlog.

At that event, Lerner decided to change the criteria by which screeners identified the cases. Using the term "Tea Party," she explained, was "pejorative" (read: politically dangerous). She ordered that the new BOLO language become "Organizations involved with political, lobbying, or advocacy for exemption under [(c)(3) and (c)(4) status]." This new, broader language had the perverse effect of sweeping significantly more Tea Party groups under the IRS radar.

She debated subjecting organizations to a new requirement—they would have to agree not to "politically intervene"—so as to "pin them down in the future." She suggested that IRS employees start looking into whether individual Tea Party groups had registered with the FEC, and if so, to ask more questions. She talked to attorneys about proposals to create new IRS rules to crack down on (c)(4) groups. All of this was unprecedented.

And she became obsessed, along with every other Democrat, with the mack daddy of conservative (c)(4) groups: Crossroads GPS. All the way back in October 2010, one of the leading Senate Democrats, Dick Durbin, had written to Doug Shulman asking for an investigation into the group, which had been cofounded by Bush political guru Karl Rove. Democratic staffers in Congress also reached out to the IRS for information on the group, and at least two outside liberal groups complained about Crossroads to the IRS. Lerner forwarded e-mails to her bosses about the organization, lamenting that Crossroads would be able to take part in the election because of a "glitch in the law" and expressing her desire that Congress pass rules to stop such actions. By June 2011 she was looking into the group personally, having requested Cincinnati's Cindy Thomas to send her the application. She supervised the case after that, and ultimately decided to deny Crossroads its tax-exempt status. In a later e-mail to a subordinate, she made clear that the decision came down to politics. "I don't think your guys get it and the way they look at these cases is going to bite us some day. [Crossroads] is on the top of the list of c4 spenders in the last two elections. It is in the news regularly as an organization that is not really a c4, rather it is only doing political activity—taking in money from large contributors who wish to remain anonymous. . . . You should know that we are working on a denial of the application, which may solve the problem." The "problem" was Crossroads' existence. Lerner's campaign to tank Crossroads was in stark contrast to efforts she'd take over the same years to expedite the approval of liberal nonprofit applications, including several done at the request of Democratic senators.

∿

By the summer of 2011, Lerner was under growing pressure from below to do something about the backlog, and so her Technical unit finally decided to perform a "triage" of the now 150 languishing Tea Party applications. It became a new method of delay. Until now, the conservative universe had heard little or nothing from the IRS. The "triage" marked the official start of the harassment. Carter Hull, despite his fifty years of agency service, was inexplicably pulled off the cases. They were reassigned to Hilary Goehausen, an IRS rookie who had only been with the agency a few months. It was a curious appointment. IRS officials later claimed that Hull was going "too slow" on the applications and that the agency wanted to train up Goehausen. Most organizations don't train newbies by tasking them with cases that their boss views as "dangerous." More likely, Goehausen got the job because she'd prove to be easier about taking orders.

Goehausen in the fall started reviewing every application, making notes on each to send back to Cincinnati. Her notes reflect an agency that by this point had completely lost the plot. Goehausen explained in an e-mail to Cindy Thomas that her goal was to separate "good" groups from those that were "just making inflammatory, emotionally charged statements without any factual support" (in her view). She later told Congress she had combed them for "propaganda," which she described as "a kind of inflammatory, emotionally charged statement" that tried to sell the public on an issue "by only being one-sided and not giving—

not discussing both sides of an issue." This was a remarkable new standard for an agency that had happily bestowed tax-exempt charitable status on Media Matters for America, an organization that has the stated mission of "comprehensively monitoring, analyzing and correcting conservative misinformation in the U.S. media."

Goehausen went to town. Some applications, she noted, were "anti-Obama." Some were "primarily emotional." Some contained "apparent political campaign activities (ie negative Obama commentary)." In communications with colleagues, Goehausen debated ways of rejecting groups that gave her unpleasant sensations. "I think there may be a number of ways to deny them. . . . This sounds like a bad org :/ . . . This org gives me an icky feeling."

As Goehausen performed her "triage," the insane pressure from liberal groups on the IRS to act against conservative nonprofits mounted. Independent groups flooded the agency with complaints. The media for its part trawled through 2010 midterm spending statistics, launching wild claims about tax-exempt abuse. Washington still hadn't finished its test cases, but Goehausen sent along her comments as well as a "guide sheet" for Cincinnati to process its backlog. The sheet laid out the types of information Washington expected Cincinnati to elicit from Tea Party groups in the process of deciding on their applications. Thomas in January 2012 assembled a team of agents, who would use the guide sheet and comments to draft long letters demanding reams of information from each of the now 170 Tea Party groups sitting in the queue. Those letters went out in February. And that's when all hell broke loose.

CHAPTER 8

Living the Lie

KAREN KENNEY sat staring at the IRS interrogatory she'd received in February 2012 and instantly decided to send it to Dawn Wildman, one of the founders of the California Tea Party movement, and a woman Kenney had been in contact with since she first revved up her own group. "Dear Dawn, this is a heads-up for an envelope I sent you tonight," ran Kenney's e-mail. She described the IRS questionnaire she'd received as "chilling, intrusive and very personal," and posited that it likely "violates at least two First Amendment rights." She asked if Wildman knew if "this level of questioning is standard practice." Kenney cautioned that she was only sending her concerns to Wildman, and not to all the leadership groups, because she didn't want to "terrify" anyone else "seeking non-profit, federal tax-exempt status."

She needn't have worried. Wildman was getting similar e-mails and calls from everyone, and not just from groups in California. By late February, in fact, the Tea Party network was alive from coast to coast with outrage and confusion over the IRS letter dump. Some particularly active Tea Party heads—Toby Marie Walker of Texas's Waco Tea Party, and the heads of several Ohio liberty groups, like Tom Brown and Tom Zawistowski— threw together a conference call for February 28 so that groups could share stories. The invitation was classic grassroots, a mixture of outrage, helpfulness, and respect for the autonomy of local groups. "Dear Tea Party and/or Grassroots leader, Recently you may have read about the IRS sending outrageously intrusive and intimidating letters to Tea Party and other grassroots organizations." They announced that group leaders across the country had realized they were under assault, and were organizing a conference call to serve as a "strategy and brainstorming session." They cautioned, "We will not be giving legal advice, we are not attorneys, or accounting advice, we are not CPA's." And they reassured, "We are not looking to form an organization or create a top down group. We are simply trying to gauge the actual scope of the problem and formulate a coordinated and effective response to it."

Tea Party leaders also immediately organized an effort to collect and collate all the IRS questionnaires. They sent out an e-mail form that requested the correspondence, noting that the goal was to put it in a "private repository with the only access being possibly attorneys, Congressmen and their staff and any other person or entity who may need to see the original documents. Since all documents received so far [have instructed] to send information to the same P.O. Box number this could be extremely relevant." Already the groups had realized that this effort appeared to be centralized.

Kenney rearranged her client appointments so she could join the conference call. She almost didn't make it on. Call organizers had made room for ninety-nine participants; they were maxed out within minutes. Outraged Tea Party leaders swapped stories and suggestions for an hour and a half. Several groups admitted they'd already responded to the IRS, on the advice of tax accountants and on fears that noncompliance might result in an audit. One participant had already mailed back a nine-hundred-page response. They broadly agreed to contact Congress, compile the repository of information, and go public to the media. And they decided they needed legal advice.

Kenney had already sent her questionnaire to radio host Mark Levin. Others reached out to Glenn Beck, and to Erick Erickson at the popular *Red State* website. Calls started to flood into House and Senate offices.

Kenney meanwhile faced a tough decision. Several groups in Ohio and Texas had declared on the call their intention to refuse to comply with IRS demands, on the grounds that they were being unfairly targeted. Others had recommended seeking out a lawyer to ask advice. Kenny resolved to put in a call to her own attorney. In the meantime, she wrote an e-mail to her leadership team, soliciting their thoughts: Should she write the IRS a refusal letter (*in all my copious spare time*)? Should she send a message to the government?

She didn't have to make that decision in the end. She jumped on a second national call, the very next day—this one featuring Jay Sekulow. Sekulow is the longtime chief counsel of the American Center for Law and Justice (ACLJ), which was set up in 1990 by evangelical minister Pat Robertson as a conservative counterweight to the American Civil Liberties Union. It specializes in taking up conservative legal causes, with a particular focus on the First Amendment's guarantees of religious liberty and free speech. Sekulow became chief counsel more than twenty-three years ago, and over those decades earned a reputation as a tough litigator, one who has had his share of trips to the Supreme Court.

Sekulow remembers his office started getting calls as soon as the questionnaires hit, and he quickly agreed to get on a national call. "The purpose of that call was to say that we needed a unified response, that we were going to stand together in pushing back against questions that were not within the scope of legitimate inquiry," he recalls. He was also interested in figuring out "who in the world was triggering this." Sekulow started his career as an IRS trial attorney, and he is familiar with tax-exempt issues. To him, "It was clear this was not coming from a local agent. No agent would look in the manual and ever see this kind of questioning. So it was clear right off to me that something else, bigger, was going on."

Sekulow on that call offered to represent those hit by the interrogatories. At a practical level, this meant that ACLJ attorneys would help to pilot groups through the process, advising them on what they did need to provide, what they didn't, and how to deal with the IRS. He also reassured participants that ACLJ's representation would help protect against IRS retaliation. He even suggested that the IRS letters might be grounds for a civil rights lawsuit, given the questions about donors and what appeared to potentially be an effort by the federal government to get access to the Tea Party's membership rolls. Because Sekulow was astounded: "In thirty-five years of law I've seen laws that were poorly written and violations of free speech because regulations were poorly imposed. But I'd never seen a deliberate case of targeting of a political group by the government in all my years. This was the NAACP; it was the same playbook."

By the time of that call, Kenney had already been sitting in her garage for hours, sorting through handouts and files, along with hours more of lugging things off to make copies and put in order so as to comply with the IRS questionnaire. She was coming up on the extended deadline and so decided to just send her reply in.

Before she'd even mailed it, she got slammed with a second round of questions. (*I kept getting this mental image of Godzilla versus Bambi. Stomp. Stomp. Stomp.*) The harassment was no less obnoxious, the amount of work required to fulfill the IRS request no less intense. But this time, with ACLJ on board, Kenney felt more confident. "What they primarily did was to help us not feel intimidated," she recalls. "They started acting as a gatekeeper, and they slowed it down. They got the IRS to back off somewhat. They couldn't stop the IRS from asking the questions, but they gave us confidence that we weren't in this alone."

Kenney went back to the garage, back to the copy machine, and got the second round of responses in the mail by the end of

March. And then she waited. Again. SFVP continued to hold its meetings, and talk about politics, and put out its newsletter. Kenney increased her correspondence with other Tea Party members about the state of the investigation, and kept her people updated on what was happening in Congress. The more she heard—about the questions groups were being asked, and their treatment by the tax authority—the more alarmed she became about the IRS's real intentions. The agency looked to be compiling a dossier that included the identification of Tea Party members, how they were selected, who they associated with, what they discussed, and even the names and contact information for their relatives.

In June, she opened her mailbox; sitting there was a third interrogatory. This one wanted the names and Social Security numbers of every person who had ever donated time or money to her organization.

Kenney was shocked. And scared. "I got it in my head that they weren't going to stop until I gave them the tax information on all of our attendees." And that, for her, was a no-go zone. She'd wanted tax-exempt status to improve her chance at grants, or perhaps have more financial ability to do public education during elections. Now the IRS was telling her that the price of that civic involvement was blowing up the anonymity of her members.

She chose her people. "I have people who show up and write tiny checks, or who give $5 or $10. They came to be involved. I had no intention of turning them over to the government."

She was also just sick of the process; she'd been hounded to breaking point. "It was such a burden, the requests, the delays. It was like, 'If you are going to grant it, just grant it—don't delay it forever.' It was like living on an eternal pause button."

Kenney pulled the plug. She wrote to the IRS telling the agency to rip up her application. The federal government had won.

∿

Kenney was right to be scared. Her decision to withdraw meant her IRS abuse ended at three questionnaires. Groups that continued to fight the process weren't so lucky.

Cleta Mitchell had without realizing it signed up to represent one that would become a national poster child for the perils of tangling with an abusive federal government and Democratic Congress. Mitchell had spent all of 2011 "haranguing" the IRS over that application she'd first filed in 2009. Nothing. Come February, her client, like more than a hundred other conservative groups, was whipsawed with a questionnaire. Mitchell dialed into that first conference call and heard Tea Party leaders recounting their experiences. "It was wild," she remembers. "There was an accountant—he said he'd never seen anything like this in thirty years. There were people saying the IRS had asked if any candidate had ever spoken at any of their meetings, and they are freaking out, saying 'Wait, we were not supposed to do that? Why?' The IRS wanted transcripts of meetings, and groups didn't have them. Everyone was so worried."

And then Engelbrecht got in touch. She'd received not one but two letters—inquiries into each of her groups, King Street Patriots and True the Vote. The KSP letter contained 95 questions and requests for documents, including copies of every page of its website, every fund-raising solicitation, every page of its training materials, every sheet of its handouts at all of its public events. The True the Vote inquiry—the IRS's second request for information from that group—contained a stunning 120 questions.

"They wanted everything: where she'd spoken, where she was planning to speak—for the next two years. Two years! When I got those letters I went insane. I redacted the identifying information about the specific clients, IRS agents, and offices, and then started stalking everyone on the Hill—staffers at House Ways and Means, House Oversight, Senate Finance. I kept saying over and over, 'Guys, something is really going on, and it's been really going on for two years,'" says Mitchell.

The lawyer started working with her clients to answer the interrogations. Only she didn't roll over. "I'd call these agents up and I'd say, 'You do realize that donor information is not public? You do realize you are telling us to disclose something that the statute says is confidential? How does *that* work?' And then they'd scurry around and say, 'Oh, you don't have to disclose the names, just the amounts.' And I'd say, 'Is that so?' And more scurrying, and then I'd get, 'Just skip that question.'"

She continues, "But that was one of the outrages of this; most people didn't have representation. And if you didn't have a Cleta Mitchell type barking at the IRS for you, you were stuck complying with a process the agency had dreamed up out of whole cloth."

Mitchell also refused to play IRS games. She had one client applying for charitable status whose only mission was to educate about the Constitution and provide constitutional discussion guides to newly elected members of Congress. When the IRS demanded to know what materials the group was using, Mitchell mailed them a free copy of the Constitution. Nothing else. "I mean, how stupid are these people?" she asks, answering her own question.

True the Vote offered its reply to the IRS questions in March. It went back into limbo, only to get a fourth questionnaire a year later. KSP's response wouldn't go out until May 2012, and totaled more than three hundred pages. It got another demand for details in October.

The IRS process, and the delays, hit both of Engelbrecht's organizations hard. The IRS's questions were so intrusive and technical that Mitchell's help was required at nearly every step. Legal bills started to pile up. At the same time, donors were reluctant to write checks to an organization that didn't have official (c)(3) or (c)(4) status, and her lack of tax-exempt status disqualified her from applying for many foundation grants. She struggled to pull in money. In one case, TTV received grant money on the condition that it would receive its (c)(3) status by the end of the year. When it didn't materialize, Engelbrecht had to hand the money back. "When I look back on this time, I get misty-eyed," she admits. "We were passing a cowboy hat around at meetings to keep going. We were getting calls from people across the whole country saying, 'Will you work with us?' And yet I couldn't legitimize our status."

And the IRS questionnaires were almost the least of Engelbrecht's problems. She appeared to have become the target of a full-blown assault by entire departments of the federal government, as well as by powerful Democratic congressional leaders and outside liberal organizations—a crackdown inspired in no small part by the president of the United States.

Democrats didn't like any conservative (c)(4)s, but they particularly hated Engelbrecht's. They'd stewed for years over state efforts to tighten up voter ID laws and to weed out voting fraud. President Obama and Attorney General Eric Holder viciously criticized the laws, suggesting they were designed to "suppress" turnout among minorities. Since True the Vote was set up to aid in educating about and implementing the new voter ID laws, Democrats instantly zeroed in on the organization as a particularly hated target.

Engelbrecht Manufacturing was founded in 1994. From that day until 2010, Catherine had no interaction with the federal government other than to file the company's annual taxes. Then she applied for tax-exempt status for her two groups.

At the beginning of 2011 the IRS showed up to audit two years' worth of business taxes. Over the course of the year, the FBI would contact Engelbrecht six times—four phone calls and two personal visits. They were inquiries both about a strange visitor at a KSP event and also about KSP's broader activities. In June, the IRS audited her personal tax returns, for both 2008 and 2009. In February 2012—the same month that KSP and TTV were hit with IRS questionnaires—the Bureau of Alcohol, Tobacco, and

Firearms showed up for an audit of Engelbrecht Manufacturing. It was a bizarre visit; the company has a license to manufacture gun parts, but doesn't actually do so. And that fact was closely documented. And yet not only did ATF show up, but as part of its audit the agents asked for a look inside a personal gun safe. "I don't necessarily have a beef with the folks that came out—they were just doing their job. But my question remained not why they came—but who sent them?" she says.

In July, the Occupational Safety and Health Administration came knocking for its own audit, grilling company employees. OSHA soon sent Engelbrecht Manufacturing a $25,000 fine for trivial infractions. In November, the Texas Commission on Environmental Quality arrived for an audit, saying it had received an anonymous complaint. The agency demanded she pay for new permits. A few months later, ATF was back again, on yet another unscheduled audit. Once is happenstance. Twice is coincidence. Three times is enemy action. (Or so wrote Ian Fleming, the famous author of the James Bond series.)

Engelbrecht didn't tell anybody about these visits for a long time. And it was only when she finally did tell Mitchell that she realized she'd fallen for the government's tricks. "I remember saying to Cleta, 'Can I run something by you? It sounds crazy, but I feel like I can hear the propeller blades of a black helicopter over my shoulder. So I just need a reality check.' And so I told her. And she said, 'Catherine, why on earth haven't you said anything?! This is unacceptable, this is orchestrated, this is outrageous,'" remembers Engelbrecht. "And it choked me up when she said that. A light switch went on. And I realized that what had been perpetrated against me had worked. I'd stayed silent. I'd just hunkered down and tried to be a better citizen. When what I needed to do was go tell the story. That was my real power."

That decision gave Engelbrecht more determination to face what was still to come—including an assault by Democratic members of Congress and the president's campaign team.

In September 2012, California Senate Democrat Barbara Boxer sicced the Justice Department's Civil Rights Division on True the Vote, writing a letter accusing it of "leading a voter suppression campaign" and nicknaming it "Stop the Vote." A few weeks later, Maryland Democrat Elijah Cummings, the ranking member on the House Oversight Committee, launched his own investigation into TTV, sending Engelbrecht an extensive questionnaire that mirrored the IRS's inquisition. Engelbrecht politely suggested that the congressman didn't understand her group's work, and offered to fly all the way to Washington to explain. Cummings responded by asking for even more documents. "I accept your offer to come to Washington and answer these allegations, but only after you provide the documents I requested." He then went on to ominously claim she was engaged in "a criminal conspiracy to deny legitimate voters their Constitutional rights." Cummings proceeded to go on TV to attack the group.

Even as Cummings launched his salvo, Bob Bauer swung into action. This was an election year, and the Obama campaign general counsel again resorted to intimidation. He issued an open memo accusing TTV of coordinating with Republicans to engage in "vote suppression." His memo was a near-identical read to Cummings's letter to Engelbrecht—leveling the same accusations, marshaling the same specific events and facts—even though the Cummings letter hadn't yet been made public. And Cummings's demands of the group were strikingly similar to those posed by the IRS.

Indeed, e-mails would later show that the IRS had helped Cummings. In January 2013, an IRS employee informed Lerner and Paz that "the House oversight committee . . . has requested any publicly available information on an entity that they believe has filed for c3 status. . . . The entity is KSP True the Vote." Lerner and Paz personally saw to it that the request was fulfilled. This Paz e-mail would later come to Congress with significant parts redacted, marked as containing confidential taxpayer information. It's a crime for the IRS to share such information, even with most of Congress, and it is still unclear what Cummings obtained. Cummings initially denied that he or his staff had even reached out to the IRS, until the e-mails showed that to be false.

"Everything," says Mitchell, "everything was a complete abandonment of the rule of law. It was all the forces of government using harassment and intimidation to shut people down."

Mitchell attends a monthly meeting of tax attorneys in D.C., a brown-bag affair at which a friendly mix of liberal and conservative lawyers discuss issues and news. Mitchell in the spring took along several redacted IRS questionnaires. "I said, 'Any of you boys getting these?' No one on the left had." Mitchell kept bringing up the issue at the lunch meetings through 2012 and 2013, inspiring a few liberal colleagues to declare her obsessed. So she took particular pleasure in showing up at the June 2013 event after Lerner's turn in the spotlight. "'We thought you were crazy, Cleta, we thought you were being paranoid,'" Mitchell recalls them saying. "And I remember responding, 'Just because I'm paranoid, it doesn't mean someone isn't out to get my clients.'"

∿

Republicans were paying attention to the calls flooding in about those February 2012 questionnaires. Before the month was even out, GOP legislators had called in Lerner to brief them on the IRS's tax-exempt process. The chief boldly told Oversight staffers that the criteria for evaluating applications had not changed—which was untrue. Lerner herself had ordered it changed the prior July. She also made reference to the guide sheet Cincinnati was using to evaluate applications and offered to send a copy. That promise prompted a flurry of e-mails back at IRS headquarters, as lawyers and leadership worried about the document's content. The IRS never did send a copy. Lerner in the ensuing months continued to insist to Congress that everything happening at the IRS was in "the ordinary course" of things.

She wasn't alone in juking Congress. Immediately following that first briefing to congressional staff, Lerner got the command from Deputy Commissioner Steven Miller to explain what all the fuss was about. In that meeting, she acknowledged that there were more than two hundred applications on ice, and that the IRS had asked for information about donors. Miller passed those details on to IRS commissioner Doug Shulman. Only a few weeks later, when Shulman was asked at a congressional hearing whether the IRS was singling out groups, he'd nonetheless reply that "there is absolutely no targeting."

This is notable, given that inside the IRS senior leaders were realizing they had a problem. The very day after Shulman's testimony, Deputy Commissioner Miller convened senior staff to get a handle on what was going on—a meeting at which he'd admit that the news that the IRS was demanding donor information was "not very good." He was alarmed enough to dispatch a trusted adviser, Nan Marks, to Cincinnati to get a bead on the situation by conducting an internal review. Marks spent weeks evaluating the Cincy operation, and in early May presented her findings at a meeting that included Miller and Lerner. She told the deputy commissioner about the Be On the Lookout list, the use of Tea Party terms, the excessive delays, the inappropriate questions, the test cases. She told him that Cincinnati had been waiting for Washington's orders. Miller, the number two official at the IRS, was therefore as of May 2012 fully aware of everything that would ultimately cause a sensation a year later. And yet in public testimony after public testimony in front of Congress, he chose not to reveal the situation—not even when he replaced Shulman as acting commissioner in November of that year. At one point in July 2012 he was worried enough about an upcoming appearance that his staff drew up sample questions he might be asked about targeting. When the testimony passed without any direct reference,

Lerner sent him an e-mail congratulating him that the hearing had "turned out to be far more boring than it might have been."

Miller knew he had a problem, though: Marks's internal investigation had made that clear. Washington suddenly had new interest in working through Cincinnati's backlog. IRS headquarters helped create a new system to process the queue, and Miller demanded weekly updates.

Lerner was nonetheless left inexplicably free to continue her war against conservative advocacy groups. She frequently referred them for audits. In May 2012, she forwarded to the manager of the auditing department an article about an "anonymous donor" who had given to the conservative American Action Network. "Let's talk," her e-mail read. In June, she forwarded a different article to the same audit manager, this one containing mentions of Americans for Prosperity, Crossroads GPS, and Citizens United.

In January, Lerner forwarded yet another story, in which the left-leaning media outlet ProPublica had fretted about the "dark money" going to five conservative nonprofits. She asked her staff for a meeting on "the status of these applications." We don't know what happened in that meeting. But we do know that two of the groups were put in the IRS's surveillance program, and three were selected for audit. In total, four of the five groups underwent additional scrutiny.

She also remained focused on trapping nonprofits. Congressional Democrats, after all, hadn't stopped demanding action. In February 2012, just as the first Tea Party interrogatories were mailed across the country, seven Democratic senators sent a letter to the agency demanding an investigation into (c)(4)s. A month later, the same seven repeated the demand.

Lerner was paying attention. In one June e-mail, she cheered on Bauer's tactic of using FEC complaints to try to force conservative organizations to disclose their donors. She also e-mailed Marks, wanting to "pick" her "brain" about a new inspiration she'd had—a way to speed up the time frame in which the IRS could force social-welfare organizations to file tax data. In July, she directed her team to put together a proposal for how to keep better track of groups receiving anonymous donations. In November, her staff compiled for her a report on the political activities of nonprofits and whether those activities had increased since *Citizens United*.

Lerner herself had absorbed the view that government needed to blow up anonymity, and then embarrass and intimidate conservative groups out of political participation. All through 2010 and 2011 the IRS kept conservative groups in limbo. The next year was devoted to hounding them for information. In March 2013, those details now in hand, Lerner got ready for a big moment: issuing the first letter denying exempt status to a conservative (c)(4) group.

Denial letters are supposed to be private, and it is up to the group to decide whether to fight the ruling. But Lerner spent precious time strategizing a way to make this first one public by immediately forcing the case to court. Even her staff was taken aback by this idea and tried to dissuade her. She was insistent: "One IRS prosecution would make an impact and they wouldn't feel so comfortable doing the stuff." She also harried her staff along: "need to move c4 denials along—really need to get one out of here."

∿

Lerner never got to issue her letter. Something—or rather someone—intervened. His name was J. Russell George, who since 2004 had served as the Treasury inspector general for tax administration, a watchdog post nicknamed TIGTA. House Republicans hadn't been fooled by Lerner's February performance, and almost immediately reached out to TIGTA to ask for an investigation. He agreed.

George spent a year looking into the scandal, and he deserves credit for bringing it to light. At the same time, his approach to the investigation left a lot to be desired.

For one, he took the highly unusual decision to allow Holly Paz (Lerner's top deputy) to sit in on every interview with ground-level employees, which had the effect of discouraging many of them from speaking freely. He also decided to update Lerner and other IRS leadership on his progress throughout the entire year, sharing multiple drafts of his report with them. This nod to fairness did not extend to Congress. He never once briefed members on the state of his investigation—an action that surely would have blown the lid off the IRS's misbehavior. That may be why George didn't—he figured Congress would break the news and potentially derail his probe. Yet his decision to keep Congress in the dark meant that the IRS was able to continue its targeting throughout 2012 and 2013, and that hundreds of conservative groups remained sidelined in a presidential election.

George's investigation, despite taking a year, was also light. He never truly grilled employees. He didn't requisition broad swaths of e-mails, or seek to truly understand how the targeting had evolved. His ultimate report instead read a bit like a statistical analysis—heavy on numbers and facts, light on blame.

The numbers and facts themselves were damning, and important to establishing from the get-go—and from a neutral source—that the IRS had behaved atrociously. At the same time, George's reluctance to go beyond a basic audit—his failure to investigate who drove the affair, or the role politics played—kept the field open for the left to make up its own narrative.

Because George traded drafts with the IRS, the agency by April knew it would no longer be able to hide what had been going on. It decided to get out ahead of TIGTA and announce the news itself. Lerner's ultimate apology wasn't some hastily concocted affair, but the culmination of weeks of plotting at the highest levels of the IRS and Treasury Department.

And it was aimed at minimizing fallout. Steven Miller, the now acting IRS commissioner, headed up that discussion, debating possible venues with his advisers throughout April. One possibility was a Georgetown University forum where Lerner was scheduled to speak on April 25; the IRS went so far as to draft her remarks. The proposal shot up the ranks at Treasury, where Obama appointees (for unknown reasons) nixed the idea.

Miller considered several other May events before settling on the ABA panel on May 10. This idea, too, was run by the chief of staff to Treasury Secretary Tim Geithner. When no objections came, Miller handed Lerner handwritten talking points he'd crafted for her to use at the event.

Miller played his part, using a closed-door session at the ABA event on May 9—the day before the big apology—to hint at the news and to blame the IRS's actions on "dumb" moves by staff and the "wave of cash" that had followed *Citizens United*.

Lerner meanwhile sought out a friendly tax attorney, Celia Roady, to deliver a planted question from the audience. And so on May 10, 2013—more than three years after the first conservative applications were segregated out and subjected to hostile treatment by the most powerful government on the planet—Lerner dropped the bomb. "So our line people in Cincinnati who handled the applications did what we call centralization of these cases. They centralized work on these in one particular group. . . . However, in these cases, the way they did the centralization was not so fine. Instead of referring to the cases as advocacy cases, they actually used case names on this list. They used names like Tea Party or Patriot and they selected cases simply because the applications had those names in the title. That was wrong, that was absolutely incorrect, insensitive, and inappropriate—that's not how we go about selecting cases for further review."

Within minutes of Lerner's talk, Washington went batshit. Cable news channels exploded, e-mails flew, staffers scrambled to write up statements. Some professed shock, some incredulity. But the overriding emotion was fury.

Congress was furious. "Lerner, and all the way up the chain—they sat here for a year and lied to us," recalls Ohio Republican Jim Jordan, who spearheaded the IRS investigation at the House Oversight Committee. "Flat. Out. Lied. And then dumped this apology, like it was no big deal." Republicans like Jordan immediately understood that not only was the IRS admitting to a crime, but to an elaborate cover-up—one that had involved duping the people's elected representatives. Speaker John Boehner summed up the general view when he asked, "My question isn't about who's going to resign. My question is who's going to jail over this scandal?"

TIGTA's office was furious. It had spent a year on its audit, meticulously working to put together a straightforward report, giving the IRS every courtesy, and the agency had messed with the release. It had gone public before George could even get the final clearances for his report. The inspector general would later testify that he'd never seen a situation in which the IRS had leaked the contents of a report before it had been made public.

President Obama feigned fury. "The misconduct . . . is inexcusable. It's inexcusable, and Americans are right to be angry about it, and I am angry about it," he said. "I will not tolerate this kind of behavior in any agency, but especially in the IRS, given the power that it has and the reach that it has into all of our lives."

Other Democrats joined in proclaiming righteous indignation. Missouri senator Claire McCaskill claimed, "We should not only fire the head of the IRS . . . we've got to go down the line and find every single person who had anything to do with this and make sure that they are removed from the IRS and the word goes out that this is unacceptable." West Virginia senator Joe Manchin railed that the IRS actions were "un-American." Montana senator Max Baucus, who'd first requested that the IRS investigate groups, suddenly decided that this was an "outrageous abuse of power."

Commentators were furious. NBC's Tom Brokaw declared, "It's time for action." ABC's Terry Moran called it a "truly Nixonian abuse of power by the Obama administration." Even liberal pundits were unhappy. MSNBC's Rachel Maddow, who rarely misses a chance to compare conservatives to devil's spawn, worried about the misuse of IRS power and said the unequal scrutiny put on conservative groups hadn't been fair. Comedy Central's Jon Stewart, in a moment of sincerity, slammed the Obama administration for its lack of "managerial competence."

Cincinnati was furious. Following Lerner's apology, Cindy Thomas whipped off a vicious e-mail to her and Paz, in which she declared that Cincinnati hadn't been just thrown under the bus, it'd been "hit by a convoy of Mack trucks."

But no one was more furious than the Tea Partiers themselves and their advocates. Mitchell processed, with mounting fury, the lengths to which the IRS had gone to hide all this and then attempted to make it a "nonstory" by chucking it out on a Friday. "All I could think was, 'Don't issue a damn apology. Issue my clients a letter of determination.'"

It'd be a very long time before that happened.

∿

To this day, many Washington politicians will insist that we still don't have the full story on the IRS debacle. That's true, to the extent that we're still missing relevant e-mails and testimony. Then again, the key to unraveling any good mystery is identifying the motive, the crime, and the cover-up.

We know the crime—the targeting of conservative applications.

We now know the motive. The Obama administration wanted

to silence conservative groups before they could harm Democrats in elections. Not all Americans noticed it, but that motive was on vivid display for years. Through most of 2009 and 2010, Democrats publicly seethed with frustration over these groups; it was their top concern.

Thanks to several years of investigation, we also now know the cover-up. The very Democrats who pushed the IRS to act would, when caught, peddle a tale based on lies and misdirection. The country was told that the IRS had been hit by a flood of social-welfare applications that overwhelmed the system; that "low-level" employees were confused by a murky law; that liberal groups had also been caught in the snare; that conservative organizations were taking advantage of tax laws; that the Washington IRS had stepped in to remedy the problems. Not a bit of it was remotely true. The effort the left put into covering up what really happened is the most damning evidence of the crime.

Here's what we do know, three years out from Lerner's apology. We know a Democratic Party, worried by the backlash to its policies, and terrified by the Supreme Court's blessing of freer speech, focused all its attention on silencing its political opponents.

We know its message was directed at an IRS that was already primed—by ideology and bureaucracy—to isolate and harass and delay the work of groups opposed to Obama.

We know that agency had already been captured by Obama acolytes, who were shifting it into an enforcer of administration policies on speech and health care.

We know the system the IRS set up was designed to capture only conservative groups, and to keep them on ice until the agency could find a way to shut them down entirely.

We know top officials contemplated other means of quieting its opposition, including a Justice Department plan for criminal prosecutions.

We know administration officials were fully briefed about IRS targeting in the run-up to the 2012 election, and kept it secret. We know that they were successful, and the effort helped to keep Obama in office and the Senate in Democratic hands.

We know that those officials then plotted a way to keep the news under the radar. We know that when it finally came out, they lied to Congress. And we know that all this went on for twenty-seven months, and swept up conservative groups that ranged from high-profile players to the Karen Kenneys of the world.

CHAPTER 9

Frosted

CONGRESSMAN JIM JORDAN was in his Ohio district, on the way to a speech, when Lerner spilled her beans. He'd known something was coming; TIGTA had given his office a heads-up that his IRS audit would go public soon, though Jordan didn't know what was in it. He saw the name of his chief counsel, Chris Hixon, show up on the phone. "I hit the button and all he said was, 'Shit, it's true.'"

Jordan's first emotion: anger, and on a lot of levels. He'd won Ohio's 4th Congressional District in 2006, bucking the anti GOP wave of that year. The 4th is Ohio's most conservative district, and Jordan's a perfect fit. He's principled, tough, in touch, and in tune with his conservative grassroots. A lot of that connection came from his years in the Ohio General Assembly and Senate. But he also has a strong affinity for the Tea Party groups and their beliefs; he and his wife homeschooled their kids, they're pro-family, anti–big government.

So he'd been tight with groups like the Sidney Shelby County Liberty Group, and highly visible conservative leaders like Tom Zawistowski, who ran the Portage County TEA Party. Those groups and others flooded Jordan's phone lines in the wake of their February 2012 IRS letters. The congressman was concerned, but also unsure of what to make of the interrogatories.

"Was it just some mistake at the IRS, was it illegal, was it something in between?" he remembers. "At the time, it was hard to know."

Now he had heard from Lerner herself that it was far worse than anyone could have guessed. It had been a vast and orchestrated targeting campaign. That made Jordan boil.

"There's plenty to be unhappy about with government. But this—this is the most fundamental right we have," says Jordan, who in an interview two years later still looks dangerous even talking about it. "I don't mean for this to sound apple pie, but this is the *First Amendment*—it is freedom of religion, freedom of assembly, and freedom of association. But of all those, the one the Founders stressed most was freedom of speech—and of that, political speech is the most important. It's your most fundamental right to criticize your government. It does not get more basic than that."

What equally upset Jordan was the mismatch—an overpowered, "cavalier," and "arrogant" federal beast, going after the little folk. "The people they were targeting are good, honest, regular American families. They are regular people, like my mom and dad, who are doing something so basic—caring about this country. We are raised to care about this country, to speak out. It's just that basic. I get mad even now just thinking about it."

Jordan's a former NCAA wrestling champion and Division I wrestling coach, still looks like one, and he does an honest mad face. He's sat on the House Oversight Committee since he was first elected, and is intense about his duty to oversee the executive branch.

And that's also what "frosted" him about the Lerner admission. Jordan hadn't known what to make of those first, February complaints, but he'd taken them seriously. Within a few weeks he'd called Lerner in front of his staff to answer questions. Jordan's team peppered many more IRS officials with questions in the eighteen months that followed. Every bureaucrat, on every occasion, insisted that there was nothing funny going on. Hixon's call set Jordan to remembering all of them. "When she gave that speech, a lot of Washington was wrapping its head around the fact that this had happened. But I'd already had all this interaction. So I was sitting in Ohio thinking, 'They lied about this.' And I thought, 'Game on.'"

∿

Democrats also shouldn't have been surprised by the news. They'd inspired the targeting. They knew that a Democratic administration and Democratic Senate and Democratic House members had called on an IRS staffed with Democratic appointees to go after conservative groups.

They now knew that the IRS had done just that. They knew the nation was outraged. They knew Republicans and the media were asking whether Obama had ordered this, whether we had a new Nixon-era level of political targeting going on. And they knew that this was no time for excuses or partisanship. So Democrats joined Republicans in expressing outrage.

Obama labeled the IRS's actions "inexcusable" and vowed to work "hand in hand" with Congress as it investigated the affair. The president was at pains to say he'd only learned about the targeting from "the same news reports" as the rest of America. White House press spokesman Jay Carney was at even greater pains to note that while the White House had been informed almost a month earlier that something was amiss at the IRS, the president had never been told.

In the Senate, Max Baucus wasn't the only Democrat who had written to demand that the IRS take action against (c)(4) groups, but who now claimed to be outraged that it had done so. There was Oregon's Jeff Merkley, who insisted that "what the IRS did was wrong" and that those "responsible" must be "punished." There was New Hampshire's Jeanne Shaheen, who claimed that the IRS actions were "completely unacceptable." And there was New York's Chuck Schumer, who maintained that "heads should roll at the agency."

Democrats in red and purple states, many of them up for reelection in eighteen months, nearly climbed over each other to produce appropriate levels of outrage. North Carolina's Kay Hagan couldn't believe how "disturbing and troubling" was the news. Arkansas's Mark Pryor took to Twitter, promising he'd "get to the bottom of this so we can fire those responsible & ensure this never happens again."

And the administration at least put on the appearance of a swift response. Four days after the Lerner event, the Justice Department unveiled a criminal investigation. Five days after the event, the IRS announced that Miller was on his way out as acting commissioner. Six days after the event, Obama appointed Office of Management and Budget controller Danny Werfel to lead the IRS, promising he'd "restore confidence and trust." Thirteen days after the event, Lerner was placed on administrative leave, having refused to testify before Congress or retire.

And yet it was all a sham.

Democrats created the environment that pressured the IRS to act. The Justice Department investigation never went far. Werfel delayed the congressional probe, and instituted policies designed to further hamper nonprofit activity. Lerner was never fired, prosecuted, or even reprimanded.

Instead, from the moment the scandal broke, the IRS and White House were spinning a yarn—setting a false narrative and minimizing the misdeeds. That yarn started only seven days after the Lerner admission, when Democratic operatives began to spread the story that the IRS had identified two "rogue" Cincinnati employees as the source of the entire problem. The entire Democratic establishment continued to weave what the *National Review*'s Rich Lowry would come to term the "Cincinnati Lie."

Just one week after Lerner's confession, Washington Democratic representative Jim McDermott used his opening statement at a Ways and Means hearing to declare, "There is a difference between stupid mistakes and malicious mistakes," and all that had happened at the IRS was that a "small group of people in the Cincinnati office screwed up." Press Secretary Jay Carney ten days after the scandal broke marked it all down to "line employees at the IRS who improperly targeted conservative groups." James Carville, the go-to Democratic defender on cable TV, wrote the affair off as just "some people in the Cincinnati office." Of course, even this Democratic telling of the scandal should have caused alarm. The idea that some "rogue" agents in Cincinnati could silence the speech of tens of thousands of Americans—and nobody noticed—is a damning criticism in and of itself.

This early slant would nonetheless prove remarkably effective. Millions of Americans would come to believe the following: that the United States has confusing tax-exempt laws (not true); that a flood of social-welfare and charitable applications overwhelmed that system (not true); that "low-level" and "rogue" agents had stepped out of bounds (not true); and that even liberal groups had been swept up in the harassment (definitely not true). It would take Jordan and other congressional investigators close to two years to unravel what had really happened. By then, not a lot of Americans were paying attention anymore.

∿

Ask Jordan how much time he's spent on the IRS investigation and he laughs out loud—a lot of time. House Oversight chairman Darrell Issa officially walked point on the IRS investigation, but much of the real work came from Jordan, who chaired the Subcommittee on Government Operations. He wasn't the only one digging deep into the IRS mess. Michigan representative Dave Camp's Ways and Means Committee did yeoman's work, as did Utah senator Orrin Hatch. (Oregon senator Ron Wyden, who worked with Hatch on the Senate report, was one of the few Democrats who showed an interest in finding the truth.) But Jordan felt a personal connection to this outrage and personally spearheaded the probe.

That's unusual for a congressman, as even his staff will admit. Jordan is gracious, and continuously gives credit to a dutiful team that diligently pieced together the IRS intimidation game. It ultimately reviewed more than 1.3 million pages of documents from the IRS, Treasury, Justice, the FEC, the IRS Oversight Board, and TIGTA. It sat through close to fifty-five interviews and did the legwork for endless public hearings. "These guys worked their tails off," says Jordan, noting that a lot of what he'd learn came from telephone briefings with this team.

But his staff in turn love to point out that Jordan was intimately involved—absorbing the information, running down questions, even personally sitting in on interviews to grill witnesses. "These are daylong affairs," says one of Jordan's aides. "And he'd be there the whole day, asking questions, picking up inconsistencies, going back on points. It's really rare to have a congressman do that. He ran this thing."

Jordan's memory burned with the meeting his staff had conducted with Lerner just following the February mailout of the IRS letters. "We had a copy of the questions the IRS had sent, and we asked her, 'Is this standard operating procedure?'" he recalls. "She lied to these guys. She said, 'This is the normal back-and-forth.'"

Prior to Lerner's announcement, the IRS had been just one thing on Jordan's to-do list; after, it became Jordan's morning, noon, and night focus. His team started from the bottom up. "We began by interviewing the guy who collects the paper in Cincinnati and opens the mail—and we went all the way up to the commissioner. And then on to people at Justice and the Federal Election Commission," remembers Jordan. He would sit at a desk in the middle of his staff office, one or another member of his group blaring on speakerphone, as the team gamed out areas of inquiry, sorted through inconsistencies, and worked out questions for interviews or hearings.

Jordan's team managed to get in a few weeks of productive work before the barriers started going up.

∿

It took Democrats less than a month to drop all their feigned outrage over the IRS scandal and to move swiftly to accusing Republicans of playing political games. As the days ticked on, the fear they felt over getting blamed for the targeting scandal paled by comparison to that they felt about losing the Senate in the 2014 midterms—or the presidency. They remained as intent as ever on shutting up conservative groups.

Two short weeks after Lerner's admission, senior Senate Democrat Dick Durbin found himself on *Fox News Sunday* being grilled by host Chris Wallace over the letter he'd sent the prior October to the IRS demanding an investigation of conservative groups. Durbin was unapologetic, and suggested that groups deserved the scrutiny. He complained that conservatives like "Karl Rove" at Crossroads were "boasting" about "how much money they were going to raise and beat Democrats." Durbin couldn't help admitting what he had been trying to accomplish—a culture of fear: "I knew that if they went to investigate this group, every other group would be put on notice."

Then there was Elijah Cummings, Darrell Issa's Democratic counterpart, the ranking member on the Oversight Committee. Cummings at the first hearing in May expressed his concern over the scandal and his hope for a "bipartisan and thorough investigation." "Thorough" in Cummings's mind was the space of one month. That's how long it took before he went on national television, in an interview with CNN's Candy Crowley, to declare the case "solved" (it was Cincinnati's fault) and to claim that "if it were me, I would wrap this case up and move on." At the time of that interview, Congress had interviewed all of five IRS employees.

When Republicans didn't take his advice, Cummings attempted to sabotage the probe. He at one point released a full transcript of one IRS employee interview, giving future witnesses a guide as to what they'd be asked in their own examinations, and allowing them to coordinate testimony. One IRS employee would later admit that prior to his own meeting with Congress, he'd been told by a supervisor to review the transcript Cummings had released.

Then again, Cummings had good reason to make this go away. The investigation would later find that his staff had been in contact with the IRS throughout the targeting scandal, going so far as to leak it information about upcoming congressional actions. In March 2012, soon after Congress started taking an interest in the IRS's actions, one IRS employee wrote to his superiors, "I got some intelligence from a senior Democratic staff member on House Oversight and Government Reform. . . . [A] hearing in May or June on 501 c 4s may be in the works."

∿

The biggest "tell" of Democrats' role in the IRS scandal may in fact be their involvement in the elaborate cover-up that followed. The left realized that Republicans very early on were beginning to blow holes in the Cincinnati lie, and Democrats wanted desperately to shut down the discussion.

Mitchell was one of the first to expose the Cincinnati scam, when she supplied to a reporter the letter she'd penned to the IRS back in October 2011—the one in which she'd asked the Cincinnati agent to forward the correspondence to the "task force" in Washington he'd mentioned. Mitchell's information ended up on the front page of the *Washington Post* five days after Lerner's Cincinnati lie.

A favorite Democratic way of undermining the probe was to claim that Republicans who wanted answers were engaged in partisan politics. Starting about the time of his Crowley interview, Cummings rarely referred to the IRS investigation without including the words "witch hunt." Liberal groups and media outlets picked up the cry, arguing that the GOP was belaboring the probe (now a whole month old) in order to gain political advantage in the next election.

The White House also took up the line, if more subtly and slowly. Obama got the ball rolling at the end of July. At an economic address at Knox College in Illinois, he accused the GOP of engaging in an "endless parade of distractions, political posturing, and phony scandals." Obama didn't specify what scandal he meant, but it was a clear reference to the tax agency uproar. Fox's Chris Wallace clarified it a few days later, asking Treasury Secretary Jack Lew if he thought the IRS targeting was just a "phony scandal." Lew's response: "There's no evidence of any political decision maker who was involved in any of those decisions. And I think the attempt to try to keep finding that evidence is creating the kind of sense of a phony scandal that was being referred to there." So, yes, the president was saying—two months after the news broke—that the whole IRS thing was just a "phony scandal."

December came, and Obama decided enough time had passed to mark the entire affair down to a government bumble. "If . . . you've got an office in Cincinnati, in the IRS office that— I think, for bureaucratic reasons—is trying to streamline what is a difficult law to interpret about whether a nonprofit is actually a political organization, deserves a tax-exempt agency. And they've got a list, and suddenly everybody's outraged," he told MSNBC host Chris Matthews. Obama's own initial outrage was clearly gone. He'd moved on to trying to reset the entire debate. His interview words suggested it was the IRS's job to weed politics out of nonprofits—which simply isn't true. And he suggested that the problem was a confusing law. In fact nothing had changed about

the law in 2010; the provision governing nonprofits had been easily and fairly enforced for fifty years. The only thing that had
changed was a new administration, with a new view of the role of
the IRS.

Obama would in later years go much further, telling Fox's Bill
O'Reilly that there was "not even a smidgeon of corruption" in
the events at the IRS. Rather, said the president, the only problems were some "bone-headed decisions."

The entire White House mobilized against the congressional
probes. White House counsel Kathryn Ruemmler in November
2013 flat-out refused to assist Jordan and Issa in questions they
had about the White House's interaction with the IRS. Specifically, the White House wouldn't let the committee interview
Jennifer O'Connor, who had worked as the top lawyer to the IRS
commissioner, and had helped lead the agency's response to congressional hearings. The committee ultimately had to subpoena
O'Connor (who'd been promoted to a deputy White House
counsel), and she stonewalled her way through a hearing.

Obama's other clever stall strategy: that Justice Department
"investigation." The probe was never real, but it allowed the
White House to claim that something was being done, and to
later declare that no crime had taken place.

Jordan grew worried about that probe early on, when FBI director Robert Mueller appeared before Congress. Mueller was
flummoxed by even the most straightforward questions about the
status of his so-called investigation. He didn't know how many
people had been interviewed. He didn't know how many agents
were working the case. He didn't know who was the lead investigator. He admitted he hadn't even been briefed on the status of
an investigation into one of the biggest scandals in Washington.
"Mueller's reaction; that set the tone," says Jordan. "It was pretty
clear there'd be no help there."

Issa and Jordan would twice in 2013 write to the new FBI director, James Comey, for updates. The law enforcement agency

steadfastly refused to give information, steadfastly refused to brief Congress, steadfastly made clear that it had little or no interest in pursuing the subject. Mueller's confusion notwithstanding, the committee found out that the lead investigator was Barbara Bosserman, an Obama donor and DOJ civil rights attorney.

Mitchell vividly remembers her own interaction with Justice "investigators" as one of the more "bizarre" conversations of her life. In February 2014, Mitchell testified in front of Congress, blasting the Justice Department probe as a "sham" and a "nonexistent investigation." Her proof was that eight months into the probe not one of her clients had been interviewed. Not a single one of Sekulow's had been interviewed either. South Carolina's Trey Gowdy, a former federal prosecutor who knows something about conducting investigations, asked at the hearing how it was that the president could declare that there had been not a smidgeon of corruption when the FBI had yet to even interview anyone targeted.

Just a few days later, Mitchell got a call from an FBI agent inviting her and Engelbrecht in for an interview. "I remember saying, 'Gee, it's been a while. I've been wondering where you are. You are probably aware that I was recently a bit critical that it had taken you so long to consider my clients.' And he admitted, 'Yes we are aware,'" says Mitchell. The attorney decided to attend that first meeting on her own. Bosserman was present, and Mitchell remembers that she said almost nothing the entire time Mitchell spoke. Only when Mitchell started talking about the national conference calls conservative groups had arranged right after the first letters hit did Bosserman pipe up. "She suddenly looks up and says, 'Were there any progressive groups on that call?' And I said, 'Why on earth would there have been any progressive groups on that call? Nothing happened to progressive groups!' What the hell kind of question is that?"

By early 2014, the administration had already leaked to the *Wall Street Journal* that the FBI planned no prosecutions in the probe. To this day, Congress has never received information about the administration's "investigation" into the IRS scandal. Jordan believes this to be as big a threat to the freedom of the country as the targeting itself. "When you have a Justice Department more focused on politics than justice, the country is in trouble. And there is no denying that is where we are."

∿

Nobody knew nothing. The IRS was a stone wall from the moment Congress started its inquiry.

Doug Shulman, who'd been commissioner until the end of 2012, declared after the scandal broke that he didn't "accept responsibility." He'd known about the backlog, known the IRS had asked for donor information, and yet had never informed Congress.

Jonathan Davis, chief of staff to Shulman, would tell investigators that he didn't really have "a background in tax law" and so it just wasn't "something I was involved with." At one point in the questioning, Davis was asked if there was anything he might have done to prevent this issue from happening. He responded, "I would leave that to the people who know a lot more about this than I do." To which the congressional questioner responded, "Sir, you were the chief of staff to the Commissioner of the IRS."

Steven Miller, deputy commissioner throughout much of the targeting, and the man who replaced Shulman, at one point considered whether he should use an upcoming hearing in 2012 to tell Congress what was going on. He decided against it. He sat on the information for another year, and then helped craft the strategy for Lerner's apology. Yet he too now claimed he didn't really understand that this was "targeting."

Nikole Flax, Miller's chief of staff, used the TIGTA investigation as her own excuse for why she felt her boss shouldn't tell Congress anything.

Then there is the elusive William Wilkins, a man who has always deserved far more attention in this scandal. The IRS—to keep up the façade that it is a "neutral" agency—has only two political appointees. One is the commissioner, the other the chief counsel. Wilkins was appointed by Obama in 2009. He'd been a counsel for the Democratic Senate Finance Committee, and then a registered lobbyist at a left-leaning law firm, WilmerHale, from which he donated to Democratic candidates. He also had another close tie to Obama: He'd led the defense team for Reverend Jeremiah Wright's Trinity United Church of Christ in Chicago when it was under investigation by (as it happens) the IRS.

Wilkins's IRS office oversaw the review of test applications in 2011, and the guide sheet that screeners received in 2012 that led to all the interrogatories. Put another way, this was a Democratic appointee's office that was filtering conservative applications. Wilkins would claim in an interview that while he was aware of "complaints" about targeting, he didn't really know what had happened until he read the TIGTA report. That was one of his more fulsome answers. Wilkins would instead recite the phrase "I don't recall" more than eighty times during his congressional interview.

To this day, we still have no evidence if the White House was directly involved in the IRS scandal. But the closest link that exists is Wilkins. The Obama appointee was at the IRS from the minute it started suppressing, through the dark days of the questionnaires, through the Lerner admission, through the aftermath. Even as every other IRS leadership role changed hands, Wilkins didn't move from his office. He's still there today.

∿

Within days of her admission and apology, Congress had invited Lerner to testify. Investigators had already realized that she was at the epicenter of the story, and Jordan knew she'd made mis-representations to the committee. Perhaps for that reason, her attorney immediately informed Congress that she intended to assert her Fifth Amendment rights and asked that she be excused from appearing. Issa was having none of it, and compelled her to attend. What followed was a spectacle, as Lerner metaphorically flipped off the nation.

Lerner showed up on May 22 having made clear her intention to assert the Fifth. The committee was ready for it. Lerner instead responded to the committee's first inquiry with a long and combative statement. She recited a potted history of her government tenure and then launched into a defense. "I have not done anything wrong. I have not broken any laws. I have not violated any IRS rules or regulations, and I have not provided false information to this or any other congressional committee." Only after this monologue did she plead the Fifth, steadfastly refusing to answer dozens of questions.

Republican Trey Gowdy, the former prosecutor, was incensed. "Mr. Issa, Mr. Cummings just said we should run this like a courtroom, and I agree with him. She just testified. She just waived her Fifth Amendment right to privilege. You don't get to tell your side of the story and then not be subjected to a cross-examination. That's not the way it works." It worked for Lerner. She to this day has never answered a question for Congress. When the Oversight Committee recalled her a year later for another attempt at information, she repeated the same Fifth Amendment response to every question asked.

Lerner only took her right to remain silent so far. Congressional Republicans would later find out that she had agreed to submit to an interview with Justice investigators. She'd agreed to do this in the context of a "criminal" probe. She'd even agreed to it with no offer of legal immunity. Lerner clearly knew she had nothing to fear from the feds. She also talked to friendly media.

Lerner's congressional performance was so outrageous that the

IRS could no longer pretend she wasn't a problem. It asked her to resign. In yet one more brassy move, she refused, forcing the agency to instead place her on "administrative leave." In the regular world—outside of the federal government—this is known as paid vacation. When a review board prepared to recommend that she be removed from her position, the Obama higher-ups instead allowed her to retire with full pension and benefits.

∿

Steven Miller was booted as IRS commissioner within a few days of Lerner's apology, and Obama tapped Danny Werfel to run the IRS on an interim basis. Werfel was serving as controller of the Office of Management and Budget, and had never worked at the IRS. But what made him attractive to the administration was that few Americans had heard of him, and to the extent they had, it was in the context of eye-glazing news stories about budgets. This allowed the Obama team to pass him off as a wonky nonpartisan, even as it installed one of its own (along with Wilkins) at the top of the agency.

Werfel immediately promised his full cooperation. His actual idea of working with Congress was noncooperation with a smile. Investigators had at the very start requested that the IRS provide them documents related to eighty-one different search terms. Mr. Werfel's team unilaterally chose to cut that to twelve, explaining that most of the terms (including vital ones such as "c3") were too "generic." The IRS kept ratcheting down the number of documents it claimed it needed to turn over. And it sat on even those documents it did admit it needed to provide, offering endless inane excuses (at one point claiming to be unable for weeks to get into a password-protected disk). Two months into the investigation, the IRS had turned over just 3 percent of the required documents, derailing congressional efforts to prepare for witness interviews.

But if Werfel was the partisan heading up the stonewall for the administration, his successor was something worse. John Koskinen, nominated in August, was so convincing in his initial vow to kick IRS ass and take names that it would be another six months before Congress realized he was fully on board with the broader Obama cover-up.

Koskinen had spent most of his years as a corporate turnaround and fix-it artist at the Palmieri Company, a management consulting firm. He later parachuted into Freddie Mac, to stanch the financial and political fallout that hit the mortgage giant during the 2008 financial crisis. The story goes that Koskinen was offered an (un-named) job in the early days of the Obama administration, but turned it down, telling the White House to call if they had some-thing disastrous that no one else wanted to manage. The seventy-three-year-old breezed through his congressional hearings on promises to cooperate fully with Congress and get the IRS back on track. He was sworn in on December 23, 2013.

Not every Republican was taken in. Koskinen presented him-self as a tough old bird, but Washington old-timers knew that he was first and foremost a tough old Democrat—and a savvy one. Freddie Mac ranks only behind Fannie Mae as one of the most politically incestuous companies in the country, and it was no accident that its board recruited Koskinen when it hit hard times. The corporate veteran had a reputation for talking tough and making sense, even as he greased the political machinery be-hind the scenes.

Jordan was highly skeptical from the start. "Right after he got confirmed, but before he testified, he came in for a meeting. He was on the edge of his chair and he just kept talking and talking and lecturing," Jordan recalls. "And I wasn't mean about it, but I made the point that in this setting, I got to ask the questions. He got ticked. So from the get-go, we weren't exactly buddies."

Jordan would relatively quickly come to the conclusion that Koskinen had obstructed Congress's investigation. He believed the new IRS head was there to make sure that the truth never came out, and to make sure the Obama administration was free to continue its war on conservative groups.

∿

Luckily for the nation, there's another guy in Washington who is never taken in by anything—not by Republicans, not by Democrats, not by anyone. Tom Fitton might count as the biggest cynic on the planet. If a fluffy, dancing unicorn with a rainbow hovering over its head smiled at Fitton on a Washington street corner, Fitton would file a lawsuit to figure out what it was up to.

Because that's what Fitton does. Judicial Watch is a conservative watchdog group, and its president starts from the assumption that nearly everyone in Washington is lying and that the only way to hold them accountable is to drag their documents into the sunshine. The group specializes in Freedom of Information Act requests. At any one time it has thousands pending. When agencies ignore or delay or obstruct these requests, Judicial Watch's team of lawyers tee up litigation. Within a few weeks of Lerner's admission, that team had filed a FOIA demand with the IRS.

Fitton despises pretty much every government agency, but he had an extra-special reason to assume that the IRS and Lerner had done the worst. Judicial Watch, way back when, had dogged the Clinton administration, and the 501(c)(3)'s reward was a giant IRS audit. Fitton remembers an IRS official telling him, "What do you expect? If you're going to scrutinize the government, the government is going to scrutinize you." As Judicial Watch pushed back against the tax agency, the IRS continued to add years to the audit—to the point that the group faced an audit pretty much every year of its existence. He also remembered who was running the Exempt Organizations unit at that time: Steven Miller. "Let's just say that when the Lerner apology happened, I wasn't very surprised by it, or to see that Steven Miller was sitting as acting commissioner," says Fitton. "We'd already had a lot of experience with these tactics."

He and his colleagues quickly plowed ahead on the Lerner case because they knew they had the best shot to expose what had actually happened. The underappreciated reality of watchdog groups is that they have far more power to obtain documents than even Congress. "It's the same dance every time," explains Fitton. "Congress nicely asks an agency for documents, gets rebuffed. Then it gets in a subpoena battle, and has to go back and forth with an administration. And then its lawyer gets with their lawyer and they negotiate—how broad, and what Congress will or won't get, and back and forth, and on and on, and all this time the agency still hasn't told Congress much of anything. And if someone isn't happy with those discussions, they have to go to court. It's endless, and spotty. We are talking about two branches of government fighting. It doesn't get more dysfunctional and slow than that."

Watchdog groups have far more power under the law. "Once a group like ours files a FOIA request, the government is obliged to tell us what documents it has, and then give them to us in a certain time frame. The burden is entirely on them, and the courts are generally supportive. It's all about disclosure from *government*—rather than citizens—and that's why it is effective."

Judicial Watch would by that summer file four FOIA requests related to the IRS scandal. The group gave Werfel time to reply, but by fall, when it was still getting the stiff arm, it went to court. Had it not, the country to this day wouldn't know the degree to which the IRS and other parts of the administration were using government to shut down their opponents' speech.

CHAPTER 10

The Unraveling

IT'S THANKS to Judicial Watch that the nation now knows that the targeting wasn't contained within the "independent" IRS. It was done in tandem with other parts of the Obama administration. Indeed, one big reason why the Justice Department showed no interest in prosecuting anyone for the IRS scandal is that it might well have been forced to prosecute itself.

Fitton was among the biggest skeptics of the Justice Department's probe. "We all know the indications of a real probe. Ask Karl Rove what a serious grand jury investigation looks like," he wryly remarks, referring to the special prosecutor investigation into the "outing" of Valerie Plame, which required Rove to testify in front of a grand jury. At least some of the documents Fitton had received from the IRS also made him suspicious about Lerner's interaction with other parts of the federal machinery. So they kept combing through the IRS documents.

Jackpot.

The Judicial Watch litigation is how the world came to find out about a May 2013 e-mail Lerner received from Richard Pilger at Justice. Lerner ultimately e-mailed Commissioner Miller, explaining that Pilger wanted to work with the IRS to "piece together false statement cases" against nonprofits. It was an idea that had come out of a hearing held by Democratic senator Sheldon

Whitehouse, she explained, and "DOJ is feeling like it needs to respond."

Miller's chief of staff was enthusiastic, suggesting that Lerner and Pilger also rope in the criminal investigations department at Justice, and the Federal Election Commission. The exchange was remarkable. It happened only two days prior to Lerner's public apology, and proved that the administration was even then working on ways to bring down nonprofits. It provided yet more evidence that the IRS (and other departments) were acting at the pressure and request of congressional Democrats. And it exposed Justice's willingness to prosecute Americans for exercising free speech.

The exchange was remarkable to Jordan for a separate reason: It was the first he'd heard about it. Justice for nearly a year had been "investigating" the IRS scandal, and had never once revealed to Congress that it had previously been in on discussions with the IRS about how to go after conservative groups.

Jordan demanded that Pilger submit to an interview. The Justice Department attorney did, and within minutes of its start fessed up that he'd in fact first reached out to Lerner about prosecutions all the way back in 2010, in the wake of the *Citizens United* decision. He also divulged that Lerner had shipped to the FBI that 1.1-million-page database of information about nonprofits, inviting the nation's G-men to go on a fishing expedition. Jordan later found out that the database contained legally protected taxpayer information that should never have been handed to FBI investigators. "So what we've got here," Jordan says, "is this interaction beginning in 2010, and building into full-fledged targeting not long after, and now the knowledge that lots of Washington was in this from the get-go."

Not that Pilger divulged much beyond this terse confession. In the rest of the interview, a Justice attorney, who had insisted on accompanying Pilger to the meet with Congress, instructed him to refuse to answer questions on at least thirty-four separate occasions. Pilger was not allowed to answer any queries about what internal discussions DOJ had about (c)(4) groups following *Citizens United*, what interaction Justice had with the FEC on the issue, or whether Pilger had talked to anybody at the IRS since the Lerner confession.

∿

Judicial Watch's lawsuit led to a second, equally damning revelation: that the IRS had destroyed Lerner's e-mail.

That's not how Koskinen put it, of course. Not that Koskinen would have mentioned the issue at all, had not the agency been caught out.

Fitton, even before he received the Justice Department e-mails, knew the IRS was playing some sort of obscene game with document production. Everything about the process was weird. "Usually we get documents from a government agency all at once, or in a rolling production. But the IRS here started giving us the material in reverse chronological order—starting with things in 2013 and working back. I can't think of a time that has ever happened," says Fitton. "Now, in retrospect, it's clear it was to help avoid anyone finding out too soon that there were missing e-mails."

Jordan began wondering why his staff hadn't been in possession of that Pilger e-mail to Lerner in 2013, or of the interaction between Lerner and Pilger back in 2010. Congress, after all, had demanded all of Lerner's e-mails. But they'd never got any of the Pilger-Lerner correspondence.

Congress in August 2013 had first issued a subpoena for all of Lerner's documents from 2009 to 2013. The IRS ignored this request, arguing over its scope, taking a months-long hiatus from its promise of biweekly production, forbidding individual IRS employees from turning over their own correspondence to Congress, and redacting tens of thousands of pages of information. Congress as a result repeated the subpoena to Koskinen the moment he was sworn in. Within a few months, Koskinen was already mocking Republicans over this request, claiming that their document demand was too "broad" and warning it could take "years" to fulfill. He nonetheless promised to hand everything over.

Jordan knew he was still missing some e-mails, but the Pilger correspondence made him take a closer look. He realized there were entire gaps in the Lerner documents. "Something was weird. The whole timeline didn't match up," he says. "So we went to the IRS and starting asking why." The IRS didn't answer him. Instead, it waited a bit. And then, in obscure language in an obscure attachment to an obscure letter it sent to the Senate in June 2014, it slipped in the news that Lerner's hard drive had crashed in June 2011. Therefore, said the agency bluntly, it had forever "lost" much of her correspondence from the early part of the targeting.

∿

Jordan couldn't believe how long the IRS had kept that news secret, and couldn't believe the way in which it had then chosen to reveal it. Koskinen had vowed in March to get Congress all of Lerner's e-mails, yet it turned out his team had already known about the hard drive crash in February. According to the IRS's story, an attorney noticed that the agency had collected sixteen thousand documents for Lerner after April 2011, but only one hundred for the period before. The IRS was in February getting ready to deliver its first tranche of documents to Judicial Watch, and Fitton thinks it was his group's lawsuit that made the IRS notice the missing records.

Koskinen, according to his own testimony, learned the documents were missing in April (as did the White House), yet took until June to inform Congress, and then only did so by burying the detail in an attachment to a mind-numbingly boring letter to the Senate. "Here's my theory," says Jordan. "I don't think he was ever going to tell us. If the IRS hadn't been called out, if we hadn't figured out something was up after that Pilger correspondence, they'd have kept this from us forever. What does that tell you about the man brought in to 'reform' the IRS?"

The IRS also didn't bother to tell the *Justice Department* that thousands of e-mails from their prime suspect in their "investigation" had gone missing. "Imagine," says Jordan, "what would happen to a corporate executive if he waited months to tell federal investigators that his company had mysteriously lost its e-mails." Justice claimed it learned about the crashed drive in the news. Hans von Spakovsky, a free-speech hero who worked for years in the Justice Department, would later point out this little detail as proof that Justice's entire investigation was bogus. "The first thing you would do if you have the FBI as your investigator [in a] situation like this is go and seize all of the documents and information the way the FBI does when they're investigating a private organization. A year and a half later, they clearly had not done that and didn't even know that all of the evidence they were supposedly supposed to be looking at, all those e-mails, didn't exist," he testified.

Koskinen would meanwhile insist, in sworn testimony, that the IRS had exhausted every means of tracking down Lerner's documents, but that all backups and copies had been destroyed. Jordan and Congress had by this point gone beyond trusting any words coming out of his mouth, and instantly asked TIGTA to look into the affair. Sure enough, "two weeks after Koskinen says he lost them all and forever, TIGTA gets in a car and in a matter of days tracks down all these tapes the IRS claims it no longer had," recounts Jordan. (The discovery would ultimately prove disappointing, as the tapes contained but a small fraction of what Lerner likely stored on her hard drive.)

Government employees do experience hard drive failures, just like private citizens. And Democrats like to claim that Republicans who bang on about the missing Lerner e-mails are engaged in wild conspiracy theories. And it is also generally the case that government bureaucrats are too incompetent to pull off intricate schemes.

Yet if ever there were a government scandal that rose to conspiracy levels, it's the IRS epidemic of hard drive crashes. TIGTA would later report that as many as eight custodians involved in the IRS scandal experienced a hard drive crash. Most were close to Lerner or closely involved in the affair. They included Judy Kindell (one of Lerner's top advisers); Justin Lowe (who briefed Lerner on aspects of the nonprofit cases); Ronald Shoemaker (who oversaw the cases that came to Washington); Nikole Flax (chief of staff to the IRS commissioner); and several determination specialists in Cincinnati. TIGTA would also later interview computer specialists who said that the method by which Lerner's hard drive had failed was "uncommon." A technician noted the presence of concentric scoring of the hard drive platters on her drive, which an expert told TIGTA would "most likely" be caused by an "impact" to the hard drive or laptop. (Lerner, in her own interview with TIGTA, "denied hitting or damaging the hard drive intentionally.")

We also know that the IRS for years was loosey-goosey in its e-mail policy, allowing Lerner to use two private e-mail addresses to conduct work, and making use of an instant-messaging system that was (in direct contravention of federal rules) never archived. Lerner in 2013 would in fact send an e-mail warning her colleagues to be "cautious" about what they put in electronic mail (because of congressional inquiries) and then asked if the agency's instant-messaging system was searchable. When told it was not, she responded, "Perfect."

The IRS's decision to hide the crash from Congress meanwhile resulted in the destruction of Lerner documents. The IRS knew in February 2014 that Lerner's hard drive had crashed. TIGTA

would find out that in March 2014, IRS employees had magnet-
ically erased 422 tapes believed to contain Lerner's correspondence. The destruction of those tapes is suspicious, given that
the IRS's chief technology officer had the previous year—in response to Congress's investigation—issued an IRS-wide directive
ordering the agency was to retain all backup tapes. No more eras-
ing. The CTO, Terry Milholland, would later tell TIGTA that he
was "blown away" to discover those tapes had been erased, and
that he believed the destruction "more significant than the loss
of Lerner's hard drive." The bigger point is that had Koskinen's
office properly alerted Washington to Lerner's hard drive crash
when it first discovered the fact—a month before the erasure—
those tapes might have been saved.

Congress still has yet to see a fraction of Lerner's e-mail—and
it may never. Koskinen spent his early months at the IRS worried
about internal "morale" and telling Congress it needed to give his
agency more funding. His appearances in front of Congress all follow the same arc: Dodge questions, jab at investigators, excuse
his agency for its misdeeds. He at one point declared that the IRS
hadn't even engaged in "targeting." By July 2014—just six months
on the job—he'd transitioned fully from reformer to partisan, joining Democrats in claiming that the Republicans calling for a special
prosecutor were doing so for political reasons. "There are some
people who don't want a straight story," he sniped, after Republicans called for an independent probe. "I'm not sure if people really
want a special prosecutor," he claimed, since Republicans preferred
to hold "all these fun hearings every week or two."

Fitton notes that the e-mail games continue to today. The IRS
at the outset created its own set of search terms for what *it* believed was responsive to Congress's request, and put all those
e-mails in a separate database. "That database is all they've ever
looked at in terms of our Freedom of Information requests," says
Fitton. "They refuse to go back to the original IRS system to
fulfill our requests. Who knows what they are sitting on?" The

watchdog chief says the IRS acknowledged in court that yet other officials "lost" their e-mail, but have refused to say who those individuals were, claiming that "people might criticize the agents in question. And apparently those government agents must be protected, no matter what happened to the Americans who employ them," says Fitton. Koskinen has so doggedly sat on records that in August 2015 a federal court threatened to hold him personally in contempt if he didn't comply with document requests.

On the whole, Fitton says, "in terms of gamesmanship and dishonesty, there is nothing comparable." This comes from a man whose group has sued pretty much every agency in government innumerable times.

Why? "What they were doing was unlawful, they knew it was unlawful, and they don't want anyone now to know the depth of their lawlessness—at least until enough time has passed to make it irrelevant," says Fitton. "That's what the pushback is about. Making time pass. Allowing people to forget their outrage."

∿

Yes, Republicans still gripe that we don't know what happened at the IRS. Yes, they have a bit of a point: Lerner wouldn't testify; the IRS lost key e-mails; the White House covered things up. But that does a disservice to the investigations, which pieced together some origins of this story, and demolished some lies.

Among the first falsehood to go was the "Cincinnati did it" line. Jordan's team interviewed those employees. One dismissed the idea of rogue agents as "ridiculous." Another agreed, "Rogue employees means doing their own acting. I don't think anybody in our team, including myself, did their own thing out of the command of chain." Hofacre, the Cincinnati employee so frustrated with the review process that she requested a transfer, told Congress that she believed the public had been purposely misled to focus on Cincinnati.

Jordan also put the lie to the administration's claim that it hadn't really known about any of this until TIGTA readied his report. The IRS commissioner and general counsel, remember, are appointed by the president. The IRS is also a branch of the Treasury Department. And the Treasury Department reports directly to the president. All the evidence shows that both the presidential appointees to the IRS and the senior political appointees at Treasury knew about the targeting of conservative groups before the 2012 presidential election, and sat on that information.

Doug Shulman admitted to the Senate Finance Committee that he knew something was wrong in the spring of 2012, during the election—and yet said nothing. He'd later plead that he did not know all the facts until the TIGTA report. But he knew enough to have stopped things, if he'd chosen to.

We know that the highest officials at the Treasury Department were aware something rotten was going on at the IRS in the spring of 2012. Russell George, TIGTA, told Congress that in the spring of 2012 he advised the general counsel for Treasury, Christopher Meade, that he was "conducting an audit of the IRS's processing of applications for tax-exempt status, and I may have advised him that we were looking at allegations that the IRS was using names such as 'tea party' to identify tax-exempt applications for review." Documents back up TIGTA's recollection. Meade would nonetheless later claim that TIGTA hadn't told him much. Similarly, TIGTA told Oversight that he'd briefed the Treasury Department's chief of staff, Mark Patterson, about the audit and the "tea party" phrase in September 2012. Patterson would later claim that he didn't even remember meeting with George that fall. When Jordan pressed him to try to remember the conversation, Patterson got testy. "All I can tell you is what I remember, okay?" he shot back. Jordan's reply: "All I know is that Russell George remembers it differently."

Connect these dots. Assuming the inspector general for the Treasury Department isn't lying to the nation (and why would

he?), both the top lawyer and the chief of staff to Treasury Secretary Tim Geithner knew about the targeting of conservative
groups months prior to the presidential election. Does anyone
truly think this information wasn't relayed up the chain?

One possible answer came on May 16, 2013, when Bloomberg
News's Julianna Goldman asked President Obama a few pointed
questions. Obama offered a careful response:

Goldman: Mr. President, I want to ask you about the IRS. Can
    you assure the American people that nobody in the White
    House knew about the agency's actions before your Coun-
    sel's Office found out on April 22nd?
Obama: [L]et me make sure that I answer your specific question.
    I can assure you that I certainly did not know anything
    about the IG report before the IG report had been leaked
    through the press.

Obama didn't say that he was unaware of targeting. He didn't
say he was unaware of BOLO lists or Lerner or donor questions. He said he didn't know about the IG report. That's a little
different.

Some in Treasury and the White House knew about the TIGTA
report an entire month before Lerner's bombshell, and in fact
coordinated with the IRS to craft the manufactured Lerner admission. As early as April 16, Treasury's deputy general counsel
informed a White House attorney about the inspector general's
findings, telling him (at the very least) that the "IG had identified
some problems or concerns with the application process as it related to conservative organizations." Miller, the IRS head at the
time, ran nearly every detail of the Lerner apology—to the time
and date and circumstances—past Treasury, which in turn informed the White House deputy chief of staff about the plan.
This was done, said a Treasury official, "so that the White House
wouldn't be surprised by the news." Some of the frantic calls in

those last days also included yet another White House lawyer and a press official. And yet Obama to this day insists he learned about the entire affair through the news.

The more Jordan, Orrin Hatch, and groups like Judicial Watch dug, the more they uncovered evidence that Democrats drove the IRS targeting from day one. From the moment Obama won the 2008 election through early 2013, the tax agency fielded no fewer than thirty-five formal congressional requests for investigations into, or new rules covering, tax-exempt organizations. Many went express to the IRS commissioner's office. Investigators also found e-mails showing IRS staffers assisting Democratic members with their own probes into conservative groups, and in turn getting "heads-up" tips about that congressional work. Miller would later admit that it was all this pressure that forced the internal IRS debate about how to handle (c)(4)s: "I mean, I think we were—we had, you know, [Michigan senator Carl] Levin complaining bitterly to us about—Senator Levin complaining bitterly about our [regulation]. . . . And, you know, we were being asked to take a look at that. And so we were thinking about what things could be done," Miller confessed.

The press put a lot of emphasis on Baucus and Durbin and other senators who'd written letters to the IRS with specific demands. Levin's own role was far more integral and direct, effectively raising him to the level of conspirator. Levin, too, signed on to those IRS letters demanding probes of conservative groups. But he was far more aggressive in his demands, handing the IRS specific target lists in the run-up to the 2012 election. In a July 2012 letter, he listed twelve groups he wanted investigated for political activity. Eleven of those were conservative organizations (he tossed in one liberal group for good form). In September, he demanded that the IRS provide him political spending figures for a list of conservative players. Miller wrote back that "as discussed" in two earlier responses to Levin (the IRS and Levin communicated a lot), the agency wasn't legally allowed to tell him whether the organizations on his list had even applied for tax-exempt status. Levin kept up the pressure, complaining that the IRS "misinterprets" the law. He at one point called the agency's failure to prosecute conservative groups "unacceptable." He also told the *New York Times* (incorrectly) that "tax-exempt 501(c)(4)s are not supposed to be engaged in politics," and vowed that "we're going to go after them." Levin in May 2013 scheduled his Senate Permanent Subcommittee on Investigations to hold hearings into the IRS's failure to "enforce the law" on nonprofits engaged in "partisan politics." He canceled it when Lerner dropped her bombshell.

What no one found out until after that fallout is that Levin's subcommittee had spent the entire year of 2012 dragging IRS officials in front of it, putting the screws to them over nonprofits. One of the officials attending those frequent meetings was Lois Lerner. Also attending was staff from ranking member John McCain's office.

Interestingly, Levin himself revealed these facts. As the IRS scandal exploded, the Michigan Democrat clearly sensed how bad it would look for Republicans to uncover these meetings, so he decided to get out ahead of the news. He released the information in an extraordinary joint letter (with McCain) to Danny Werfel a few weeks after Lerner's announcement. The letter began as a full-throated call to suspend Lerner from the IRS. Levin and McCain explained that among the reasons for why this should happen was that Lerner had failed to disclose the targeting to them in the course of their own "investigation" into nonprofits and the "statute." That's how Levin and McCain cleverly slipped out the news that they'd conducted "a year's worth of correspondence between the Subcommittee and the IRS, as well as document productions and repeated consultations with IRS staff." The letter was carefully worded, designed to reveal yet minimize the committee's pressure on the IRS. McCain undoubtedly had the Keating scandal in his mind. Twenty-five years earlier he'd got rapped for pressuring a regulator in the banking sector. He didn't now want to be accused of bullying the IRS. (It didn't help. McCain would later be accused by conservative groups of taking part in the targeting, an accusation he reacted to with a furious press release, calling it "demonstrably untrue.")

It was Judicial Watch, again, that obtained papers documenting Lerner's attendance at one of those Levin meetings. "We don't know exactly what happened at that meet-up," notes Fitton. "But suddenly you have these two senators—after the sugar hits the fan—claiming to be outraged by the IRS's actions. And doing so in a letter designed to exonerate them from their own roles."

Investigators also quickly demolished what had become a favorite Democratic claim: that liberal groups had also been targeted. TIGTA himself had undercut this baloney in his report, simply listing the numbers. The IRS targeted 292 conservative groups, and all 292 were put under review. It subjected 6 liberal groups to review. And while it's true that the term "progressive" was later found on the infamous BOLO list, it was in a section of that spreadsheet that ultimately wasn't used by screeners to isolate targets. Only one side got the IRS treatment.

CHAPTER 11

The Fix Is In

JIM JORDAN, Orrin Hatch, Dave Camp, Russell George, dozens of staffers, and Judicial Watch toiled along, unraveling the affair bit by bit. They were joined by yet one more powerful force in the sleuthing. The targeted Tea Party groups might have been molested by the IRS, but they refused to surrender to a victim's mentality.

The targets spent three years in turmoil—first in suspended animation, then confusion, then fear. The consequences were very real. Democrats wanted the IRS to shut these groups down, and at a crucial time—the elections of 2010 and 2012. They got their wish.

Fitton notes that it wasn't as clear-cut a victory as some on the left would have liked, but it worked all the same. "Lerner had been at the FEC. She knew the law inside out. And she knew that any formal action would likely get slapped down by the courts. So rather than reject applications, she did the next best thing. She kept them in limbo, so that the groups couldn't fully operate." He throws in an additional irony: The only reason why Lerner could do this was because conservative groups were trying to do the right thing. "The truth is, the law doesn't require you to immediately file an application to get (c)(4) status. The smart groups on the left sure weren't doing it. It was just the poor suckers in the

Tea Party, who, because they tried to cross the T's and dot the I's, the whole movement was shut down."

Lerner hadn't hit full operational speed by the 2010 midterms, and the "shellacking" that Obama received in that election was in no small part due to Tea Party groups spreading the words on issues and getting out the vote. By the estimates of one study, the Tea Party pushed an additional 5.8 million additional Republican voters to the polls in 2010. But the IRS muzzling took its toll on the movement in the two years that followed. Grover Norquist, president of the influential Americans for Tax Reform, makes a compelling argument in his own book on the IRS, *End the IRS Before It Ends Us*, that Obama's siccing of the agency on conservative groups saved his presidency. He intimidated them out of the game.

Many groups pulled their applications, tired of the hassle. Others couldn't get funding from donors and dwindled away. Some got hit by a weird fillip in the law that subjected them to an automatic revocation of their application if it dragged on too long—an issue that Lerner was aware of, and made use of. Some, wary of the delays, and the stories they were hearing, and the questions they received, pulled back on their activities and toned down their work. "They couldn't handle the onslaught," says Jordan. "These were people doing this in their garage. Or part-time. Or in the spare minutes, away from their real job, when they had a moment to send out an e-mail. And that's the part that most bothers me. I despise the bully picking on the weak kids in the playground. This is the sophisticated, powerful IRS going after folks hand-painting signs in their backyard."

The targeting was hardest on the small groups, but it also hurt the big (c)(4)s—even the ones that could afford sophisticated lawyers. Steven Law, the president of Crossroads GPS (which Lerner was especially determined to bring down), explained to me that the hit to his own group was financial. Among the many reasons groups like Crossroads pursue tax-exempt status is to qualify for special mailing rates that nonprofits receive. And Crossroads does a bucketload of issue-related mail. Yet the group had to wait five years to finally get its nonprofit status, costing it a small additional fortune every time it went to the post office.

Obama won in that regard. Then again, his IRS couldn't have chosen a more ornery or knowledgeable group of people to pick on. The Constitution is the Tea Party's bread and butter. And that Constitution had been violated. So as congressional investigators set to interviewing and issuing subpoenas, conservative groups set to documenting the horrors and seeking justice.

At the epicenter of that movement was Jenny Beth Martin, the charismatic leader of Tea Party Patriots (TPP), a national umbrella group for the movement. Martin served double duty during the scandal. She had to cope with the IRS interrogatory of TPP (it was on the targeting list), but she also became the go-to organization for other groups under assault.

"Our own accountant got our first IRS letter, and it was at just the same time as everybody else. But we were the only national organization targeted—the other groups, they were small, they were local—and so we started doing everything we could to help them out," says Martin. She started weekly webinars, where people could tune in and get general advice from an attorney about how to approach the interrogatories. Sometimes the local groups would find their own counsel, sometimes Tea Party Patriots helped arrange for counsel—and paid the legal bills. Martin remembers through all that crazy time—before the targeting was revealed—that she felt the need to be very careful about what she said, to not make accusations. "That was another whole part of this. We all knew something was going on. But if you went to a major donor and said you thought the IRS was targeting you, they would think you were crazy. 'Look at all those Tea Party people, out with signs and conspiracy theories.' And also, the IRS still held the cards, nothing had yet been revealed. And none of us wanted to say anything that might derail our approval. So we did our best, and found counsel, and answered many of the questions."

After the targeting was revealed, all bets were off. Martin also had Cleta Mitchell as counsel, and when the Lerner news broke, they were ready to go live to the nation with the stories of what had happened to groups across the country. She also reached out to her network and within days had arranged and paid for a group of dozens of local Tea Party members to come to Washington and tell about their experiences.

TPP arranged the meetings and made introductions to legislators. It arranged for video crews to document their stories. And it arranged press conferences.

It also started going back to groups, collecting information, making a record of the abuse. Martin remembers the Albuquerque Tea Party sending her a photo of the "stacks and stacks" of boxes of information they had sent to the IRS. "That image will always be burned into my memory," she says. TPP started demanding that government departments hand over documents. Her organization also funneled local parties over to Jay Sekulow, who was preparing a lawsuit. Tea Party Patriots ended up doing a documentary about the IRS that featured many of the stories of average Americans who had been harassed into silence.

Martin appeared in front of Congress in July 2015, to sum up everything her group had done to record and unravel the IRS dishonor. "Two people on our support team made over one thousand phone calls in the spring and summer of 2013 to make sure we had the details necessary to provide various congressional committees with the information and evidence they needed," she told Congress.

"We arranged town hall meetings to discuss the issues, and we coordinated and paid for travel for our local coordinators to come to Washington to testify and/or talk to committee staff.

"We filed FOIA requests, and we paid for smart lawyers to help understand the gibberish and thousands of redacted pages of paper we got in response.

"And, of course, we had to spend precious man-hours filling out all those crazy questionnaires from the IRS in the first place."

Martin overall estimated that her group spent at least forty-five hundred man-hours working on IRS targeting–related issues. As she explained, "Think about that for a minute: forty-five hundred man-hours. That's the equivalent of one employee working two and a half years on this issue alone—just since 2013."

Karen Kenney was among representatives from twenty groups whom the Tea Party Patriots underwrote to come to Washington to tell their stories and meet with congressmen in late May 2013. She was happy to join, though less than impressed by the city and its occupants. She spent one day talking to staffers, and has good memories of meeting with California representative Tom McClintock, who personally came to hear the stories of abuse. Mostly what she remembers, though, is a lot of staffers, and few informed members. And also that she wasn't allowed to use the drinking fountains because of lead in D.C. pipes. (*Where's the damn EPA when you need them?*) She got dehydrated and missed meetings, sick in her hotel room.

Kenney took a second trip to D.C. in June, funded by the grass-roots organization FreedomWorks, when she testified. That was when she had her adventure finding the bathroom. (*I felt like a Christian in the coliseum in Rome.*) Even years later, she looks nervous recounting the moment, and that look is a vivid reminder that most Americans are not called upon to tell their ugly tales to millions of TV critics, to face the withering questions of haughty congressional members. Starting a Tea Party organization was, in Kenney's mind, an act of civic duty. Testifying in front of Congress was, in Kenney's fluttering heart, a supreme act of bravery.

Kenney remembers sending a silent thank-you to Michigan representative Dave Camp, who introduced her by noting that she worked with veterans. She believed he'd deliberately included that fact in an effort to shield her from nastier Democratic questions. She remembers Wisconsin representative Paul Ryan genuinely welcoming the witnesses to Washington. She remembers that every Republican member sat fixed in their seat for the duration of the hearing. She remembers that every Democratic member got up and left at some point and didn't bother to come back until it was their time to ask questions. She remembers looking down the line at the four other Tea Party witnesses and thinking, "I'm not alone."

Kenney might have been nervous, but didn't look it come showtime. Her five minutes on the stage were a ringing retelling of her experience and a condemnation of government power. It was rebroadcast from coast to coast.

∿

Within a few weeks of Lerner's admission, Sekulow had filed a lawsuit against the IRS that would grow to represent thirty-eight groups in twenty-two states. It accused the Obama administration of violating the First and Fifth Amendments, as well as the Administrative Procedures Act (which lays out how government must produce regulations) and the IRS's own rules. Mitchell filed litigation. Individual Tea Party groups filed litigation. Kenney's group to this day remains active in the Sekulow suit, even though she is no longer seeking tax-exempt permission. "The people need to know what happened," she explains. "And that suit gives a reason for discovery."

Several of the lawsuits are still winding their way through the courts, but they have in the near term served an important purpose: They've pressured the IRS to get applications approved. Mitchell sued on behalf of True the Vote, and on the day the federal government was supposed to respond to her lawsuit—in September 2013—it conveniently explained to the court that the IRS had just granted (c)(3) status to the group and was therefore moving to dismiss the suit.

Mitchell says congressional pressure also helped. The House in February 2014 publicly announced that Jenny Beth Martin of the Tea Party Patriots would soon testify about her own still-languishing (c)(4) application. Mitchell remembers telling Martin (who is also her client), "Wait for it. You will have it before you testify." Sure enough, the day before that testimony, the IRS called to say it had granted the Tea Party Patriots tax-exempt status. "Coincidence?" asks Mitchell. "Hardly."

Sekulow witnessed the same behavior. Only after he launched a lawsuit did his groups begin getting approval. As of the end of 2015, he had only two clients that had yet to receive tax-exempt status. "The reality is that without that litigation, we'd still be fighting for all those exemptions. They didn't want to give anything," he says.

The Tea Party movement also jumped to hold lawmakers accountable. Obama was beyond their reach; he'd encouraged the IRS in every way possible, but he'd been careful never to outright call for action. And executive privilege keeps most White House documents beyond the reach of FOIA requests or congressional subpoenas.

Congressional Democrats never felt such constraint, however, and were on record vigorously and openly demanding that a federal agency go after their political enemies. How that pressure is any different than that exerted by the Keating Five against the federal bank regulator (and which cost senators their jobs) is hard to fathom. Conservative groups didn't miss the comparison. Since May 2013 they've filed dozens of ethics complaints against Democrats involved in the targeting. Congress is still an old boys' club, and reluctant to take aim at any of its own. So nothing has come of any complaint.

Nothing likely will.

∿

It took Cleta Mitchell very little time to figure out that the Obama administration had no intention of stopping its campaign to silence its opponents. It had been caught unofficially targeting conservatives, in secret. That would clearly have to stop. It instead moved swiftly to a new phase of the operation: officially targeting conservatives, in the open.

Werfel debuted the first piece of this on June 25, briefing reporters about his thirty-day report on the scandal, which included his new "plan of action" for dealing with the conservative application backlog. One highlight was a new optional "expedited" process for obtaining 501(c)(4) status. Werfel's "fast track" deal boiled down to this: The IRS would finally, begrudgingly, do what it should have done from the start and quickly grant tax-exempt status. The hook? Groups would have to agree to give up their freedom of speech.

Those organizations taking the deal had to agree to limit to 40 percent the amount of money and time (calculated by employee and volunteer hours) they would spend on future political activity. The official legal amount was 49 percent, and the IRS had never before used time as a component of that calculation (it had always just been based on spending). By including the new time measure in the calculation, the IRS could significantly lower the amount of real political work that groups could engage in.

Mitchell spotted the scam immediately. "It was just a new way to screw the same groups they'd been screwing," she says. "And all under the guise of being 'helpful' and 'solving the problem.' It was so blatant, so in-your-face."

Unfortunately, few in the movement saw what Mitchell so quickly did. Her phone started ringing, clients wondering if this "fast track" deal was their ticket to legitimacy. Mitchell cautioned that the IRS had purposely chosen not to define anywhere how it would calculate "volunteer" time. "If Mitchell volunteers, and a high school student volunteers, does our time count equally? Or do you factor in my hourly lawyer rate? Who is a volunteer? What kind of services count? It was vague on purpose, so that they could define you down to zero politics, with the right criteria," was how Mitchell explained it to callers.

Some groups took the deal, not knowing any better. Some took it because they didn't do politics anyway and just wanted out of IRS purgatory. But many, groups like Jenny Beth Martin's, outright refused to be assaulted twice. It wasn't right, Martin told me in 2014, that "every other 501(c)(4) [including liberal groups] would get to live under a different standard than those of us who had been targeted and had been waiting for a determination for years." She let the deadline for using "fast track" pass.

Her reward: Later that summer, Tea Party Patriots received another round of interrogatives from the IRS, with demands for information Martin had already supplied, as well as new details— such as her fund-raising letters from 2012. She wasn't alone. It is a little-known fact that many groups that declined fast track continued to get hit with IRS question letters, long after the agency targeting had been exposed, and well after Werfel was supposedly "fixing" the problem.

The fast-track idea meanwhile didn't spring out of nowhere. The nation would find that out later in the year, in a bit of news dumped in the quiet of the Thanksgiving Day weekend. (The Obama administration has always made a specialty of slipping out controversial news at times when it hopes nobody is watching.) By that November 2013 day, Democrats were already hip deep into their argument that the IRS mess was nothing more than an unfortunate mistake, brought about by confusion over a complicated law. That groundwork laid, the IRS and Treasury on November 29 announced a new regulation for (c)(4)s.

It wasn't so much a regulation as the full expression of everything Democrats had been hoping to do since Van Hollen and Schumer first dreamed up the DISCLOSE Act. It essentially barred social-welfare groups from participating in any politics. The regulation prohibited candidate-related election activity—banning even the names of active politicians or political parties on an organization's website. It prohibited the use of words such as "oppose," "support," "vote," "defeat," and "reject." It prohibited voter registration drives and voter guides. It prohibited hosting candidates at events, even nonpartisan ones. It restricted the leaders of social welfare groups from talking about judicial nominations. It declared political activity as contrary to the promotion of social welfare. (Apparently a well-faring state is one in which nobody talks about politics, and that receives all its political information from the government.) It formalized the use of volunteer hours in calculating political activity. And, of course, it applied all this only to (c)(4) groups. Labor unions were exempt. They would still be able to support Democrats politically to the full extent of biased IRS law.

The particular insult was that Werfel presented the new regulations as the *fix* to the IRS targeting. The prior regulation had been unclear and had confused IRS agents, went his argument; the new regulations would provide clarity. The administration went so far as to claim that it was resolving problems identified in TIGTA's report. It was a brilliant strategy: Use the unsanctioned silencing of the IRS as an excuse to create a system of sanctioned silencing. Obama meanwhile rushed out the rule in November 2013 to ensure that conservative groups would be out of action prior to the 2014 midterms.

Only TIGTA hadn't recommended that the answer to the IRS's stifling of speech of those opposed to Obama should be a rule that would stifle the speech of those opposed to Obama. And the IRS hadn't just started working on those rules after Lerner spilled the beans. As congressional investigators kept digging, they found that IRS and Treasury officials, spearheaded by Lerner, had first started this legal shutdown strategy in 2011. That strategy was far enough along that by 2012, Treasury tax official Ruth Madrigal was asking an IRS lawyer about the agency's "off-plan" work on a (c)(4) regulation. "Off-plan" means the IRS hid the effort, not publishing it on the public schedule of upcoming rules and actions. Around the same time, IRS chief counsel (and Obama appointee) Wilkins met with the staff of Democratic senators to talk about the regulations. By 2013, IRS officials considered such a rule change the agency's top priority.

In short, the Obama administration had been planning this for ages, and one question is whether Lerner wasn't sitting on those (c)(4) applications as a way of keeping them quiet until the administration could get the rule in place. Whatever the motivation, Werfel's claim that the regulation was in response to IRS misbehavior goes down as one of the bigger lies in the IRS affair.

That planning was why Werfel had been able to roll out his fast-track proposal so quickly. The agency already had in place the outline of counting "volunteer" hours and caps. Mitchell goes so far as to note from documents produced in a FOIA case that the IRS had been preparing to issue the rules on Labor Day weekend 2013, only it got derailed by the Lerner confession. "We have a FOIA lawsuit, which is another way of saying I now have binder upon binder of pieces of paper that the IRS has blacked out before it sent them to me. But the one thing I have been able to ascertain is that those regulations were already set to roll in the early fall," she says.

The proposed rule caused another Washington explosion. Only this time it wasn't just conservatives howling. Obama wanted conservative (c)(4)s shut down; he accepted that the collateral damage would be liberal (c)(4)s, which would also be restricted in their activity. The administration soothed itself with the knowledge that a turbocharged labor movement would still be on its side.

The liberal nonprofit community didn't take it quite so well. Comments poured into the IRS, mounting by the minute. Everyone hated the regulation. Conservative groups like Americans for Prosperity and Crossroads and Tea Party Patriots and True the Vote and the Heritage Foundation hated it. Hobby and special interest groups like the American Motorcyclist Association and the Home School Legal Defense Association hated it. Trade groups like the National Association of Manufacturers and the Solar Energy Industries Association hated it. Liberal groups like the Sierra Club and the NAACP and the Alliance for Justice hated it.

The American Civil Liberties Union slammed the proposal in a twenty-six-page comment, saying it "threatens to discourage or sterilize an enormous amount of political discourse in America." It astutely noted that the rules opened the door to even more of the sort of political targeting that had caused the scandal. The NAACP pointed out in its comment that most of its work fighting racial discrimination "would be illegal under the proposed regulation." Even the mighty Service Employees International Union wrote in to oppose the rule. It had been spared this round of regulating, but it worried that the speech restrictions might have a snowball effect that would ultimately roll up organized labor.

Brad Smith's group, the Center for Competitive Politics, quickly pointed out that the rule was in fact a twofer for the left. It largely barred conservative social-welfare groups from engaging in political speech. Those groups that wanted to continue actively doing so would have to register as 527 organizations with the Federal Election Commission. Which would require them to . . . disclose their donors. Which would then tee those donors up for retribution. Game, set, and match. As the center's Allen Dickerson testified in front of Congress, "The reason 501(c)(4)s do not disclose their donors is because Congress said so. When the Internal Revenue Code was passed, it created criminal penalties for the unauthorized disclosure of the donors to these organizations. And the reason for that is that it has always been understood that 501(c)(4)s are the beating heart of civil society. These are the organizations, like the NRA and the Sierra Club, which go out there and take unpopular positions and move the national debate and make this a vibrant and functioning democracy. Requiring unpopular organizations to give up their donor list to public scrutiny is not only contrary to Congress's intention in the Internal Revenue Code, it is contrary to constitutional law."

The commentators might as well have been beating their heads against a wall. The White House had dropped this rule in the dead of night, acting like it was just one more little regulation, just a small effort to provide a bit of "clarity" to IRS rules. In fact the (c)(4) regulation had become the greatest priority of the Obama administration. This became clear in December, as Congress and the White House brawled over an omnibus bill to continue funding the government. The fight was high-stakes; if funding legislation wasn't passed by Congress and signed by Obama before year's end, the government would shut down.

The administration had a long wish list of dollar priorities: more money for the International Monetary Fund, money for the president's newly proposed pre-kindergarten program, more funding for Obamacare. Republicans later told me that House Appropriations chairman Hal Rogers wanted only two things in return: protection for groups that morally opposed Obamacare's contraception coverage requirements, and language that would put a hold on the IRS rule.

Democrats wouldn't budge on the IRS. They were willing to throw over everything else the president wanted, so long as they kept the IRS crackdown on conservative speech. "They were willing to shut down the entire government for this," says Fitton. "The entire government. That tells you how important it was to the left." Faced with a shutdown scenario, and worried about getting blamed for it, the GOP retreated, and the rule continued.

By the end of the IRS's public comment period for the rule, in February 2014, the agency was nonetheless sitting on 150,000 public statements. "I'm told if you take all the comments on all the Treasury and IRS regulations for the last seven years, double that number, you are close to the number of comments we have on this single regulation," Koskinen later admitted. An analysis by the Center for Competitive Politics found that 87 percent of the comments opposed the rule outright, and 94 percent opposed it in whole or part.

And yet Koskinen became the rule's biggest advocate, sullenly refusing to budge in the face of overwhelming opposition. Jordan found himself so frustrated that at one meeting with the commissioner he says he spat out, "What was this, like a quid pro quo? We'll nominate you if you continue the rule, no matter what?"

The only reason the rule isn't in effect today is that the White House miscalculated. Liberals had convinced themselves the IRS was a linchpin to retaining the Senate in the 2014 midterms. As *The Hill* reported in February, "Senate Democrats facing tough elections this year want the Internal Revenue Service to play a more aggressive role in regulating outside groups expected to spend millions of dollars on their races." But the White House hadn't counted on much of its base—groups that would be crucial to supporting its candidates in November—revolting over its rule.

The White House was worried the rule would backfire. Koskinen got new marching orders, and in April 2014 he announced that the agency was pulling the rule, for now, and updating it based on comments. He suggested it wouldn't be reissued before the end of the year. Conservatives were nonetheless worried enough about it that the Republican Congress in December 2015 inserted a ban on the rule into the year-end spending bill.

∿

Three years on from the public outing of its abuse, the IRS continues to operate as it did on May 10, 2013—the day of Lerner's admission. Little has changed. The agency is just as dysfunctional; the administration is just as determined to use it to target its political opponents. Nobody has been held accountable.

The House Ways and Means Committee in April 2014 sent a letter to the Justice Department outlining its case for why Lerner should face criminal prosecution. It provided documents showing at least three different ways in which Lerner criminally violated statutes. One, she helped to target only conservative organizations, thereby robbing them of equal protection and due process. Two, she may have impeded TIGTA's investigation by giving misleading statements. Three, she risked exposing (and may have exposed) confidential taxpayer information by using her personal e-mail address to conduct official business. The Justice Department never responded. In October 2015, it closed its IRS investigation, with no charges.

The House on May 7, 2014, in a bipartisan vote, found Lerner in contempt of Congress, for offering testimony (by reading out her statement) yet still refusing to answer questions. The citation went to U.S. Attorney for the District of Columbia Ronald Machen, an Obama appointee. The contempt statute in question explains that the U.S. attorney's only "duty" "shall be" to "bring the matter before the grand jury for its action." Machen instead sat on the citation for eleven months. On March 31—the day before he retired from his post—he informed Speaker John Boehner that he'd unilaterally decided not to investigate Lerner. So much for accountability.

The House also on May 7, 2014, passed a bipartisan resolution calling on the Justice Department to appoint a special prosecutor to look into the IRS scandal. Some twenty-six Democrats joined Republicans to demand that Attorney General Eric Holder do something to restore credibility to the agency. Fitton points out that the textbook argument for a special prosecutor is any situation in which Justice has a conflict of interest in an investigation—say, if it had been working with the IRS to go after nonprofits. That call for a special prosecutor has never been answered.

By the end of 2015, Obama had taken to blaming Congress for the IRS targeting of conservatives. In an appearance on *The Daily Show*, he explained, "You've got this back office, and they're going after the Tea Party. Well, it turned out, no, Congress had passed a crummy law that didn't give people guidance in terms of what it was they were trying to do. They did it poorly and stupidly. The truth of the matter is that there was not some big conspiracy there. They were trying to sort out conflicting demands." So much for presidential outrage.

∿

All stories have endings, but the IRS scandal hasn't yet reached its last chapters. In many ways, that's depressing. It's been three years since Lerner's admission. We know the contours of the assault, but the details may well already be lost to destroyed IRS hard drives.

Then again, the lack of an ending is also inspiring. Because if there is one noteworthy American quality, it is tenacity. The players in this drama aren't giving up.

Jordan feels he knows generally what happened. "They saw this coming. The context is 2010. They'd done a bazillion dollars of crazy spending, stimulus, they were doing Obamacare, they saw the wave coming. They realized these groups are organized and focused and ready to vote. Democrats are hounding the IRS after *Citizens United* to act; Lerner gives a speech at Duke acknowledging she knows they are asking for just that; we have e-mails showing they were working on a (c)(4) project. It was all driven by raw politics and liberal ideology. No mystery there." While Jordan has changed subcommitees in Congress, he's still investigating the IRS.

Fitton and his colleagues at Judicial Watch have done more than anyone to pry out damning information here and damning information there, and they're still doing it. He's still sitting on a mess of FOIA lawsuits, and still playing cat and mouse with the government. Judicial Watch has recently been attempting to get hold of Justice Department documents that expose the political nature of the Bosserman nonprobe. Justice continues to conveniently say that turning over any documents would compromise its investigation. Fitton's team of attorneys keep filing.

Mitchell still has clients dealing with the IRS. She's still involved in the movement, and still just as ripshit. She dialed in not long ago to a Tea Party conference call to answer questions about the IRS regulation. The call also featured a Tea Party member who had been tasked with explaining to the group the ins and outs of interstate health compacts. "And that's what pisses me off," says Mitchell. "Here are these American citizens, calling in on a Sunday night, when they might be watching a movie, because they want to understand interstate health compacts. I'd love to know how many officials at the IRS, the ones holding the power to delay and deceive and make everyone jump, understand interstate health compacts." Mitchell is still litigating.

Engelbrecht finally received her determination approval for True the Vote in September 2013, three years after filing. She received approval for King Street Patriots in December 2013, three and a half years after she first set out on that journey. Jordan calls her the "real hero" of the scandal, "a woman who suffered every form of government assault, and kept pushing to the end." He remembers saying to her in a committee hearing, "You do know why they were coming after you, right? They were coming after you because you were doing a good job, and making a difference."

Her voter-rights group work matters more to her now than ever. "I've realized this is no longer about Republican or Democrat," she says. "This is about government versus the people. And at the end of the day, government will not correct itself. And so it has fallen on us, all of us, to speak out. It is on our watch. Otherwise, we are complicit and far worse will fall on our children. Whether or not you feel that the government has dealt you a short straw, you put that aside. You engage. You keep engaging. You be a part of this country."

Jenny Beth Martin keeps growing the Tea Party movement. The IRS didn't kill that spirit. At the end of 2014, she had 599 active groups in her network. By the end of 2015, she had more than 700. Hundreds of volunteers every Sunday night call in to webinars to talk about policy and politics and the direction of the country. Hundreds more volunteers call in every Monday to talk about what's happening on Capitol Hill, and upcoming action. And she notes that the level of involvement these days "is just so much more sophisticated. We have people showing up in big numbers at events. We have people getting involved in campaigns—sometimes even running for office themselves. The level of engagement is maturing. People understand more than ever that they have to stand up."

She's still demanding that someone be held accountable. "I to this day have people come up to me across the country. They are holding some letter from the government—maybe from the IRS, maybe from the Census Bureau, maybe something else— and they are shaking," she says. "They think they are being targeted. Why wouldn't they? This goes to the foundation of our government, to the trust. There is a crack, it is deep, and it will only widen if someone isn't held responsible."

Karen Kenney gave up on her application in 2012. But she too has never wavered in her belief that her group matters and needs to keep on. "There are reasons why each of us are here," she says, "and even if I don't know the exact purpose, I'm going to have some meaning. And they can't stop millions of Americans who feel the same way." After withdrawing her application to become tax-exempt, Kenney went through the process of filing to pay IRS taxes. It was at that point that she experienced the ultimate eye-opener. "Turns out we make so little money that we don't owe federal taxes anyway. We don't make enough. So we did all this. We went through this whole process to be tax-exempt, and we have zero liability to the feds. Can you believe that?"

(*One of God's little jokes. God, I do love your little jokes. Really, I do.*)

The Albuquerque Tea Party—the organization started by a West Point grad and Army Cavalry veteran, the group the IRS funneled aside as the "test case" in 2010—it hasn't given up on obtaining tax-exempt status.

It's been six years.

CHAPTER 12

Waiting for Disco

IN THE SUMMER of 2008, Don McGahn arrived at his first day of work, and the security guard nodded a familiar hello. McGahn had been coming to this little building for years, always as a visitor. Now the guard scanned McGahn's new ID and gave him a look. "Wait, you're one of the new ones," the confused guard mumbled. McGahn shrugged: "Guess I'm official now," he said. "Do you have any idea where I'm supposed to go?" The guard shrugged himself, and offered, "Guessing you go straight to the top floor."

McGahn did go straight to the top floor, because that's where the chairman of the Federal Election Commission sits, and McGahn was now that guy. The political lawyer had visited the FEC's nondescript headquarters on E Street hundreds of times, always to defend a conservative politician or political group that had been dragged in front of the commissioners on some charge or another. He'd been a frequent witness in front of Congress and the FEC—usually along with Bob Bauer—testifying about McCain-Feingold rulemakings, trying to preserve free speech. George W. Bush had noticed, and the administration finally convinced McGahn to work from the inside. So back he went to the building, only this time with an office.

And a weird place it was. "It was such a different culture; it had an entirely different point of reference," says McGahn, who at the time had just turned forty years old. A fraternity-like feel permeated the bureaucracy, complete with its own language, and a smug belief in purpose. When McGahn was appointed, the FEC hadn't had enough confirmed commissioners to function in months, and the staff had taken over the joint. "All these people kept coming up and saying, 'We're so happy to have you join us,'" he remembers. "And I'd tilt my head and think, 'I'm not sure what you mean. I'm not *joining you*. That's not how it works. I was appointed to be a commissioner. And I don't own a rubber stamp.'"

McGahn would serve what FEC observers say was one of the more consequential tenures in the agency's forty-year history. He'd reform procedures, drag FEC proceedings into the daylight, and help put the accountable people back in charge. And in the process, he'd realize—and expose—that the IRS wasn't the only part of the Obama administration that was going after conservatives. The intimidation was happening government-wide, including at an independent, bipartisan agency that had been purposefully designed to stay above politics.

∿

The Federal Election Commission is one of the Watergate reforms, created in 1975. It exists to enforce campaign finance laws: the Federal Election Campaign Act, McCain-Feingold, and plenty more. Most "independent" agencies in Washington have five board members, a majority (three) of which belong to the president's party. Congress, in a rare moment of wisdom, realized that the FEC needed strict political balance. The agency sits six commissioners—three Republicans and three Democrats. And the law requires that at least four members vote affirmatively to take any action.

This frustrates the left and campaign finance believers, who feel that the FEC ought to begin from the assumption that money in politics is a bad thing. They have long been frustrated that some Republican FEC commissioners stand up for free speech and often do not approve action against election players. That's one reason why this community turned to the IRS—out of frustration with the FEC. Lerner had referenced that in her speech at Duke in October 2010: "Everybody is up in arms [about the flood of money to 501(c)(4) groups]." The "Federal Election Commission can't do anything about it; they want the IRS to fix the problem," she said candidly.

The left also hates that the law puts all the power of the agency in the commissioners' hands. The FEC is, after all, staffed with bunches of lawyers and bureaucrats who were all drawn to the agency out of a desire to get money out of politics. They are primed to make new regulations, go after political actors, and tamp down on speech.

Yet what good are those bunches of bureaucrats when Congress really did put the commissioners in charge? When the FEC receives a complaint, for instance, it falls to the general counsel's office to first issue a report on the merits of any alleged finance violation. The commissioners then look, and vote on whether there is "reason to believe" a violation occurred. Staff is barred from conducting investigations or proceeding further without this green light. Staff is barred from liaising with law enforcement. Staff is barred from digging into or harassing the accused in complaints.

The FEC bureaucracy chafes under these restrictions, and over the years its response was to begin ignoring the law and slowly take over the agency. An early ringleader in this effort was none other than Lerner, who in her time at the FEC had pursued groups like the Christian Coalition. Lerner kept her ties to her old FEC haunt even when she moved to the tax agency. She remained a key contact for an FEC bureaucracy that shared her desire to stomp out speech.

∿

The Lerner link would play a part in the FEC's own harassment of conservative groups. That link began in mid-2008, as the Obama-McCain presidential race raged and Democrats filed complaints with the FEC against all and sundry. One of these came from Bauer, as part of his unprecedented campaign against the American Issues Project (AIP) over its ads highlighting ties between Obama and Bill Ayers. Democracy 21, Fred Wertheimer's speech police outfit, also filed an FEC complaint against AIP.

The commission tends to work at a slug's pace, and it wasn't until February 2009 that an FEC general counsel's office attorney, William Powers, went sniffing to the IRS about AIP. He found Lerner. FEC documents (dug up by Judicial Watch) show that the bureaucrats were frustrated. They wanted to know what percentage of AIP's money it was spending on politics, but all it had were figures on the one Obama ad, and AIP hadn't yet filed any tax forms. Powers wondered to Lerner whether the IRS had issued an exemption letter to AIP? He also requested that the IRS Exempt Organizations chief share "any information" about the conservative group. He appeared to be fishing for Lerner's opinion on whether the group was out of bounds. He also put in a request about another conservative organization that had been singled out in a complaint, the American Future Fund. Nine minutes after Lerner received this request, she directed IRS attorneys to get on it.

Lerner shipped back information in March, and Powers happily exclaimed in an e-mail that it "looks as if it will be very useful." One of Lerner's deputies would send another 150 pages about the two organizations later that month. By April, the FEC general counsel's office had recommended that the commission pursue AIP. In total, the general counsel's office issued three separate reports—each arguing a different legal theory for prosecution—as part of a four-and-a-half-year effort by FEC staff to bring down a group that had been singled out by Bauer for having criticized Obama.

~~~

Political operatives are a quirky breed. Maybe it's because they spend days trying to elect people who should be by any measure unelectable. Maybe it's because they spend too much time worrying about the FEC. Whatever the reason, some of them have fascinating alter egos. When McGahn came in search of his office that 2008 day, he sported shaggy longish hair, in keeping with his off-time persona as an accomplished lead guitarist for a band that covered Guns N' Roses classics at mid-Atlantic venues. He owns thirty guitars and once told *Wall Street Journal* reporter Brody Mullins that he'd strum on one as he read election-law filings and complaints.

McGahn was born into political savvy. He grew up in Atlantic City, and his uncle Joe McGahn in 1971 beat in an election Hap Farley, a thirty-four-year state legislator and the "boss" of the city's infamous Republican machine. The whole extended family was steeped in politics, and the future FEC chairman stepped into his first campaign headquarters when he was three. His first memories of Thanksgiving were dinner discussions about how to get the senior vote.

He went to Notre Dame, starting as a "delusional pre-med." He remembers "dumping Calculus 2 and finding a sudden passion for history." He ended up at a regional law school, Widener, and after a judicial clerkship landed at the powerhouse D.C. law firm of Patton Boggs. Unlike so many political attorneys, McGahn practiced what he called "real law"—litigation, antitrust, copyright, trademark—but when a senior lawyer asked for some help with a few campaign finance briefs, he jumped at the chance. Given his family background, representing politicians came naturally.

By 1999 he was the general counsel to the National Republican Congressional Committee, and he kept assisting that operation even when he began his own law practice. He made a name for himself, and is credited with developing many of the techniques still employed by party committees. There were always rumors that McGahn was about to be appointed to the FEC. But the stars didn't align until 2008, by which point nobody took the rumors seriously anymore. When his nomination finally came through, it sent a little bolt of outrage through some Democratic circles, egged on by the campaign finance "reform" lobbyists, who viewed him as a die-hard partisan Republican. (In reality he's a die-hard reformer, and a precursor to the more recent and more vocal variants of libertarian-leaning Republicans.) After a fairly brutal confirmation process, he got that office.

McGahn's a crack lawyer, and would have known that the American Issues Project complaint was nonsense. His political side would have told him the first general counsel's report against the group was fishy. But he never had to deal with most of it. The Supreme Court's *Citizens United* ruling made most of Bauer's complaint irrelevant, and the staff withdrew its proposal.

McGahn nonetheless noted that the level of "chatter" within the FEC about *Citizens United* increased dramatically. Maybe the FEC needed more coordinated investigations with other agencies? Maybe it could force more disclosure? McGahn noticed, too, that the "commissioners on the other side of the aisle became much more vocal about these nonprofit groups, and started mirroring the talking points that were being circulated by self-styled 'reform' lobbyists at Public Citizen and similar groups." The chatter increased in the early part of 2011, when House Democrat Chris Van Hollen, smarting over his DISCLOSE Act loss, filed a lawsuit to try to force the FEC to require more donor disclosure. "I call it 'disclosure-mania,' where Democrats and the leftists decided to use the pretext of disclosure to undo *Citizens United* and intimidate and silence opponents," says McGahn.

McGahn would only later find out about the staff's early, unauthorized dealings with the IRS about AIP. The staff hadn't received permission to commence an investigation, and shouldn't
have had that contact. And he'd only later discover that this was
just the start of the staff's behind-the-scenes efforts to get conservative groups.

Citizens United should have ended the whole AIP affair; Bauer's
complaint was no longer valid. Instead, the general counsel's
office went digging. E-mails show that only a few weeks after
Obama started complaining about *Citizens United*, in early 2010,
Powers got back in touch with Lerner to see if she had any new
AIP information. She responded the next day that the group
hadn't filed anything more. More digging. It took the staff eighteen months, but it concocted a new rationale for prosecuting the
group, circulated in a second report in September 2011.

Further changes in the law made *that* report moot. It too was
withdrawn. The general counsel nonetheless made one last, novel
attempt to nail AIP. Its third report, another eighteen months on,
in March 2013, contained an entirely new theory about how such
nonprofits should be judged. Taking cues from the disclosure-
mania Democrats, it declared that AIP should have filed voluminous disclosure reports.

The FEC, for the purpose of measuring nonprofit spending,
looks at the overall spending of a group. That makes sense. An organization might spend $50,000 during an election year on direct
campaign activity, but $100,000 the following, nonelection year
on education. Looked at over the span, the group is only spending
33 percent of its money on direct campaigning, well below half.
Looked at in a single year, it's spending 100 percent of its money
on campaigning.

And yet that's precisely the standard the FEC staff now wanted
to impose on AIP. The nonprofit clearly had spent the majority
of its money from 2007 to 2010 on its primary purpose of "educating and informing the public of conservative principles." It

poured money into an online advocacy project designed to promote grassroots outreach, and on a national education program
on taxes, national defense, and climate change. Over two years,
it spent less than one-third of its money on direct campaign
expenditures—well below the bar. Even the staff couldn't argue
otherwise. So instead they invented the brand-new "calendar
year" theory, under which AIP broke the caps. The FEC staff
really wanted to get this group.

   The Republican commissioners were appalled. McGahn wrote
for all three in their statement opposing prosecution in July 2013,
in a scathing takedown of the staff's reasoning. He essentially accused them of malpractice and political bias. McGahn pointed
out that the FEC staff had always taken a multiyear view, especially when it came to evaluating liberal groups such as the
League of Conservation Voters or the MoveOn.org Voter Fund.
"Here," he wrote in the statement, FEC staff "could be seen as
manipulating the timeline to reach the conclusion that AIP is a
political committee. . . . Such after-the-fact determinations create
the appearance of impropriety, whether or not such impropriety
exists."

   He also shellacked the staff for attempting to impose this standard after the fact. "Due process ought to prevent such shenani-
gans," he railed. Had AIP thought or known it would be subject
to a different standard than the rest of the universe, it would undoubtedly have operated differently. And McGahn excoriated the
staff for thinking it could implement such a dramatic change without asking any input from its bosses, the commissioners.

ᴧᴧ

The FEC bureaucracy spent nearly five years trying to take down
AIP. But it was hardly an isolated case. McGahn had been keeping
track of other examples of unauthorized staff actions.

   In March 2012, a Democratic operative filed an FEC complaint against Rick Santorum's presidential campaign. McGahn noted that the complaint was "scant at best"—a whole two pages. It claimed that Santorum had received an impermissible "in kind" contribution from the Michigan Faith & Freedom Coalition (MFFC), since the coalition had allowed Santorum to appear at one of its forums. It also claimed illegal "coordination" between that organization and Santorum's campaign, since the president of the MFFC had volunteered for the Santorum campaign. FEC staff recommended prosecution.

McGahn and a fellow GOP commissioner later dismantled the accusations one by one, in a document rejecting action. It turns out the MFFC had invited all the GOP candidates to speak at an event, but the candidates did not want to speak together. So the group had arranged different venues and invited each separately. Santorum was the only one who agreed to this arrangement. The event was about faith issues, it featured other speakers (clergy members and a doctor), and it did not allow any campaign signs or campaign literature. It was the furthest thing from a Santorum campaign rally. As such, it was entirely legal.

The invitation to all the candidates had meantime been sent out prior to MFFC head Glenn Clark's endorsement of Santorum. Clark endorsed in a personal capacity, not as the head of the group. And he volunteered his time for the campaign, receiving no compensation. There was also no evidence of any coordination.

"Scant" was a polite way of describing the complaint. And "flimsy" was a polite way to describe the staff's recommendation of prosecution. The case wasn't even a close call. Yet McGahn discovered that the staff had in fact spent five months and gone to extraordinary lengths to nail the Santorum campaign with something, anything. And it had once again engaged in an investigation without permission from the commissioners.

As McGahn wrote in his statement opposing prosecution, the staff had "performed extensive research during an extra-statutory investigation," in which it dug up left-wing news articles that were critical of the Santorum campaign. These included a posting from a blog associated with the far-left *Talking Points Memo Muck-raker* website. Staff nonetheless compiled these into a thirty-five-page dossier and shipped them to the Santorum campaign, demanding a response to the accusations.

The counsel for the Santorum campaign (who happened to be Cleta Mitchell) responded to the FEC that she was flummoxed as to why she'd been sent a pile of left-wing talking points. McGahn wasn't so much flummoxed as annoyed. As he wrote, "For almost five years we have asked [the FEC general counsel's office] to provide the authority, even a scintilla of information that would authorize what has become their ever-growing habit of gathering news clips and other materials (that now includes openly biased blog posts) in an effort to supplement the complaint and sending them to respondents long before the Commission considers the matter. Simply put, OGC has been unable to provide authority for their actions."

These extralegal investigations always seemed to revolve around complaints against conservatives. So too did the unauthorized FEC staff reach-outs to Lerner and the IRS. And so too another form of interaction. McGahn during his time discovered that the FEC staff maintained a policy—undisclosed to the commissioners—that granted itself at-will authority to interact with the Justice Department.

That connection really got rolling after September 2011, after Tony Herman was hired as FEC general counsel. He was joined in early 2012 by Dan Petalas, who was appointed head of the agency's enforcement section. Petalas had spent nearly a decade at the Justice Department. FEC rules make clear that a bipartisan majority of commissioners must vote to refer unlawful conduct to law enforcement. Yet it appears that information was increasingly shipped to Justice without informing the commissioners, much less asking permission.

Much of this content arrived at Justice in the form of confidential reports. As noted, when a complaint is filed against a political actor, the general counsel's office is tasked with writing a report for the commissioners advising them on whether it believes there is a violation. These reports are never made public until a case is closed. Yet FEC staffers blithely handed them over to Justice. On at least one occasion, they sent the report to Justice before they had even sent it to the FEC commissioners.

McGahn publicly highlighted another case, in which Herman's office tipped off Justice to a potential criminal violation by a Louisiana trucking company owner named Arlen Cenac Jr. Cenac was indeed found to have made illegal campaign contributions in other people's names. It was nonetheless up to the commissioners as to whether to refer him to Justice. Instead, the staff made that decision on its own.

It's still unclear exactly what drove some of these abuses at the FEC. They were happening at the same time that the IRS was building its scandal. There are e-mails showing that IRS and FEC staff were talking about similar cases, and Lerner kept ties back at the commission. Once the IRS scandal was exposed, a lot of investigators began wondering just how much unsanctioned, two-way cooperation between Obama agencies was taking place in opposition to conservatives. If the FEC staff was funneling tips to Justice, was Justice influencing FEC staff reports? Was Lerner influencing FEC staff?

McGahn explains that what makes the situation even murkier is the basic character of FEC staff. They are naturally biased. "The place in its early days was staffed by followers of Ralph Nader—Naderites who believed that all politicians are corrupt, and that both parties are awash in too much money," he says. A younger generation is now in town, but the ghosts still linger. Says McGahn, "Much of that early thinking is still baked into the fabric of the FEC." The FEC general counsel's office still tends to only hire a "certain kind of person," he notes. These aren't people "who have practiced law in private practice for any length of time. They aren't people who served as an in-house corporate counsel. They aren't people who have had to help real clients. They certainly aren't people who have campaign experience. They are people coming out of fancy law schools, where they had written an article or two on campaign finance reform and the evils of money. They'd already signed up for a certain way of thinking, and they are true believers." McGahn recalls, "I didn't see any counterpoint whatsoever. Put them in the right environment, and they'd go and go."

Evidence of this popped up in later documents that showed the FEC staff had in 2010 reached out to the IRS to provide it formal comments on the FEC's (then) proposed regulations on charitable 501(c)(3) groups. An IRS employee in an e-mail noted that her colleagues were "not aware of a prior instance in which we have sent a formal written comment to the FEC on proposed regulations." The IRS chief counsel's office nonetheless worked directly with Lois Lerner to draft the document. A majority of FEC commissioners might not have been willing to target certain nonprofits, but a majority of FEC staff was clearly interested in going the same route as the IRS.

Because FEC staff were true believers, they also refused to accept the changed legal environment. "There were cases, like *FEC v. Wisconsin Right to Life* that severely limited the reach of what the FEC could do," says McGahn. "And there were other cases, in my early years there, that strongly suggested what was going to come in *Citizens United*. But it was like operating in a flat-earth society. Folks at the FEC weren't even close to understanding what was going on, and how much of what they believed was being rejected by the courts. The staff was clinging to a lot of things that had since been thrown out, like a guy in 1982 thinking disco was going to come back."

Far from embracing reality, McGahn said the staff viewed themselves as a "plaintiffs' advocacy shop, whose job it was to push the envelope, test the law, expand the reach of the statute. If they lost in one court, they'd just go to the next circuit and try again. It was so wholly inappropriate for a federal agency to be doing that. It's not our job to be forging new law."

The background is why McGahn to this day remains unclear how much of what happened to conservatives at the FEC was deliberate targeting like that at the IRS, and how much of it was plain institutional bias against groups that push for more free speech. "When 99.9 percent of the bureaucracy is obviously Democrat, it's tough to figure out if what they are doing is for partisan gain as opposed to some deep-seated ideological bent. But as a practical matter, it all becomes one and the same, since the ideological policy choice seems to always tilt left and silences the right," he says.

He's undoubtedly got his stats right. In 2014, the Office of Special Counsel, which investigates illegal political activity by federal employees, settled a case with an FEC lawyer named April Sands, who had spent 2012, according to the OSC, posting "dozens of partisan political tweets, including many soliciting campaign contributions to President Obama's 2012 reelection campaign." She'd done this despite federal laws against such fundraising. She'd also "participated in a Huffington Post Live internet broadcast via webcam from an FEC facility, criticizing the Republican Party and then–Presidential candidate Mitt Romney." Hans von Spakovsky, the former FEC commissioner, would point out that Sands had once worked for Lerner at the FEC. "Quite a 'coincidence' that an FEC lawyer who was illegally using government facilities to try to get Barack Obama reelected used to work for the lawyer who headed the IRS office that apparently tried to stomp on conservative organizations critical of the same president's policies," wrote von Spakovsky in the *National Review*. "If there is any agency in the government where employees need to take extra steps in being nonpartisan and politically circumspect, it is the Federal Election Commission."

Both Brad Smith and Don McGahn make similar points. The left might wish the FEC were more powerful, but in truth the place is plenty powerful already. It freaks out even seasoned campaign lawyers. The mere suspicion that the FEC is gunning for one side and running unauthorized investigations is enough to alter actions and chill speech.

McGahn says that to him the bias is as concerning as outright targeting. "The hard-left elites think regulation is always the answer, and that people need to be controlled. And in their view, whatever the left does is for the greater good, whereas the people who aren't playing by the rules are the people on the right. Those folks annoy and scare them. Lots of the lawyers who end up at the FEC are typical ruling-class elites who view conservatives as backwoods simpletons who aren't smart enough to appreciate all that leftist progress can offer. I was certainly treated that way—because I am Republican, I was dumb, I was a rube, unable to grasp their 'big thinking.'

"And in a way that is more scary. I'd love to say what goes on is simple partisanship—a desire to 'get' the right. But it's deeper than that. It's a way of thinking, and in some manner, that's far more troubling, and a worrisome use of government power."

This was McGahn's insight: that the institution itself needed an overhaul. He'd already witnessed that the staff was primed for action, and willing to take it when nobody was looking. He worried that it might not take much for the place to ramp up into a full-scale IRS-like targeting operation.

∿

A lot of Republican commissioners arrive at the FEC hopeful of getting rid of this or that stupid finance regulation. They quickly discover that getting four commissioner votes to change existing regulations is usually impossible, and whatever change happens quickly disappears after they leave. McGahn decided to focus on the FEC itself. He knew he could expose the FEC staff's behavior; he knew he could tell them not to do it. But given their overwhelming belief in their rightness, and given that bureaucracies operate in the dark, he knew it would just happen again. So instead of focusing on this rule or that enforcement case, McGahn did something very un-Republican (and more like what Democrats do): He focused on reforming the process.

And so he began a years-long battle to change internal FEC procedures. He won several victories, at least on issues that Democrats struggled to defend against. By the time the Republican left the FEC in 2013, the agency had far greater requirements for transparency and due process. Groups that were audited were finally allowed to formally tell their side of the story—which they'd never been able to do before. Groups that were the subject of the complaints were finally allowed to answer queries from commissioners in real time—rather than watch them talk, which is how it had always been.

But McGahn never got his top priority. He sweat blood and tears, working for years to revise the agency's official enforcement manual, thereby putting the reins back on the staff and the commissioners back in control. It was an effort to get "a hold of the process, which was simply rigged," he says.

His push for a new enforcement manual set the left howling that he was attempting to "block enforcement" and "weaken the agency." The Republican notes that he didn't want to stop investigations or even stop interaction with Justice. As he says, his only goal was to clarify *who* got to make the decisions: "The presidentially appointed, Senate-confirmed commissioners, who answer to the public, or an unaccountable staff?" The left wants the latter, since it provides more running room to harass conservative groups that engage in free speech.

McGahn's drama over the enforcement manual hit fever pitch in the summer of 2013, in the wake of the Lerner scandal. The Republican gave it one last hurrah, ramping up his reform efforts internally. His new manual proposed to halt staff's unsanctioned interaction with other agencies and require Justice to file written requests or subpoenas to the FEC if it wanted to lay hands on internal documents—which was simply a return to the process of years past. It also would have truly limited staff's ability to launch sweeping investigations without the commission's say-so.

The push inspired Herman, the general counsel, to write a long memo opposing McGahn's changes, a document quickly made public. Herman, hilariously, argued that the staff was *better placed to make decisions than the commissioners.* His precise words were that sensitive FEC decisions were best left in the hands of "non-partisan, career leadership." The nonpartisan bit practically had McGahn rolling on the floor.

Outside "reform" groups jumped in to back up the bureaucrats, accusing McGahn of wanting a staff "gag rule," and of engaging in a "lame-duck power play." So McGahn started publicly releasing some of the details of staff misbehavior and pushing back against the liberals complaining that he was trying to dilute FEC enforcement. "This isn't a power grab," he at one point told a *Washington Post* reporter, explaining that the reform went to the FEC's basic credibility. "You just can't have an agency where the staff is sort of left to their own devices to come up with lists and do their own thing, because it creates such an opportunity for people to accuse the place of playing political games."

Herman was so bitter that McGahn was questioning staff's right to run the asylum that he took the extraordinary step of publicly complaining about a sitting commissioner. The lawyer essentially called McGahn a liar, claiming that his portrayal of the general counsel's office was "not true." He brushed off his Justice chumminess as nothing more than a routine FEC practice of responding to prosecutors' requests, and airily noted that until recently no commissioners had objected. He confessed himself "perplexed by the allegation."

Democratic commissioner Ellen Weintraub also jumped to the

defense of the staff's right to walk all over her and the rest of the commission. She insisted that the real worry was that staff "had become cowed by commissioners and it may be coloring their independent judgment." As the debate raged, Herman up and quit. While he never gave a precise reason for leaving, the timing seemed designed to look like a protest resignation.

The Democratic commissioners refused to budge on the issue (even though they had previously said in a House oversight hearing that a manual was a good idea), and McGahn wasn't able to get the requisite four votes. When he left his office for the final time in September 2013, it was to widespread applause from free-speech and due-process advocates on both sides of the aisle for what progress he had made. Brad Smith from his perch at the Center for Competitive Politics praised McGahn for "following the law and the Constitution, not treating the FEC as a roving, unbounded, political police force."

Still, the FEC staff retains plenty of power and ability to target and intimidate. And the Obama administration has also upped its efforts to make the FEC into a more openly partisan weapon. Democratic chairwoman Ann Ravel landed there in 2013, straight from a job running California's FEC equivalent, the Fair Political Practices Commission. She arrived with a mission to turbocharge the FEC's powers. She's proposed greatly expanding disclosure rules. She wants to give the FEC power to regulate Internet content. Most disturbingly, she wants to get rid of one commissioner, to end tie votes, and allow one party (presumably hers) to steamroll the other. With the IRS on ice, the left has turned its attention back to using the FEC against its opponents.

As Cleta Mitchell put it to the *Washington Examiner* in August 2015, "[Ravel] and Lois Lerner are peas in a pod. She wants to weaponize government agencies to shut down and chill free political speech."

Government intimidation wasn't confined to the IRS.

CHAPTER 13

Government Shutdown

SENATOR SUSAN COLLINS is a Republican, but she's a Maine Republican, which means she's something a little different. The Pine Tree State is tough territory for conservatives, and Collins has held on to her seat by bucking her party on key issues. One of these is campaign finance law. She voted with Democrats on McCain-Feingold, and she has long publicly embraced greater "transparency."

Collins was also one of those rare Republicans who, at least in the early years, expressed a willingness to try to work with Obama. So it was something in the spring of 2011, still early in the Obama tenure, to see Collins fuming and rallying the entire Congress to oppose a presidential action. It isn't easy to get her that mad.

The catalyst came on April 20, 2011. White House press secretary Jay Carney took to the podium. Yes, the rumors were true. Obama was contemplating (yet another) executive order, this one to force any federal contractor to disclose its donations to groups that participated in politics.

Those rumors had started the day before, when Hans von Spakovsky, the former Justice and FEC Republican, posted an explosive blog on *PJ Media*. "An impeccable source has provided me with a copy of a draft Executive Order that the White House is apparently circulating for comments from several government agencies," he wrote. That order would seek "to implement—by executive fiat—portions of the DISCLOSE Act." He quoted his source as saying, "It really is amazing—they lost in the Supreme Court, they lost in Congress, they lost at the FEC, so now the president is just going to do it by edict."

Von Spakovsky went on to detail the contents of the order. It would require any potential government contractor, and its directors and officers, to divulge as part of its bidding process any contributions made to political parties or organizations. Even more intrusive, it would require contractors to disclose any money to independent groups that might use that money for political ads. Von Spakovsky pointed out that the focus on "transparency" for companies was largely a ruse, since federal contractors had already long been barred from making any contributions to political parties or to candidates.

No, this was a backdoor way of delving "into the personal political activities of their officers and directors—and require them to report political contributions those employees have made, not out of corporate funds (which is illegal), but out of their personal funds," wrote von Spakovsky. It was also a way of outing otherwise anonymous corporate donations to nonprofit groups. The backlash would then intimidate companies out of such speech.

Carney was quick to spin this as "reform" and "transparency" and to suggest that U.S. taxpayers had a right to know how federal dollars being paid to contractors were being used in campaigns. Free-speech advocates rolled their eyes. The order didn't cover federal employee unions, which negotiate contracts—paid for with taxpayer dollars—far in excess of government contracts. The White House wasn't forcing them to explain how they used their dollars. It also didn't cover any of the many liberal groups (such as Planned Parenthood and environmental organizations) that suck up millions in federal grants.

The executive order brought instantly to many minds the

infamous John Dean memo of that era. The point of Nixon's
"enemies list," Dean had said, was to "determine what sorts of
dealings these individuals have with the Federal Government and
how we can best screw them (e.g. grant availability, federal contracts, litigation, prosecution, etc.)."

The Obama order was in fact far more than just intimidation.
It was a partisan threat. Federal contracts are supposed to go to
the lowest bidder. But for many this was the federal government
making clear that a new standard held: Contracts would go to
those who were on Obama's side of the political aisle. Companies could bid and lose out for the sin of donating to Republican
groups. Or they could protect their livelihoods by halting donations to the GOP altogether. It was a new twist on an old phrase.
It was "not-pay to play." And it was a win-win for the White
House.

Yet Obama's penchant for issuing law-defying executive orders
and regulations wasn't yet fully honed in 2011. He still needed
to get reelected. He was still courting some Republicans. He was
more cautious in those days.

And the blowback to the proposed executive order was extraordinary. Anger from the usual free-speech advocates wasn't
necessarily a surprise, although their outrage was palpable. In an
interview with me at the time, Minority Leader Mitch McConnell called the order the "crassest" political move he'd ever seen.
"This is almost gangster politics, to shut down people who oppose
them. . . . I assure you that this is going to create problems for
them in many ways—seen and unseen—if they go forward."

More eye-popping was blowback from Collins. She was all on
board with transparency. But she's also no dummy. And she has an
old-fashioned definition of government corruption. She'd spent
many of her Senate years trying to weed out the potential for that
corruption. What she saw in the Obama order was naked politics, and an order that would roll back seventy years of efforts to
get politics out of government contracting.

Collins was so affronted, she spearheaded a GOP letter to the president, and at a policy lunch briefed Republican senators on its implications. The otherwise calm senator was keyed up. The whole reform language was "Orwellian," she told me. The administration's argument that this was about disclosure was a "fraud." The very notion "offend[ed]" her "deeply."

It was, she said, "the equivalent of repealing the Hatch Act"— the 1939 law designed to weed out federal pay-to-play. Collins noted that it had taken decades to create a federal contracting system based on "best prices, best value, best quality." The Obama order blew this up overnight. Quite aside from the intimidation aspect, the order might cause companies not to bid, reducing competition and raising government costs. It also, she noted, put "thousands of civil servants" who oversaw contracting "in an impossible situation."

Other Republicans noted the surreal aspect of Obama floating this order—designed to dry up Republican donations—at a moment when he was holding fund-raisers at breakneck speed and when his supporters were bragging that he was on track to break the $1 billion reelection threshold.

Collins likely saved the day. Obama was still in a period where he was hoping to nab some Republicans for his budget and other priorities. Collins was a prime target, and her wrath over the executive order made an impression. The White House went mum on it, and it faded from memory. But it is no doubt sitting in a drawer somewhere.

Government intimidation wasn't confined to the IRS and the FEC.

∿

The Federal Communications Commission has since the 1940s had a whole host of rules requiring disclosure by groups taking responsibility for running political ads. Those rules were pretty clear. McCain-Feingold added to the requirements, including the new demand that politicians declare on air that they "approve" of their campaign messages. These too were pretty clear.

Andrew Schwartzman, the senior vice president and policy director of a liberal outfit called the Media Access Project (MAP), in March 2011 nonetheless argued in a petition filed with the FCC that a whole world of smart people had in fact for decades been incorrectly interpreting all these requirements. The laws, he claimed, demanded far more: They required not just disclosure of the group taking responsibility, but of those who actually *paid* for the advertisement.

MAP's petition was specific: It wanted the FCC to force groups to list in public filings with the agency any financial backers who contributed more than 10 percent of the budget for a TV or radio ad. Groups that took more than 25 percent of their TV commercial budget from one donor would have to publicly identify those donors' names, on air, as part of the commercial. Schwartzman tied all this into the controversy that in 2011 was raging over nonprofits, and said the rule change was necessary to expose the shady characters behind "front" groups. "I would argue it's a relatively modest change in existing practices," he disingenuously told the *Washington Post*.

It was far from modest. It was another part of the growing war against conservative speech. MAP, like Van Hollen, like Schumer, like Lerner, like Bauer, knew that corporations and individuals were sensitive to having their names broadcast in politics, for fear of retribution. Threaten to put their name in a commercial, and it would increase the likelihood that they'd bow out of political participation altogether.

The FCC moved cautiously—at first. In April 2012, its majority Democrats voted to force broadcasters to post online records about political advertising sold by the station. Republican commissioner Robert McDowell, in a partial dissent, pointed out that financial details about political ads had been available for inspection by the public in individual broadcasting offices around the country since the 1960s. He added that the commission, and Congress, had long felt that political information in particular should be kept locally, in order to protect broadcasters from having to divulge commercially sensitive information about the rates they charged for TV ads. And he pointed out the unfairness of the requirement, in that it only applied to broadcasters, and not to cable or radio stations or to newspapers or direct mail, which would not have to disclose the pricing of their services.

This mattered not one bit to the commission Democrats, whose only goal was to get all the spending and pricing information in one central database, the better for liberal groups to troll for targets. And indeed, the Sunlight Foundation, a nice-sounding organization that exists to beat up conservatives (it is also funded by George Soros) immediately began calls for volunteers to help it put together a "searchable, sortable database" of ad buys nationwide.

Media outlets like ProPublica were soon using the records to publish stories like one in 2012 that ran under the headline "Revealed: The Dark Money Group Attacking Sen. Sherrod Brown." Brown is a Democratic senator from Ohio, who was running for reelection in 2012 and who had his public record highlighted in TV ads by a 501(c)(4) organization called the Government Integrity Fund. ProPublica used the FCC records to track down the man listed as the nonprofit's chairman and treasurer, who happened to be a Republican, who happened to run a lobbying firm, which happened to employ among its staff a man who happened to have worked a year earlier for Brown's Republican opponent, Josh Mandel. ProPublica cast this noninformation as a giant conspiracy, without ever explaining why there was anything nefarious about a group of Republicans running ads against a Democrat. By 2014, the Sunlight Foundation was bragging that the information had allowed it to begin to "unmask the donors behind political ad buys."

The groups were so tickled by their progress in identifying more donors that by the end of 2014 the Sunlight Foundation

(Soros money), Common Cause (Soros money), and the Campaign Legal Center (Soros money) wanted the FCC to expand its rule. McDowell, the Republican commissioner, had worried in 2012 that the broadcast disclosure rule was unequally applied. The liberal groups were happy to fix that. They wanted the FCC to expand the disclosure requirement on ad buys to cable and satellite. Advocates argued that the FCC needed to get this in place before the 2016 election. And congressional Democrats did an IRS redux, applying pressure on the agency. California representatives Anna Eshoo and Henry Waxman, along with Florida senator Bill Nelson, wrote a letter explaining that it was "imperative" that the FCC sweep everybody under new disclosure rules. By the end of 2014, the commission had formally proposed just such an expansion.

These victories were but the prelude. No one on the left had forgotten MAP's original demand, and all through 2012 and 2013, Democrats kept pushing the FCC to do what Congress wouldn't: require the full disclosure of all the financial contributors to political ads. In an early 2013 Senate Commerce Committee hearing, Florida's Nelson, joined by West Virginia Democrat Jay Rockefeller, demanded the FCC, extralegally, impose the requirements of the DISCLOSE Act. Nelson tied the issue back (yet again) to *Citizens United*, and told the FCC commissioners, "You have the statutory power. You don't have to do what we failed to do four years ago, to pass the disclosure act." Then–FEC chairman Julius Genachowski seemed enthusiastic about the idea, calling it a "First Amendment–friendly, powerful tool."

Republicans grew alarmed, and thirteen of them led by Senate minority leader Mitch McConnell in April wrote a letter to the FCC putting it on notice that they were watching. The DISCLOSE Act had been among the "most politically charged, partisan issues in recent Congresses," they said, because it raised "grave constitutional concerns for speech protected by the First Amendment." Any action in this direction by the FCC would "seriously undermine" its "integrity." Texas senator Ted Cruz was worried enough to put an indefinite hold in the fall of 2013 on Obama's nomination of Democrat Tom Wheeler as chairman of the FCC.

Wheeler, a wealthy venture capitalist and lobbyist, had raised hundreds of thousands of dollars for the Obama election, and was clearly an Obama loyalist. Cruz in confirmation hearings demanded to know whether the nominee thought the FCC had the authority to unilaterally impose such a disclosure regime. The Democrat ducked the question, claiming he didn't know enough about the issue. Mr. Cruz informed Mr. Wheeler that he wouldn't be getting a vote until he educated himself. Cruz only lifted his hold after a meeting with Wheeler, after which the senator announced he'd been given assurances that the soon-to-be chairman had no intention of making the political disclosure issue a "priority."

Wheeler has held to that agreement. In the summer of 2015, he argued the FCC had plenty else on its to-do list, and wouldn't be pursuing the left's disclosure wish list anytime soon. That position earned him the wrath of liberals like Marty Kaplan, a left-wing professor who wrote a scathing column in the *Huffington Post* that same month. The 2016 election would bring more anonymous ads, he wrote, and the pity was that "we'll get good and mad at the dog crap soiling democracy's lawn, but we won't even know whom to shame."

The shaming would be easier, wrote Kaplan, if Wheeler would just understand that "we don't have to wait for the president to send a disclosure bill to Congress that won't go anywhere; we don't have to wait for Congress to bite the hand that feeds it. The FCC can do that rulemaking on its own, and after a 120-day public comment period, if you conceal who's paying for those ads, you'll get nailed." Kaplan complained that as "important" as Wheeler's other priorities were, only his taking up the disclosure mantle would "rescue" democracy.

If Kaplan had substituted the word "Democrats" for "democracy," the piece would have had a whiff of honesty. It was nonetheless revealing. The pressure on the FCC to join the targeting brigade will continue.

Government intimidation wasn't confined to the IRS, the FEC, and the White House.

∿

Democrats wanted corporations out of politics. The White House had tried doing it to a discrete group—government contractors. A scant few months after that failed, the left debuted a bigger, better fallback plan. They'd get the whole corporate world in one big swoop. And luckily for them, they had yet another agency, one with control over public companies: the Securities and Exchange Commission.

The SEC on August 3, 2011, received a petition from an odd if purposefully named organization: the Committee on Disclosure of Corporate Political Spending. It was in reality a collection of ten liberal academics, many of them high-profile scholars who frequently parlayed their putative research into calls for more and bigger rules on the financial sector.

They were back, in force. Their petition asked that the SEC "develop rules to require public companies to disclose to shareholders the use of corporate resources for political activities." This was a reprise of the Larry Tribe idea.

The broader argument for the rule was cast in all sorts of fancy scholar-speak. The petitioners insisted that the law gave the SEC the authority to require such a rule. They cited a new trend in shareholder proposals that demanded that companies divulge their political spending. They referenced the *Citizens United* decision, claiming that the Supreme Court had backed just this type of disclosure.

Their *Citizens United* meditation was actually the most revealing part; it was yet more proof that what drove the petition was the left's new focus on outing companies, teeing them up for reprisal. The scholar-speak was designed to cloak what was a naked partisan play.

Citizens United focused the left's attention on nonprofits. But it was equally frantic about the new free-speech rights of corporations, which now had greater freedom to run their own issue ads. It was also worried that companies would give more money to nonprofits that would also engage in the political system. The DISCLOSE Act had been its initial attempt to immediately shut down the freedoms *Citizens United* had restored to companies. When that failed, the left crafted a sweeping multipronged campaign to embarrass companies out of civic participation.

Liberal groups had been going from company to company, trying to pressure them into disclosing their political giving, but that plan wasn't yielding quick results. The petition was an attempt to get at the same end by a faster, bigger, all-encompassing means—namely by getting the SEC to impose the same requirement from above.

The idea initially went nowhere. Obama's SEC was busy, now that his Democratic Congress had passed the gigantic Dodd-Frank financial straitjacket. But the left wasn't about to let go; it kept pressing and pressing. In December 2012, the patience paid off. The Office of Management and Budget released its list of potential regulatory actions. It included that the SEC's Division of Corporate Finance was deciding whether to recommend to the SEC a rule requiring companies to disclose political giving.

We don't know precisely what SEC chairwoman Mary Schapiro thought about this plan. The left's problem was her professional staff. Turns out the agency still contained a few serious career lawyers—attorneys who held the quaint view that the Securities and Exchange Commission's job was to regulate trading, not political speech.

According to documents obtained by Congress, one of these

was Eric Spitler, counselor to Schapiro and the director of SEC's Office of Legislative and Intergovernmental Affairs. Only a few months after the scholars filed their petition, Spitler used one of their arguments against them, in an e-mail to Schapiro. Plenty of groups were indeed filing shareholder proposals about disclosure with companies, he wrote. And thanks to existing SEC rules and regulations, those proposals were getting a fair hearing and vote. "I think a key point for us to make is that the mechanisms already exist, and as their letter points out, people are using them."

In January 2012, Spitler sent another e-mail, this one flatly highlighting the left's motivations: "Ironically, it is that fact that Congress cannot act in this area because the votes are not there that is causing them to put more pressure on the agency so they can show something can be done." Another staffer was far more blunt: "This is an issue for Congress to address." Staff noted that acting outside of Congress could cause a troubling situation. The SEC can only regulate public companies. An SEC disclosure rule would force public firms to release all sorts of information that their private counterparts didn't have to. Practically speaking, only Congress could require uniform disclosure.

It was more unfair than even that. The SEC could only look at companies. It could not require disclosure from unions, which also spend directly on elections and give money (anonymously) to nonprofits. Which is precisely why the left was asking the SEC, rather than Congress, to regulate.

The staff also had the temerity to point out that even were the SEC to obnoxiously ignore Congress, another agency still had a first and better claim. In December 2012, employees in the office of Meredith Cross, the director of the SEC's Division of Corporation Finance, prepared a memo that made this point: "FEC is the primary federal regulator of political activity disclosure," it lectured. "Formulating a SEC disclosure rule that is not duplicative of other federal and state law requirements and does not raise First Amendment issues may be challenging."

In April 2012, Schapiro infuriated Obama's liberal base by voting with Republican commissioners to move ahead with an SEC agenda that did not include a disclosure rule. The timing had the left seeing red. It was an election year, and they'd been counting on getting a corporate-disclosure win. At the very least, they had wanted the promise that the rule was coming. They had hoped the mere possibility of it would cause companies to think twice about spending that election year.

E-mails and letters poured into the SEC. Groups demanded meetings and explanations. One SEC e-mail recounted a May meet-up between Schapiro, members of outside pro-disclosure groups, and a former Democratic congresswoman. When Schapiro asked, "Why not the FEC instead of us?" the congresswoman responded, "Because the FEC is even more broken than you." A congressional Republican memo on the exchange pointed to this as glaring evidence that even supporters didn't believe this was a legitimate SEC job. They were just looking for any means to an end.

Congressional Democrats—as they had done with the IRS and the FCC—jumped in to push a rule. Barney Frank—the other half of "Dodd-Frank"—was in the summer of 2012 still the ranking member on the House Financial Services Committee. In July, his deputy chief counsel e-mailed the SEC Office of Legislative and Intergovernmental Affairs to make a request. It read, "We have gotten a question from leadership about SEC authority to require disclosure on corporate charitiable [sic] contributions. There is particular interest in what the authority is for disclosure of 501(c)(4) contributions (political contributions)."

The request was remarkable. The summer of 2012 was also the height of the IRS targeting of conservative nonprofits. Frank's office was essentially asking if the SEC would zero in on corporate money to those same nonprofits. And it made clear that the demand was coming from the top, from the Democratic "leadership"—likely Nancy Pelosi's office.

The e-mail was forwarded to numerous higher-ups at the SEC, with the following (somewhat snarky) note: "I suspect the answer to the actual question is relatively easy," it read, "but I'm including all of you on the email so you'll be aware that House Democratic Leadership is interested." One SEC lawyer almost immediately answered: "There is no specific authority." The attorney explained that for the SEC to move ahead, it would have to think of some way to argue that the provision fell under some broader existing disclosure rule.

Schapiro and her two fellow Democratic commissioners ultimately sat in at least eleven meetings with liberal groups demanding disclosure. Many of these meetings were with Public Citizen, the same organization that had been busy filing requests with the IRS to target 501(c)(4) groups. And Public Citizen openly explained that it wanted the SEC rule for the same reason—to expose "electioneering front groups."

Another three meetings were with an organization formed in direct response to Citizens United, called the Coalition for Accountability in Public Spending. It was founded in 2010 by then–New York City public advocate Bill de Blasio (who is today New York City's liberal mayor). The organization admitted that its main goal was to force companies to disclose all their political spending. The meetings also featured all the other usual suspects: Common Cause, People for the American Way, etcetera.

The staff remained resolute. When in September 2012 the agency started working on its next-year agenda, Cross's office was asked for its opinion on disclosure. It brusquely stated, "The Division would not recommend adding it to the agenda at this time unless requested by the Commission."

Which is precisely what the commission, or at least one commissioner—Luis Aguilar—proceeded to do. The Democrat began a campaign to get the disclosure rule included, sending formal requests to both Schapiro and the agency's other liberal, Elisse Walter. By the end of September, Schapiro had been made to see the liberal light. Congress did not obtain any documents explaining why she chose to ignore all the wisdom of her staff, but a little more than a week after Aguilar's demand, the general counsel sent around a draft agenda for the upcoming year that included the disclosure rule.

The staff, at the wish of political masters, now switched gears. It feverishly attempted to cook up some good excuses for why the SEC needed to act as speech police. The Division of Corporation Finance in January 2013 produced a draft argument in favor of the rules. It even creatively came up with a way to make Barney Frank and the Democratic "leadership" happy. It read, "A substantial amount of corporate spending on politics is conducted through intermediaries not required to disclose the sources of their contributions.... There are cases, such as corporate contributions to intermediaries that spend a large fraction of their funds on politics, for which inclusion within the scope of the Commission's rules seems warranted." The SEC, at Democratic leadership's request, was advocating a backdoor way of blowing up nonprofit anonymity. This is an example of how Congress makes agencies do its bidding.

In the end, the blowing up happened on the other side. The SEC had terrible timing with its proposal. Not long after it indicated that it intended to proceed, the IRS targeting scandal was exposed and put new focus on other agencies that were pursuing nonprofits. The scholarly community also rained down scathing criticism on the disclosure idea, pointing out just how far the SEC had to stretch to find a legal rationale for inserting itself in the debate. The corporate world uncharacteristically pulled together to beat up on the idea. House Republicans called hearings, warning new SEC chairman Mary Jo White that she risked derailing her tenure at the agency with an uproar over a highly partisan rule, an issue that would overshadow and stymie the rest of her agenda.

White, a straitlaced former federal prosecutor, decided that she had no interest in wallowing in a partisan mudhole. In

October 2013, she disparaged the whole idea, saying that the disclosure rules pushed by activists "seem more directed at exerting societal pressure on companies to change behavior, rather than to disclose financial information that primarily informs investment decisions." A little more than a month later, the SEC circulated its list of upcoming priorities. Disclosure was gone.

Democrats haven't given up. In August 2015, forty-four Democratic senators signed a letter to White demanding that she get on their disclosure train. It was threatening. "We ask that you make this a top priority for the SEC in the near term, and inform us of the basis for your decision should you not plan to include it on the commission's agenda for the upcoming year," it read. The "upcoming year" part is important. It includes a presidential election.

ᴧᴜᴖ

Government intimidation wasn't confined to the IRS. The service was simply the agency that most fully succumbed to a pressure campaign the left waged across the vast sweep of the Obama apparatus. As soon as the DISCLOSE Act failed in Congress, liberal activists and Democratic politicians instituted a broad and coordinated campaign to get the IRS, the SEC, the FEC, and the FCC to hassle conservative nonprofits. Americans were outraged over the IRS, but they didn't know the half of it.

The left got more than it hoped for when the IRS outright muzzled nonprofits. The left's campaigns at the FCC and SEC, and via the White House executive order, had all been aimed at one thing: disclosure. The activists wanted lists of names. Because they were already fine-tuning a new method of cowing conservative players out of politics.

CHAPTER 14

Star Chamber

BRUCE JOSTEN has been at home at the U.S. Chamber of Commerce for more than forty years. And for about thirty-five of those years, he had pretty obvious jobs.

Josten is on paper the executive vice president for government affairs, making him the second-ranking officer at the nation's largest and oldest trade association. In reality, he's the chamber's chief strategist, chief lobbyist, chief policy expert, chief go-to guy. For thirty-five years, Josten has done battle with the trial bar. For thirty-five years, Josten has pressured and educated and lectured Congress on trade and health care and immigration and taxes and spending. For thirty-five years, Josten has put together coalitions of businesses to fight for (largely) free-market legislative priorities.

In January 2010, the Supreme Court issued *Citizens United*, and Josten got a new job. Not one he'd asked for. Not one he expected. And not one he likes. In addition to all his other jobs, he has added, in his words, the title "chief defender of the business community's right to open its mouth."

The trade association became the left's foil for everything supposedly wrong with corporate spending. And Josten's days became all new. He found himself testifying in front of Congress against the DISCLOSE Act and other speech-suppression ideas. He found himself defending against endless attempts by the left to force the chamber and companies to disclose their political funding and political spending. He found himself researching the complex web of liberal groups that then used that disclosure to jointly target and harass companies engaged in politics. He found himself calming nervous CEOs whose companies came under pressure to leave the chamber and withdraw from political speech. He found himself educating entire C-suites on the left's game plan, and the perils of giving in to the intimidation.

"Somebody had to get out in front of this as a spokesman," says Josten, who credits a whole team of people at the chamber who have for several years now made it their mission to respond to the assaults. "And the mad, mad, mad thing of today is that somebody *had to*. We thought *NAACP v. Alabama* was the definitive answer— that there are rights to freedom of speech and association. The business community, and business owners, they are a foundation of this country. They represent every worker in America. Of course they must be allowed to speak about our country's direction. And of course that voice is healthy for debate.

"But look at these groups. Look at this campaign. Look at the stakes. These folks are very clear: They not only want to silence business during a political campaign season, they want to move the business community entirely out of the legislative process in Congress, in the states. They want us silenced entirely. And they've got a game plan."

∿

That game plan hinges on disclosure.

One thing that drives the left nuts about the chamber is that it is a trade association. Companies are barred by law from giving directly to parties and candidates. And they must disclose a lot of their political giving. But the chamber as a nonprofit is allowed (just like unions) to keep its donors anonymous, and to directly spend money on political campaigns.

And the chamber has been spending money in campaigns—growing amounts of it. Josten went to Harvard, and he gives off the appearance of a swanky lawyer. In reality, he's a scrapper. It makes him a good fit with chamber CEO Tom Donohue, whose prior job was as the combative head of the powerful American Trucking Associations. When Donohue took the top chamber job in 1997, one of his goals was to ramp the organization into a far more powerful lobbying and political voice in defense of business and free markets. Pre-Donohue days, the chamber spent little if anything on politics. In recent cycles it has spent an average estimate of $35 million, much of it in support or defense of Republicans and free-market ideas. This amount pales compared to the regular union spending blowouts on elections. But the left would rather the chamber spent nothing at all.

Obama shared that dislike, and came to office intending to take out the organization. Not that he showed his cards at first. Obama was still acting as a uniter, and he maintained a wary but cordial relationship with the trade association for about six months. His moment came in the summer of 2009, when the chamber dared to oppose his budding proposal for a single-payer health system, running ads correctly warning that such a policy would lead to higher taxes and "government control over your health."

The White House reaction was swift, and in keeping with the sort of intimidation the Obama team had practiced in the 2008 campaign—against the Hillary super PAC, and against conservative groups like the American Issues Project. Obama began meeting privately with dozens of CEOs, sidelining the chamber and letting it be known that their association with the group might cause them problems. On October 9 he elevated the campaign, using his podium to slam the chamber in front of the entire press corps, berating it for opposing his agenda. The president had opted out of the presidential financing system so that he could accept unprecedented campaign contributions. Yet here he was griping that the *chamber* spent money on lobbying.

These days, Obama routinely calls out opponents by name. It's commonplace. But early in his tenure it was still a bit shocking to see a president—one who'd taken an oath to represent all Americans—use his power to demonize a specific organization. Activists took the president's cue and mobilized against companies allied with the chamber's campaign against single-payer care. Some staged unpleasant protests outside the homes of insurance CEOs. They showed up at CIGNA CEO Edward Hanway's house outside Philadelphia. They showed up in Indianapolis, outside the home of WellPoint CEO Angela Braly. They showed up in Wayzata, Minnesota, at the home of UnitedHealth CEO Stephen Hemsley. In September, they staged some 150 demonstrations at insurance headquarters nationally. The joint activist-presidential attacks provoked publicity, which was Obama's aim. It sent a powerful message to every CEO that the chamber was a political risk.

It was part of a broader effort by left-wing organizations, which had for more than a month been targeting individual chamber members. This was 2009, and one of the hot topics in Washington was climate change. Democrats had failed miserably in prior efforts to pass climate legislation, but Obama had reelevated the issue and promised to ram through a bill. Corporate America was still highly sensitive to the topic, worried about what would happen if it opposed Obama. As Jim Rogers, the CEO of Duke Energy, said in that era, "If you don't have a seat at the table, you'll wind up on the menu." Some thirty companies had even formed a new organization, the U.S. Climate Action Partnership (CAP), to try to demonstrate their interest in reducing greenhouse gas emissions.

The left was aware of this sensitivity, and pounced when the chamber came out in late summer against the Obama suggestion that it might use the Clean Air Act to impose climate regulations. The chamber wasn't opposed to steps on global warming. It instead argued that Congress was the only appropriate body to impose such a massive shift in the energy economy, and that the United States should consider it only if the world's biggest polluters—China, India—also took steps.

Liberal groups didn't have a roster of chamber donors, but they did have at the ready a list of company executives who were formal board members of the chamber—including a short list of those they felt most susceptible to pressure. Thus began a campaign against select boards and CEOs, in which they labeled any organization that stayed with the chamber a climate denier. Weak-kneed companies started folding like accordions. Two California utilities, PG&E and PNM Resources, both announced their withdrawal from the chamber. Also nuclear-power generator Exelon. Nike was a particular profile in noncourage, issuing a statement complaining that it "fundamentally disagrees with the U.S. Chamber of Commerce's position on climate change and is concerned and deeply disappointed with the U.S. Chamber's recently filed petition challenging the E.P.A.'s administrative authority and action on this critically important issue." (Nike skipped over the small detail that EPA had no administrative authority.) The company withdrew from the chamber's board, though kept its (useful) membership. Apple got in on the action, noting that "we strongly object to the chamber's recent comments opposing the E.P.A.'s effort to limit greenhouse gases." It issued a resignation letter, effective immediately.

Josten points out archly that not one of the corporate members of CAP ever endorsed Waxman-Markey, the Democrats' proposed cap-and-trade bill. They all knew how bad it would be for the economy. Yet several CAP members were happy to make a spectacle out of their resignation from the chamber, in an effort to curry greenie points. "We were brutalized as an organization simply for pointing out a few obvious realities, like that no climate action would make a difference unless all countries participated," he remarks.

The pressure was so successful, liberals couldn't wait to replicate it. They got their next chance in January 2010, only a few weeks before *Citizens United*. The *National Journal*'s Peter Stone broke the news that the chamber ads of 2009—the ones that had slammed Obama's plan for single-payer health—had been funded in part by six large health care insurers. Since this was money to nonprofits, the donations were legally anonymous. But two health care lobbyists had divulged the insurers' names to the reporter.

Liberals were thrilled to have a new list of corporations to attack. Nineteen Senate Democrats almost immediately called for legislative retribution, demanding that the insurers be stripped of their antitrust exemption in the coming health care bill. Obama joined those calls. Another round of protests ensued. In early March, thousands of union and liberal activists bombarded the insurance industry's annual conference, held at the Ritz-Carlton hotel in Washington, issuing "citizen's arrest" warrants for health care CEOs, engaging in civil disobedience, and unrolling an oversized yellow police tape reading "CORPORATE CRIME SCENE." Later that month, nine protestors were arrested in downtown Manhattan on charges of disorderly conduct while protesting at WellPoint's corporate offices—blocking the entrance, chanting "Arrest the Profiteers." It was part of a dozen similarly riotous sit-ins across the country. They were all designed to target the companies and direct public animosity against any organization that opposed Obama's health care agenda.

∿∿

Obama signed his health care bill that same month, and conservatives got a powerful issue. *Citizens United* also gave them a voice. As the midterm season rolled along and Democrats faced a tidal-wave defeat, they escalated their campaign against corporations and nonprofits—and made the Chamber of Commerce a unifying target for the whole campaign.

Congressional Democrats pursued their DISCLOSE agenda,

and Josten spent days in hearings, attempting to get members of the most democratically elected institution in the world to remember the Constitution. Democratic operatives filed complaints about conservatives with the FEC and the IRS. Activists started petitioning other federal agencies to impose disclosure, and unleashed shareholder proxy wars against companies. Obama began his public campaign against "shadowy" groups, echoed by the liberal establishment and powerful Senate Democrats, spurring the IRS to action.

But the president had a special and ugly attack waiting for the chamber, which the White House still blamed for the agony of, and anger over, its health care law, and Dodd-Frank, and its prospective climate bill. And for the millions of dollars the chamber was spending against Democrats in the midterm. Obama's goal was twofold—to silence the chamber, and to get more names of companies to target.

Obama let loose that attack in early October, about a month before the election. A little-known researcher by the name of Lee Fang at the liberal Center for American Progress crafted a highly irresponsible posting for its *ThinkProgress* site. It pointed out that the chamber accepted foreign "dues money" and on the basis of this argued that the trade group was "likely skirting longstanding campaign finance law" against foreign spending in U.S. elections. It cleverly dropped in the names of some Middle Eastern countries that hosted chamber chapters—Bahrain, Egypt, Abu Dhabi—to make it all sound a little more sinister. Fang's "likely" was proof that he had no idea what he was talking about and was engaged in pure muckraking.

That muckraking was good enough for the president of the United States, though, who two days later in a public rally complained bitterly about a new round of ads that were running against his Democrats. "Just this week, we learned that one of the largest groups paying for these ads regularly takes in money from foreign corporations," Obama railed.

The rapid response from the rest of the liberal establishment was almost impressive. The Democratic National Committee rushed out ads repeating the libel, claiming that "it appears" the chamber has "even taken secret foreign money to influence our elections." Liberal activists put out releases and statements claiming that foreign corporations were stealing our democracy by funneling illegal money through the chamber. MoveOn.org made up a dollar amount, claiming, "Foreign corporations are funding some of the $75 million the U.S. Chamber of Commerce is spending to defeat Democrats." It also imagined up donors, claiming the lobby was getting the money from foreign corporations "in countries like China, Russia and India, the same companies that threaten American jobs." In Bauer style, it urged its members to call on the Justice Department to investigate.

Josten, who was growing accustomed to this White House's tactics, was nonetheless floored. "I won't even call this guy a reporter, he was a hack, at *ThinkProgress*—which isn't even a news organization—and he tries to convince people we're using foreign money in campaigns. And amazingly, within a week he had the president of the United States citing it. I couldn't believe it."

Josten and the chamber flatly denied the charge, and explained that the organization received only a small amount of money from foreign sources and that none of it went into domestic ads. The lie was so large that even the left-tilting mainstream fact-checking organizations had a field day. FactCheck.org, a project of the Annenberg Public Policy Center, ran a long piece under the headline and tag "Foreign Money? Really? Democrats peddle an unproven claim." The writer, Brooks Jackson, explained that "Democrats, from President Barack Obama on down, are trying to turn an evidence-free allegation into a major campaign theme." Jackson noted that the FEC allows organizations to take in foreign money and still make donations, so long as they have a "reasonable accounting method" and enough money from U.S. sources to cover the donations. Jackson ended, "Accusing anybody of violating the law is a serious matter requiring serious evidence to back it up. So far Democrats have produced none."

The *New York Times*, hardly a chamber cheerleader, ran its own well-researched story, concluding, "There is little evidence that what the chamber does in collecting overseas dues is improper or even unusual, according to both liberal and conservative election-law lawyers and campaign finance documents." The *Times* noted that plenty of liberal groups, like the Sierra Club and the AFL-CIO, also have international units and also spend money domestically. Other groups pointed out that the real offender in terms of foreign money was the union movement. According to the Center for Competitive Politics, close to half of the unions that are members of the AFL-CIO are international. And they presumably pay union dues.

The whole episode marked a height in cynical and unaccountable politics. The president of the United States singled out and accused a political opponent of a crime, on the basis of an undocumented and untrue slur. Josten is still stunned years later. "We have 114 American chambers of commerce physically located abroad. Their membership is composed of U.S. multinationals doing business abroad. We have an entire vetting process, whenever a new one is formed, to make sure it is not a phony government organization in some third-world country, but rather a legitimate chamber formed by U.S. money," he notes. "The amount of dues that flow up to the U.S. Chamber of Commerce is about $100,000 a year. That goes into our international division, which services them. $100,000 a year. Seriously. We have a more than $250 million budget."

Yet Obama stubbornly kept repeating the claim. Then, as the president confronted growing press criticism for spreading misinformation, the White House abruptly changed tack, claiming that the real problem was "anonymity." This was 2010 and it fit in neatly with Obama's campaign at the time against "shadowy" nonprofits. White House press secretary Robert Gibbs declared that the better chamber discussion needed to be about disclosing "the identities of [its] donors." Obama Svengali David Axelrod also cleverly attempted to use the uproar to force the chamber to hand over the names the left so eagerly wanted. "I guess my answer to the chamber is just disclose where your money is coming from and that will end all the questions," he told ABC News's Jake Tapper. *Time* magazine in a follow-up story wrote, "Such calls, says the chamber's executive vice president for government affairs, R. Bruce Josten, amount to an attempt to intimidate donors with the implicit threat of boycotts and harassment." Josten was speaking from experience, having watched the coordinated activist campaigns against companies that spoke out against health care or climate.

The episode moved Bob Schieffer, the no-nonsense host of CBS's *Face the Nation*, to call bullshit on Axelrod during a Sunday appearance. "They do spend heavily on politics," said Schieffer of the chamber. "But this part about foreign money, that appears to be peanuts, Mr. Axelrod. I mean, do you have any evidence that it's anything other than peanuts?" Axelrod, rather than answer the question, attempted to turn it around and force the chamber to prove a negative. "Well, do you have any evidence that it's not, Bob?" Schieffer didn't appreciate the dodge. He finished the segment with a withering appraisal: "I guess I would put it this way. If the only charge three weeks into the election that the Democrats can make is that somehow this may or may not be foreign money coming into the campaign, is that the best you can do?"

It was. And from Axelrod's perspective, it was good enough. It was generating ugly headlines against the chamber, and keeping focus off the miserable Obama economy and track record. And the strategy was proving far more fruitful in other contexts.

∿

One of these was the Minnesota governor's race. It was a made-to-order example of the financial pain and headache the left could inflict on any company that it knew was engaged in politics and then targeted. It explained why the chamber immediately dismissed Axelrod's suggestion that it list its corporate donors. The trade association had only just witnessed what liberals like Axelrod had done to Target Corp.

Target, the retail giant, is based in Minneapolis. It opened its first store in the state in 1962. Unsurprisingly, it has an abiding interest in a positive state business environment. In 2010 it saw an opportunity to further that via Republican gubernatorial candidate Tom Emmer. Emmer, who'd served in the Minnesota House of Representatives, was running on lower business taxes and more jobs. That sounded good to Target, which in July 2010 gave $150,000 to an organization called Minnesota Forward—created by the Minnesota Chamber of Commerce and the Minnesota Business Partnership—which was running ads for Emmer.

The left tried to suggest that the Target donation was an example of the evil forces *Citizens United* had unleashed. It was a silly claim. None of this was secret; Minnesota Forward disclosed the contribution under state law. And none of it was new or outrageous. Target had a history of giving in state and local races. Its own political action committee, TargetCitizens, tended to spread donations evenly between federal Republicans and Democrats. And Target pointed out that its support for causes and candidates was always laser-focused on its "retail and business objectives," which included "economic growth and job creation."

Target's donation was clearly aimed at electing a governor with free-market priorities that would benefit consumers, workers, and retailers. But left-wing activists didn't care about this truth; they wanted to make Target an example. They combed through Emmer's record, looking for a politically sensitive issue, and landed on the candidate's opposition to gay marriage. At the time, Emmer wasn't out of the mainstream in that position. In 2008, the majority of Americans still opposed gay marriage, as did, for the record, Barack Obama.

But it's all in how you phrase it. In the activists' hands, being pro–traditional marriage was but a short hop and skip to being actively "antigay"—which Target now stood accused of, by virtue of its support of Emmer. MoveOn.org immediately organized a national boycott of the store, crafting a petition on its website. It was at least honest about its goals. It called on signers to agree, "I won't shop at Target until it stops spending money on elections. Companies like Target should stay out of elections, period." The left leveraged social media platforms to turn the boycott into a nationwide cause. Facebook buzzed with fan pages such as "Boycott Target Until They Cease Funding Anti-Gay Politics." YouTube videos featured former Target shoppers professing outrage. One, showcasing a mother telling her story of how she returned more than $200 of Target goods in solidarity with her gay son, went viral. "I'm going to boycott Target until they make this right," she declared. Best Buy, which had also given money to Minnesota Forward, came in for the same treatment.

And what did Target need to make right? That was the joke. The Human Rights Campaign, an organization that supports gay rights, maintains what it calls its Corporate Equality Index, which annually ranks companies on its gay-rights policies. Target in 2009 and 2010 boasted a 100 percent score. The company was already offering domestic partnership benefits for employees. It had sponsored gay pride events around the state.

Yet Target couldn't withstand the assault. By August it had formally apologized for giving money to benefit Emmer. CEO Gregg Steinhafel meekly announced that the company would revise its entire policy on political donations. One major change: Target would henceforth require any trade association to which it gave money to refrain from using those dollars for campaign activities. This was exactly what the left had hoped for; it was a stunning victory. And it had won it, by the way, with a Minnesota disclosure law that had required Minnesota Forward to divulge Target's donation. Democrats were soon pushing that law as a model for the nation.

ᑎᘛᑎ

The left's decision to focus on Emmer's position on gay marriage was calculated and deliberate. It was part of a strategy that would later be disclosed by a man named Eric Burns. Burns had in a prior life been a staffer to Chuck Schumer, the New York senator who warned that his DISCLOSE Act was designed to make companies "think twice" about voicing an opinion. Burns became president of Media Matters, a Soros-funded outfit founded by liberal activist David Brock. It's a heavyweight in the left-wing universe, and in 2010 Burns and Brock released a strategy memo for a coalition of liberals, much of which was focused on their new tool, "disclosure." The goal, said the memo, was to root out the names of corporate donors, which the left would use to "create a multitude of public relations challenges for corporations that make the decision to meddle in politics. Working with allied organizations we will utilize the database's information to provoke backlashes against companies, shareholders, employees and customers, and the public at large." The memo explained that the coalition would use anything and everything to tar a business; it would not draw distinctions. "When businesses back candidates, Media Matters Action Network will portray it as a complete endorsement of everything that given politician has said or done." (Media Matters Action Network is a 501(c)(4) group. It does not disclose its donors. And despite its active involvement in politics, it never ended up on a Lois Lerner list.)

When Josten says that "somebody" had to step up, this was why. The left had a very deliberate and organized plan after *Citizens United*—to get the federal government to harass and disclose the names of political actors, and then to use that information to isolate, humiliate, and intimidate those players out of politics on the back end.

Josten finds the attacks particularly frustrating, because, contrary to propaganda, *Citizens United* never did set off a rush of corporate spending. Even prior to the Supreme Court decision, more than half the states had no bar whatsoever on companies contributing directly in state and local elections. Yet even then, few did. Companies are nervy by nature. Some give; many don't. They are always wary of bad PR.

So while *Citizens* did give them more rights, it didn't result in a tidal wave of money. Even what corporate spending there is remains pathetic by comparison to union and liberal activist dollars. That goes even for the chamber. Yes, Donohue and Josten pumped up the political-spending budget. But the chamber's $35 million in 2012 expenditures has to be compared to $1.7 billion that the National Institute for Labor Relations Research estimates organized unions spent in that cycle. "We are an eat-what-you-kill organization; we have to beg people to make contributions," says Josten. "Companies tend to give money to their specific trade association first. We are about fifth in everybody's line."

Josten muses that what the left also always misses is that money never matters as much as ideas. He remembers billionaire casino magnate Sheldon Adelson giving millions to Newt Gingrich's unsuccessful presidential run. Or Linda McMahon, World Wrestling Entertainment magnate, who spent $100 million on two failed bids for the Senate in Connecticut. "Endless money. But did they win? No," says Josten.

Josten these days spends phenomenal amounts of time educating corporate executives—about DISCLOSE (which Democrats continue to push); about *Citizens United*; about proxy battles; about campaigns like those against Target and Best Buy and the chamber. "It's something that has to be done, because those executives get nervous. They are responsible for the bottom line. And now politics has become more than civic debate; they worry it is a business risk."

He also spends an inordinate amount of time educating Congress on the laws of the land. "Think about it. We've had enormous turnover. About 60 percent of Congress—they've only been here since the 2010 election. What the hell do they know about McCain-Feingold? Not much, is the answer," he says.

Josten notes that he has on occasion gotten lucky; the left has slipped and made his job easier. The Media Matters memo is one example. He also references a 2013 article in the liberal publication *Mother Jones*, entitled "Revealed: The Massive New Liberal Plan to Remake American Politics." In it, the reporter blew the lid off a private meeting attended by three dozen of the largest liberal organizations. The meet-up was by "invite only and off the record," but it included the "top brass" of every influential left-wing organization in the country, from the NAACP, to the Sierra Club, to the unions, to Greenpeace. One goal of the meeting was to formulate a game plan to harass and intimidate companies. The attendees even listed a few targets, like Chevron, that they were already teeing up for particularly rough treatment. Another target was Google, which the group wanted to pressure out of its association with the chamber.

"You get a document like that, and it helps," says Josten. "You take it to the C-suite and you say, 'Don't take my word for it—this is what they said in their own words. So consider yourself warned. The whole game here is to embarrass you and create a backlash and damage your corporation.'" His advice to these executives is always the same: Stay strong, stay clear, stay the course. Giving in just encourages them; they sense weakness.

But he acknowledges that it is "really hard to fight." He circles back to the campaigns against the chamber by Obama and leading Democrats. "What do you do when you are on the wrong side of demagoguery? How do I knock down a completely untruthful statement, when it is the president of the United States saying it? These are people with a title. People that, rightly or wrongly, the public holds in some respect. We are so very small compared to that. And yet, to listen to them, we're the one that needs silencing."

CHAPTER 15

Shakedown

IF YOU'VE never been to a corporate shareholder meeting, you've likely never heard of Justin Danhof. If you ever have been to one, you'll likely never forget him.

Danhof runs something called the Free Enterprise Project, part of the National Center for Public Policy Research. NCPPR was founded in 1982 by Amy Ridenour, and its mission, as Danhof describes it, is to "build up the conservative free-market voice wherever we see it most quiet." That's how the think tank came to run Project 21, a black political outreach group. It's why NCPPR formed a health care reform task force, after witnessing just how lazy so many Republicans were on health policy. ("That's how we got Obamacare," quips Danhof.) And it is how it came to own the Free Enterprise Project (FEP), which by self-description "exposes efforts by left-wing interest groups to divert businesses away from best practices and into left-wing advocacy."

It's a big mandate, and FEP over the years has done everything from exposing corporations that partner with left-wing activists in favor of bad regulation to publicly demanding that companies hold true to free-market principles. Danhof's job in recent years has nonetheless come to center on just one issue: shareholder proxies.

Those proxies are today, alongside public pressure campaigns against the Chamber of Commerce and CEOs, the left's favorite means of intimidating corporations into silence or submission. A sophisticated left-wing infrastructure exists to run the project, a sprawling collection of social investment funds, unions, public pension funds, online activists, and liberal brain trusts. Perhaps nobody in the universe knows more about this network and its tactics than Danhof, a thirty-three-year-old dynamo who took over FEP about four years ago, not long out of law school. Every spring proxy season, he's a one-man proxy watchdog, jetting from corporate headquarters to corporate headquarters, trying to hold back the intimidation tide.

The left's interest in proxies dates back at least fifteen years, and was spearheaded by the labor movement and some Soros-funded outfits. The strategy went on turbodrive after *Citizens United*. The idea is to seize control of the corporate proxy process, using public pressure, shareholder sentiment, and the fear of bad publicity to force companies to bow out of politics.

Activists manage this by abusing Securities and Exchange Commission rules on corporate governance. The SEC requires every public company to annually hold a meeting for shareholders— the true owners of companies. In the olden days, a company's few shareholders would attend in person, voice their concerns, and vote on changes. Today's shareholders are spread across the globe, so in-person voting is impossible. Shareholders instead vote by "proxy." Think of it as absentee voting. Prior to the annual meeting, a shareholder is sent a list of proposals to be considered at the annual meeting; the shareholder votes the proxy ballot and returns it to the company.

Here's the rub: According to SEC rules, any shareholder who has held at least $2,000 in stock for a year can introduce a proxy proposal. These proposals go through an SEC vetting process to ensure that they are relevant to corporate governance. The SEC has an incredibly indulgent view of "relevant." This has allowed a slew of so-called social investment funds—organizations like Walden Asset Management, NorthStar Asset Management, and Trillium Asset Management—to buy a minimum of stock in targeted companies for the sole purpose of standing up proxy proposals that embarrass the companies out of politics or force them into liberal positions. These groups are supported by and tied to liberal outfits like As You Sow, a nonprofit that supports "corporate social responsibility."

Most of the proposals are aimed at forcing disclosure, with the goal of creating more Target-like situations and pushing companies out of politics altogether. A successful disclosure proxy forces a company to be open about any donations to any politically active nonprofits (like Minnesota Forward). Employing the Media Matters strategy, the left then follows that money to politicians, and highlights the giving as a corporate "endorsement of everything that given politician has said or done." PR nightmares, boycotts, and falling share prices ensue. Companies stop giving money.

"Social" investor groups like NorthStar justify their proxy work with the usual guff about a broader need for "transparency." But since the SEC requires proxy proposals to have at least *some* relevance to actual business practices, Danhof explains that the most popular form of liberal proxy is what he's nicknamed "political incongruency" proposals.

He explains, "So they start with some opening salvo about how awful *Citizens United* is, the floodgates are open, blah, blah. And then they say, 'We want a list of all your political donations and political activity over the past year. And we need an annual report of this so that we can identify any of those donations or activities that are "incongruent" with your stated corporate policy.'

"What do they do then?" Danhof continues. "They get the disclosure information and then they go to the corporate site and say, 'Hey, look here. You claim to be an environmental steward. However, in 2008, you gave $5 to an organization that supported this Republican senator, who voted against cap-and-trade legislation. Therefore you are "misaligned," and you need to stop such donations.'"

Danhof finds the entire process insane. "It really is that attenuated. And the amazing thing is that the SEC accepts that bullshit. The activists argue that these proposals are somehow relevant, because the company is lying to shareholders, lying to the public. And it's all about making companies go quiet."

Danhof spends his day riffling through mountains of these proxies, and since *Citizens United* the mountains have grown taller. Activists in 2011—the first year after the Supreme Court ruling—filed a record number of shareholder proposals on political spending. According to the Manhattan Institute's Proxy Monitor, 92 percent of these were sponsored by social investment funds or labor union pension funds.

The phoniest argument the activists use is that companies need to adopt disclosure policies in order to minimize their "risk." One 2011 proxy fight came courtesy of Boston's NorthStar, which was bitter that Home Depot and Procter & Gamble had given money to the reelection efforts of Ohio Republican senator Rob Portman and Ohio Republican representative Steve Chabot. As with Target, P&G's donation made sense. The company's headquarters is in Cincinnati, and it has an interest in economic policies that would help shareholder value and employment.

Home Depot isn't based in Ohio, but it also cares about free-market policies. In its demand for new rules, NorthStar told Home Depot that it was necessary the company adopt disclosure to reduce the "risk to the firm's reputation and brand through possible future missteps in corporate electioneering." Left unsaid was that the only groups ever likely to try to hurt Home Depot's brand over politics would be NorthStar and its left-wing allies in the union and environmental and Democratic political movement. NorthStar wanted Home Depot to adopt NorthStar policies to save it from NorthStar.

Or take it from that same 2010 Media Matters memo, which

laid out the exact strategy for the proxy battles. "The data in [our database on corporations] may also be used to launch shareholder resolution campaigns to prevent corporations from making these types of expenditures," it read. "Working with partner organizations such as yours, we will help to make the case that political spending is not within the fiduciary interest of publicly traded corporations and therefore should be limited. In fact, our efforts to expose spending will enable us to make the case that a corporation's political efforts have the potential to irreparably damage its brand and bottom line." Media Matters made clear that its goal was to entirely shut down the opposing argument: "Over time, we believe these efforts will dissuade corporations from interfering in our democracy."

The groups the left rely on to really make progress with proxies are union pension funds. Groups like Walden and NorthStar keep raising the bar for what they want from companies, but they lack clout. Walden's senior vice president in September 2011 sent a form letter to corporations laying out his group's ultimate wish list. It wanted not just the names and amounts of donations, but details of "direct or indirect lobbying," as well as the "decision making and oversight processes related to direct, indirect and grassroots lobbying activity." Yet these activist investment firms often hold the minimum number of shares necessary to participate, which makes them easier to ignore.

The unions are a different story. Groups like the California Public Employees' Retirement System (CalPERS) or the California State Teachers' Retirement System (CalSTRS) are investment giants, with hundreds of billions of dollars under management. These groups are also usually overseen by liberal state politicians, who are on board with the activists' strategy and have the pension-fund money and proxy votes to force change.

The politicians who run those huge pension funds began in 2011 by exerting pressure on companies from the investment side. In June 2011, California state treasurer Bill Lockyer and

New York City public advocate Bill de Blasio—both die-hard Democrats and both charged with overseeing the investment of pension-fund money—wrote letters to their respective pension funds calling on them to use their heft to demand corporate political spending disclosure. Both CalPERS and CalSTRS quickly moved to formally adopt policies to do just that.

De Blasio went even further, delving back into the Target fray. The pol was a trustee of the New York City Employee Retirement System, which owned shares in Target. The left had already forced Target to cease using money in campaigns via trade associations. Yet the retailer hadn't been able to shake the assault; activists sought to continue making an example of it. They scored a particular hit in 2011, when pop star Lady Gaga very publicly ended a deal with Target for her newest album due to its "continued political activity." Target's share price kept dropping.

De Blasio skipped all the preamble about disclosure and went right to the Media Matters chase. He wanted Target—and all companies—out of politics altogether. And so he asked his $40 billion fund to directly vote against any Target director in the absence of Target's promise that it voluntarily cease all political donations. No more politics, period. The de Blasio demand came on the eve of Target's annual meeting, which was being held at a store in Pittsburgh. Common Cause, the United Steelworkers, and a pro-gay-rights group helped organize a rally outside, while activist shareholders mobbed the meeting, to demand more changes. The activists so overwhelmed the event that at one point Steinhafel asked, "Does anybody have a question relating to our business that is unrelated to political giving? I would love to hear any question related to something else."

The unions also began to pressure support sectors in the financial industry, groups like Institutional Shareholder Services, an influential and otherwise well-respected firm that advises hedge funds and mutual funds on proxy resolutions. ISS usually evaluates proxies on a company-by-company basis. But in 2011, under torturous pressure from unions, it issued a general guideline recommending that shareholders vote in favor of proposals to disclose political activity. Having ISS out on the side of the activists only increased pressure on companies to make concessions.

Danhof's job is to halt the concessions, to fight the proxies— and to do it by beating the left at their own game. Through FEP, he also buys shares in companies that are under assault, thereby giving him a voice at shareholder meetings. FEP is tiny—it has nowhere near the funds of a Walden—and Danhof admits that sometimes his organization is forced to draw on the individual portfolios of its handful of NCPPR employees in order to meet the share requirement.

FEP then begins to educate. It distributes information designed to inform the board, shareholders, and consumers about the left's tactics. "We put out a press release, we alert investors. We explain that this has nothing to do with good governance. We explain what it is all about—silencing free speech. We're trying to change the narrative," he says.

Every spring proxy season, Danhof is on airplanes crisscrossing the country to show up at annual meetings in person. At them, he tries to encourage corporate boards and shareholders to ignore the disclosure proxies and think about what does matter—public debate, good economic policy, a return on investment.

He takes special care trying to get through to the corporate executives. "Inside the FEP, we call it the Backbone Project. We're trying to get them to man up. You kind of feel for them. The left is always coming, saying that if you keep doing what you are doing, we'll be running ads against your board members. It nerves them out." Danhof remembers one moment a few years ago when he got a phone call from an executive of a major company. Danhof had planned the next week to go to that company's annual meeting and applaud the leadership for sticking to its political guns. The executive thanked him, but also begged Danhof to stay away, stay quiet. "He basically said, 'Please. We don't need the attention,'" and that if the firm received any more focus, it might have to cave.

Danhof feels for them, but only to a point. The free market is under assault. Organizations like his have worked tirelessly to uphold the constitutional right of these corporations to speak. To not do so is civic and business malpractice.

And a lack of corporate backbone isn't the only problem. Some companies perform a very simple, if cynical, cost-benefit analysis. Target will never know what benefits might have accrued to it had Emmer been elected governor (he lost). But it was able to look at its pummeled stock price and see very clearly the up-front cost of its donation. Companies also build into that cost-benefit analysis groups like Danhof's, or the chamber, or other free-market advocates. "They know that we won't stop, that we'll keep fighting for a free market, keep fighting on their behalf. And if they don't even have to put any money into us doing it, why take that risk? That's the tricky part. It's where our fight gets particularly hard," he says.

FEP might be a lonely voice, but it's been an effective one. For all the drama, the left's proxy strategy has broadly been a flop. Big institutional investors have generally continued to support an investment in smart policy and economic growth, as well as speech. While corporate management tends to get freaked out by activist campaigns, shareholders are a step removed, and a bit steadier.

Every one of the shareholder proposals on political disclosure in 2011 failed. The left ramped up its efforts in 2012. Among the 150 Fortune 200 companies that had held their annual meetings by the end of May, 21 percent of shareholder proposals were related to political disclosure or lobbying—the largest proxy category. That number of proposals was up 50 percent from the prior year. Yet again, the effort failed. The average proposal received about 20 percent of the vote, down from 22 percent the year before. Not a single resolution passed.

While liberal activists would undoubtedly like to win some of these proxy fights, they are also sanguine about losing them. They know that, at the very least, they have managed to harass companies, eat up executive time, worry corporate boards, and send a chilling message of what may come. And they know the real fight doesn't happen in public. It happens in back rooms. The left is sophisticated about corporate pressure. The proxy fights are in aid of building up what can only be described as a behind-the-scenes protection racket.

~~~

At the epicenter of this is a 501(c)(3) charity (also never targeted by the IRS) called the Center for Political Accountability. CPA was founded in 2003 and these days is run by Bruce Freed, a former Democratic staffer. Freed sits back and lets the activist thugs rough up companies, mob their meetings, threaten boycotts. Then the man in the suit, representing an organization with an anodyne name, slips in to make the deal. Freed explains to CEOs that it really is good "corporate governance" to disclose political spending. He shows them a little list—called the Zicklin Index—that CPA maintains with the Wharton School of Business. That index benchmarks the best "political disclosure" and "accountability" practices of big U.S. companies.

He points out the names of other big firms that have "voluntarily" decided to adopt "best practices." He points out how lovely and pleasant life is for these corporate "leaders." No raucous shareholder meetings. No protests. No ugly ads. No boycotts. Freed smiles his smile and encourages them to get on board. Because, well...if they don't, there's just no telling what his friends at Common Cause, and the unions, and As You Sow, and MoveOn.org, and Media Matters will do in response.

Tony Soprano couldn't do it better, and Freed gets results. While most of the news media spent its ink on the proxy fight battles raging in 2011, the far more interesting fact was this:

Going into that proxy fight year, fifty-seven of the S&P 500 companies had already chosen to forgo political spending or to disclose their political spending on their websites. They'd already been gotten to.

That number has grown. The CPA's 2015 report on its Zicklin Index proudly announced that 124 of the S&P 500 companies, or 25 percent, these days place some form of restriction on their political giving—including restrictions on issue ads, on contributions to candidates and parties, on money for 527 groups, nonprofits, and trade associations, and on support for ballot initiatives. It also bragged that "most" companies now have policies addressing political spending, and that more than half maintain a dedicated web page addressing the topic. A lot of this is Freed's doing.

The Zicklin Index is Freed's favorite tool. He gives his spiel to a company and gets them to voluntarily give up their speech rights. He then flags them on the index and uses it to gull yet more companies into following suit. Everybody is doing it, says Freed, and if you don't, you risk looking like a corporate-governance Neanderthal. "Once again, the CPA-Zicklin Index demonstrates a growing trend among major American companies to disclose their political-giving activities," bragged the most recent report.

In 2013 the *Weekly Standard*'s Michael Warren wrote a piece featuring a letter sent to Ronald Robins Jr., a senior vice president at Abercrombie & Fitch. The Ohio-based clothing retailer barely spends a dime on politics. Warren wrote, "Nevertheless, the letter informed Robins that companies like his 'face increasing pressure' to support political groups and candidates that 'threaten corporate reputation, bottom line and shareholder value.' This 'secret political spending,' the letter continued, 'threatens not only the health of our democracy but also the reputation and integrity of companies.' Half the companies on the S&P 100 stock market index, the letter said, have 'recognized the dangers' and have 'demonstrated leadership by disclosing the details of and implementing board oversight of their spending. The signers added that they 'hope' Abercrombie will follow the lead of these exemplary companies." The letter was signed by Freed.

What Freed presumably doesn't admit is that the process is rigged. The index has Wharton's backing. But both Freed and his group's general counsel, Karl Sandstrom, have enormous influence over the process. They both sit on the advisory board of the Zicklin Center and help craft the index. The index alters its scoring procedures from year to year, and companies that scored high drop lower—which gives the impression that everybody ought to be providing yet more disclosure.

Nor does Freed admit that his organization is a left-wing shop masquerading as a good-governance, nonpartisan watchdog. CPA, like everything, has lived off Soros money. Freed came out of Democratic politics. Sandstrom once served as general counsel for the Democratic National Committee. CPA's chief financial officer, Michael Novelli, was an Obama campaign director in Maryland in 2008. Peter Hardin, one of CPA's writers and editors, also works at the Soros-funded Justice at Stake.

Companies that don't take Freed's advice are left to the tender mercies of his friends. In 2011, Trillium, another "social" investment fund, put particular emphasis on a disclosure proxy it had filed with the Boston financial firm State Street. The proxy ended up getting a surprising 44 percent of the vote, and State Street lost its nerve. Trillium and As You Sow later bragged that the activists had graciously withdrawn their proposal after the firm agreed to prohibit its trade associations from using company dues for political purposes and to reveal any giving to 527s and nonprofits.

Proxy season 2013 brought yet new record numbers of shareholder disclosure proposals, many of them filed by unions like the American Federation of State, County and Municipal Employees. Among the arguments activists make for these is that shareholders ought to know—and have some say—in whether and how a company spends on politics. It's a demand the unions have never imposed on themselves. AFSCME is estimated to have spent $50 million in 2012. Its thousands of union members had no voice in this decision, and no input over how the money was spent.

Proxy season 2013 also brought a new, far more disturbing tactic. Liberals have lots of friends, and many of them in high places. Among the most powerful are Democrats with the power to sue—state attorneys general or state comptrollers, for instance. One such person is Tom DiNapoli, a Long Island Democrat who became New York state comptroller in 2007—a position that makes him a trustee of the New York state pension fund. In early 2013, DiNapoli filed suit against telecommunications company Qualcomm, demanding to view its private records of political donations.

Qualcomm's founder, Irwin Jacobs, and other Qualcomm leadership were big-time Democratic donors. In 2012 alone, Jacobs poured some $2.3 million into Democratic super PACS, including one to reelect Obama. And he was transparent about it. But DiNapoli wanted proof that the company wasn't fraternizing with the political enemy on the sly, giving money to trade associations or conservative nonprofits. He claimed that as the sole trustee to the pension fund, which was a big investor in Qualcomm, he had a right to see any donations, since they might pose "financial risk" for shareholders.

The suit relied on a Delaware "books and records" law that gives shareholders some rights to inspect corporate documents, but that is usually used to prove mismanagement. The *New York Times* crowed that it was a "novel and potentially significant tactic in the running battle over corporate political spending in the post–*Citizens United* era." As if offering proof for why this suit was necessary, the *Times* noted that Qualcomm scored "relatively" low on the CPA-Zicklin Index, which the newspaper innocently described as a product of a "nonprofit watchdog organization."

Up to now, corporations faced risk from angry liberals, or consumers, or maybe shareholders. DiNapoli made clear that they
also risked legal jeopardy from the state. DiNapoli unleashed
the most powerful tool of government—prosecution—on Qualcomm, with all its prospects of legal costs and adverse consequences.

Qualcomm did a State Street. It folded. DiNapoli a month
later "was pleased to announce" that he had "decided to withdraw
the lawsuit" following Qualcomm's decision to "implement a re-
vised political spending disclosure policy," in which the company
would now make public all contributions to political candidates,
parties, trade associations, nonprofits, and ballot measures.

Qualcomm's crumble was especially unfortunate given the
DiNapoli argument that disclosure mitigates corporate risk. That
has it backward. "All it does is increase it," says Danhof. "Now
the details are out, and the left has a game plan for attack. And by
virtue of the fact a company gave in, the left also knows that it is
susceptible to pressure. So disclosure is an invitation for them to
come back again and again."

The stats prove it. And they come courtesy of that very same
CPA-Zicklin Index. A 2014 analysis by the Center for Competitive Politics (Brad Smith's organization) found that about 36
percent of companies whose disclosure "scores" ranked in the top
quarter of the 2013 CPA-Zicklin Index received activist proxies.
By contrast, only about 23 percent of companies ranked in the
lowest quarter of the index received activist proxies. The better
a score on the index, the more likely a company was to get hit
again. That pattern holds, year after year. These companies aren't
"rewarded" for their "best practices"; they are teed up for further
abuse.

Conversely, there is zero proof that voluntarily adopting a disclosure provision helps a company in any material way. Research
in 2011 by Roger Coffin, the associate director of the Weinberg
Center for Corporate Governance, looked at companies that had

voluntarily signed an "anti–*Citizens United* pledge" in the after-math of the 2010 Court decision. They did not see a material increase in their firm's value. They did, however, lose their ability to take part in public debates that might grow their business and share prices in the long run. When government of one kind or another controls 40 percent of the private economy, any business that doesn't participate directly or indirectly is begging for finan-cial and economic harm.

After I wrote a column about Freed and his racket in 2012, the *Wall Street Journal* received a surprising letter, which we pub-lished. It came from John C. Richardson, who was a cofounder of CPA, and had led the group until 2007, when he left in disgust. "While I reluctantly concur with Ms. Strassel's depiction of the corporate shakedown that the CPA has essentially become, I am less bothered by its venality than by its irrelevance," Richardson wrote. The real problem out there, he said, was corporate *corruption* that was "dressed up as free speech." He cited the example of corporations that transfer huge sums of money to politicians who regulate them. "I fought to keep the CPA focused on its core objective but left in 2007 when it had become clear that sub-stantive solutions took a back seat to showboating. . . . My former colleagues at the CPA have sadly chosen to pick the low-hanging fruit of corporate shakedowns, wrapped in the dogma of good governance," he wrote. Richardson is a rare soul these days: a man who believes that disclosure is supposed to provide some public good, not provide a means by which to silence debate.

Danhof these days is trying to beat the left at its own game, by proactively filing his own proxy resolutions, which are designed to refocus corporate minds on the free-market bigger picture.

He's filed resolutions with Google and Apple asking them to be "transparent" with investors about the high costs of their alterna-tive energy and climate investments, and about the risks if Wash-ington pulls the plug on subsidies. He's filed resolutions with McDonald's and Coca-Cola demanding that they better educate their consumers about the safety and benefits of using genetically modified food. He's questioned insurers to explain their continued support of a failing Obamacare regime. He's filed resolutions pushing dozens of companies to adopt policies to protect employees from workplace discrimination over their political actions and beliefs.

Those last resolutions followed the hounding out of Mozilla CEO Brendan Eich, for the supposed crime of donating to a campaign in support of traditional marriage. Companies like Visa moved quickly to take such a positive action. Companies like Costco, which may top the list of liberal corporate sellouts, went so far as to ask the SEC to disqualify Danhof's proposal.

This is one of Danhof's big frustrations—that the SEC often turns down his proxy resolutions. The SEC usually allows anything that is considered a "significant policy issue" to go through. The problem, says Danhof, is that "significant policy issues in the eyes of the SEC is anything the left creates. Just tick them off: political lobbying, disclosure, diversity in the workforce, gay rights, fracking reports, renewable energy, global warming, net neutrality, childhood obesity. But when I come along with a proposal related to political speech and the First Amendment, well, that's apparently not a significant policy issue."

He's also been shot down on his attempts to ape the left's proposal arguments. "I once filed nearly a dozen resolutions with health care companies. I made the *exact* same argument they had. The liberal proposals asked corporations to support a socialist health care platform. I said, 'You say you support free markets. But you also belong to an organization that lobbied for Obamacare. You can't both support the free market and support Obamacare. You are misaligned.'" The SEC wouldn't allow it.

Danhof remains convinced, however, that this business pressure is the key to creating more "backbone" and free-market policies. "What the left has understood forever is that big business and big government go hand in hand. They use the growth of big business to expand the growth of big government, and vice versa. What they also understand is that business is far more susceptible to pressure than government. So they devote a lot of time to pressuring business. We on the right, we ignore that. We sit here and we throw little pebbles at big government and get all frustrated when things don't change overnight. What we need to be doing is using the model the left created, and attacking this symbiotic relationship from the business side."

∿

The DiNapoli tactics and continued pressure also provoked a trio of the nation's top business leaders to act. In April 2013, Chamber of Commerce president and CEO Tom Donohue, Business Roundtable president John Engler, and National Association of Manufacturers president and CEO Jay Timmons coauthored a letter to business leaders nationally. It was intended as a full-scale exposé of the left's intimidation operation, highlighted by three of the most influential business leaders in the country. They explained that this proxy season, CEOs would be getting letters from "groups claiming to represent your investors." They were in fact "activists," whose "goal is to limit or remove altogether the business voice from the political and policymaking processes." They laid bare the "multi-faceted strategy" on the left—proxies; the campaign to get the SEC to impose disclosure; the books-and-records litigation.

They also laid out the four "key myths" of this movement: "1) disclosure of corporate political activity has broad support among investors; 2) a lack of disclosure regarding government relations activities (as the activists define it) is risky for investors; 3) most companies are satisfying activists' demands for disclosure; and 4) disclosure is the activists' only goal." They then demolished each myth.

The three largest mutual fund companies in the country, they pointed out, had never supported a disclosure proxy. The authors referenced comprehensive 2012 research by former Clinton official and Harvard PhD Robert Shapiro, who found "no credible evidence" that political activity harms shareholder value. They ran through Freed's Zicklin Index ruse. They quoted from the Media Matters memo about the left's real goals, and included a revealing statement from New York's Bill de Blasio: "We will use every tool, whether it is actions among consumers up to boycotts, whether it's shareholder actions, whether it's work from pension funds—to use the pension funds to direct Corporate America to change its ways—legal action, you name it, it's on the table."

The three business leaders concluded, "These groups will not stop until business' ability to engage in political and policy advocacy is eliminated altogether. The good news is that the old saying is true: Knowledge is power. We believe that your company can benefit by knowing the facts."

Republican politicians are also speaking to the issue more, even within the 2016 presidential campaign. In October 2014, as she was preparing for her own bid, Carly Fiorina, the former head of Hewlett-Packard, penned a piece in the *Washington Post* calling on businesses to grow a pair. Corporations, she said, need to "understand the source and purpose of activist pressure. Caving on an issue only invites more attacks. If a company is a good steward of customer and shareholder interests, pursues appropriate policy and delivers on its brand promise, there is nothing to fear. We need more business leaders who are willing to stand up and contribute to our public discourse."

The Chamber of Commerce's Bruce Josten is hopeful, too. Somewhat. Only a few days before I interviewed the business chieftain for this project, in the early fall of 2015, the chamber received a letter. That letter also went to the CEOs of all 108 member companies of the chamber's board of directors. Its authors were twelve Democratic senators. It demanded information about the chamber's "denial efforts." The senators had heard that the chamber and companies were mobilizing to oppose President Obama's (extralegal) climate regulations. It slammed the chamber as a "partisan enforcer for industries whose activities threaten public health and undermine the public well being."

The left-wing Senate caucus demanded that every company submit responses (within three weeks) that clarified their position on the chamber's legal efforts to oppose the Obama regulations; whether they'd been informed by the chamber of this effort; whether they'd been given an opportunity to express a view; and whether they'd told their own board of directors and stockholders of the chamber's efforts against "climate action."

Donohue immediately sent out a letter to the same CEOs clarifying all the misrepresentations of the senators and offering a pep talk about "standing up to pressure." But Josten remains unsure where this will go.

After all, he's seen it before. This was a repeat of the left's intimidation tactics against an influential conservative group called the American Legislative Exchange Council. It had nearly destroyed ALEC.

CHAPTER 16

Corporate Blackmail

TO THIS DAY, Lisa Nelson refers to it as the "corporate blackmail" letter. It arrived in the early spring of 2012 at her Visa office in D.C. Nelson at the time was in the government relations department for the credit card company and had seen her share of bare-knuckle political activism. But this letter was bigger, meaner, scarier.

The letter was officially addressed to Visa CEO Joseph Saunders and every single member of Visa's board; Nelson had been cc'ed. It came from a black advocacy group known as Color of Change, cofounded by liberal activist Rashad Robinson and by onetime Obama adviser Van Jones. The letter was very clear about what it wanted Visa to do. And it was very clear about what would happen if Visa didn't do it.

The prior month, a seventeen-year-old African American in Sanford, Florida, Trayvon Martin, had been fatally shot by a neighborhood-watch volunteer named George Zimmerman. The circumstances of the altercation proved confusing, but the black community instantly became angry over the police's decision not to arrest Zimmerman. Florida has a "stand your ground" law, which authorizes a person to protect against a perceived threat. Within a few weeks, Color of Change was blaming this law on a center-right organization known as the American Legislative Exchange Council.

Visa was among a number of corporations that gave money to ALEC, in support of its efforts to foster a pro-business environment at the state legislature level. Color of Change's letter was as direct as could be. Visa's board must immediately pull all money from ALEC. If it did not, the advocacy group would commence airing radio ads in the hometowns of every single Visa board member, holding each of them personally accountable for the death of a young black man. Color of Change helpfully included the menacing script of the ad that would rain down on their communities if they didn't comply, and quick.

"So imagine this," says Nelson, a spunky fifty-four-year-old dirty blonde. "Here you are, a former CEO of a company. You now sit on the board of Visa. You are semiretired. You are trying to enjoy the rest of your life, while still doing some good, giving back, corporate governance. And you get a letter being told that you are about to be held responsible—among your friends and neighbors—for Trayvon Martin being shot. The calls, as you might imagine, started raining down on the CEO."

The Visa board members weren't alone. More than a few Fortune 500 companies had made the mistake of revealing, at an event here or there, that they gave money to ALEC's work. The threat letters flew out to board members at McDonald's, John Deere, Coca-Cola, Pepsi, Amazon, Wendy's, Procter & Gamble. They all contained the same message: Keep donating to that free-market group, and you will experience character assassinations, consumer boycotts, and a political migraine that no prescription medicine will fix.

Nelson, both at Visa and at her former job at AOL Time Warner, had witnessed the rise of the proxy disclosure-and-pressure movement—the boycotts, the campaigns against companies, the attempts to hound them out of free speech. But she'd never seen anything as aggressive as this. She also knew well of ALEC's important work. She immediately arranged a conference call with her CEO where she conferred this message: "You need to understand that this is corporate blackmail. And if we give in to it, they'll just want more and more and more."

Nelson felt from the start that "I needed to keep making the case that, as a company, we could not be put in a position where we could be told who we could work with." Her CEO agreed. She was successful, and Visa kept on with its ALEC donations.

At least for a time.

∿

It was just a little meeting in Chicago, in September 1973. Among those around the table were Illinois state representative Henry Hyde (who'd go on to become a prominent member of the House), Paul Weyrich (who'd go on to cofound the Heritage Foundation and Moral Majority), and Lou Barnett (who'd go on to run Reagan's political action committee). The three were all active conservatives, united for free markets and limited government, but they also held the belief that the best government is local. They felt that state lawmakers needed a forum where they could exchange ideas, build on best practices, and coordinate efforts.

And so ALEC was born. Membership was voluntary, and state legislators from both parties paid a small annual fee to belong. The group held regular meetings, and by the 1980s had created more than a dozen task forces: on civil justice reform, health care reform, telecommunications reform, and more. Legislators join task forces of choice, and help create "model policy" that other members take back to introduce in their own state chambers. ALEC's model policies are always free-market, always aimed at a better business climate, often revolutionary. ALEC helps create the ideas and spread the gospel from state to state.

It quickly proved a vibrant alternative to the official National Conference of State Legislatures, which is taxpayer-funded and includes every state legislator by definition—which means it is often captive to liberal, blue-state interests. ALEC subsists on member dues and contributions from foundations, companies, and nonprofits. The 1994 conservative wave fueled membership, and by 1995 ALEC boasted three thousand out of the country's seventy-five hundred state legislators. Its membership included thirty-two state legislative speakers and thirty-four majority leaders. In that year, at least twelve governors were ALEC alumni.

It was also bipartisan. ALEC was a way for pro-business Democrats, especially those from the South and the West, to talk with like-minded Republicans and hash out smart policy and workable compromises at the state level. The 1994 election left a lot of closely divided statehouses, and ALEC proved the glue in many of the bipartisan state reform successes that followed. Democrats also felt a real stake in the organization, which has a practice of rotating its chairmanship each year between Republicans and Democrats.

ALEC is also effective. In any given year, an average of a thousand bills based on ALEC model policy are introduced in state legislatures. In any given year, an impressive average of 20 percent of those become law. ALEC is a reason states have cut taxes on income and on corporations; reduced unemployment insurance; shored up private property rights; instituted medical savings accounts; reformed public pension plans; cracked down on trial lawyers; and enacted sunshine laws. Few Americans have heard of ALEC. But there's a case to be made that no one policy organization has touched the daily lives of more Americans.

ALEC's success quickly earned it the ire of the left. Public sector unions dislike ALEC's success at government pension reform. Spend-happy Democrats dislike ALEC's success at tax and budget cuts. Environmentalists dislike ALEC for its opposition to green mandates and subsidies. Naderites dislike ALEC for its policies that give individuals, rather than government, more choice over their health care or appliance buying. Teachers' unions dislike ALEC for its support of vouchers and charters and school choice. Liberal governors and legislators dislike ALEC for its annual state rankings, which often show that their fiefdoms have miserable business climates. Trial lawyers dislike ALEC for its triumphs in asbestos reforms, medical malpractice reforms, and punitive damages reforms.

They dislike that it is bipartisan, because that helps ALEC's model bills to pass in state legislatures and emerge with more credibility. They dislike ALEC's whole philosophy of state power. Democrats like things centralized. It's easy to lobby and influence one bill in the nation's capital. It's hard to put out fires in fifty states. It's harder still to stop those fires from spreading. ALEC proves Supreme Court justice Louis D. Brandeis's famous 1932 idea that states are "laboratories of democracy." ALEC need only get a successful model reform passed in one state before ten more are competing to do the same. National politicians see those reforms work and start advocating them at the federal level.

And they dislike that so much of ALEC's work exposes their own ties to special interest groups, and their feeding at the public trough. Eliot Spitzer, the onetime New York attorney general, pioneered the tactic of attacking businesses for headlines and state (settlement) profits. His fellow Democratic attorneys general across the country adopted those tactics and refined them. They'd also file questionable suits against business, earning headlines and profits. But many added the twist of handing the state's legal work to their friends in the trial bar, who would in turn donate some of these taxpayer payments back to the AG's reelection. ALEC helped expose this scam, and more than a decade ago started pushing a model Private Attorney Retention Sunshine Act, which mandates public disclosure of the contracts between a state and the trial bar. At least twenty states have already adopted that law, making it much harder for AGs to blatantly pay off their plaintiffs' attorney campaign donors. The left dislikes that.

So most of ALEC's forty-year existence has been dogged by liberal abuse and attack. For the most part, though, it was the usual political cut and thrust. Left-wing groups issued press re-leases condemning ALEC model legislation. They ran lobbying campaigns against ALEC-inspired bills in statehouses.

A favorite tactic was to impose anti-ALEC litmus tests on Democratic politicians. In 2003, the liberal People for the Amer-ican Way sent a warning letter to Anthony Williams, then the Democratic mayor of Washington, D.C. PFAW president Ralph Neas bemoaned that Williams had recently embraced school vouchers, and told him he'd better not go through with a planned appearance at an ALEC workshop devoted to school choice. Wil-liams's presence, complained Neas (who also, of course, released the letter to the press), would provide a "veneer of bipartisan re-spectability to a group whose goals are destructive to the public interest and the people you serve." The sight of a disconnected, liberal Hollywood club lecturing a black mayor on the needs of his constituency was something to see, and Williams clearly thought so too. He attended the ALEC event.

The attacks were endless, but also expected and manageable. They required an ALEC statement here, some pushback there. Few intruded on ALEC's growth or success. And as the organiza-tion expanded, it began to develop an interest in areas outside of its traditional focus. In the mid-2000s it created a new organiza-tion that came to be known as the Public Safety and Elections Task Force, and that dealt with noneconomic issues. In retrospect, it was a mistake.

∿

In the spring of 2005, Florida state senator Durell Peaden and state representative Dennis Baxley worked through their state legislature what they called "stand your ground" legislation. The law protects a citizen's right to defend their life against real or perceived threat. The bill was a policy and political winner, pop-ular among state residents—in part on liberty grounds, in part on the belief that it would reduce crime. Former Florida governor Jeb Bush signed the bill into law in 2005.

Baxley was proud of the legislation. He was also a member of ALEC. He brought it back, and worked to help turn it into model legislation. Within a few short years more than thirty states had a version of "stand your ground" on their books. The bills were immensely popular, and many were signed by Democratic governors, including Arizona's Janet Napolitano (who'd become Obama's secretary of homeland security) and Michigan's Jennifer Granholm.

On February 26, 2012, Trayvon Martin was shot. And Martin was the hook, a new way to go after ALEC. The left had always despised the group, but post–*Citizens United*, they had new reason to target it. The electorate in 2010 had revolted against a bevy of liberal and unpopular policies and programs. Democrats sustained staggering losses at the federal level, but they'd suffered even bigger ones at the state level. The electoral disaster gave Republicans unprecedented control over state legislatures and governors' mansions, and a new ability to green-light reforms of the sort that ALEC proposed.

The shooting was a tragedy; the death of any seventeen-year-old is something to mourn. But the left only viewed it that way for a short time. The sadness quickly gave way to outrage, and then to something appallingly cynical. In an interview with Bloomberg in May 2012, Common Cause spokeswoman Mary Boyle explained that her group had been waiting for months for the right moment to file a complaint with the IRS to strip ALEC of its nonprofit status. "The Trayvon Martin thing was like a gift," she said, in an extraordinary, if horrifying, moment of honesty.

Getting Americans outraged over school vouchers or pension reform—that's tough. Getting them outraged over a young black man's death, getting them to believe it is the fault of a racist organization, fueled by heartless companies—that's a lot easier.

In the space of a few weeks, the liberal coalition mobilized against ALEC, elevating an organization few Americans had ever heard of to the status of national pariah, responsible for dozens of laws that the left now refers to as "kill at will" statutes. By the end of March a rogues' gallery of left-wing groups had organized a riotous rally outside ALEC's D.C. headquarters to demand that the group "disclose" its funding. The National Urban League. The NAACP. MoveOn.org. The AFL-CIO and Service Union Employees International unions. Common Cause. People for the American Way. The Center for Media and Democracy. Color of Change.

Color of Change was a newcomer to the ALEC fight, not really focusing on the group until the end of 2011, when it started pummeling it for its support of voter ID laws—claiming (incorrectly) that the statutes suppress minority turnout. But the Martin shooting gave Robinson and Jones cause to dramatically elevate the group's attention on ALEC, and gain attention for itself. It also allowed them to go after their real targets: all those companies providing "dark" money to the organization.

Robinson's group had helped popularize anticorporate boycotts. Color of Change in 2009 pressured dozens of corporations to yank their ads from Glenn Beck's Fox News show, and had repeated that blackball maneuver against conservatives such as Andrew Breitbart, who was dropped from ABC's 2010 election-night coverage.

As a 501(c)(3), ALEC doesn't have to disclose who gives it money. But over the years, some corporations had acknowledged their ALEC partnership. Color of Change tracked down these names and cranked up its machine. A letter to eighty-five thousand members urged them to insist that companies like Coca-Cola stop supporting ALEC. The letter listed voter ID laws and "kill at will" laws as the reason for the protest, though it also couldn't help but complain that ALEC supported "private education" and worked to "break unions." Next up were the "blackmail" letters. Coca-Cola got an early one. Kraft followed. Wal-Mart. Amazon. Procter & Gamble. McDonald's. Wendy's. Pepsi. Intuit. Blue Cross Blue Shield. Visa. And on and on.

The group didn't even try to hide that its goal was to embarrass and intimidate companies out of supporting ALEC in any way, shape, or form. As National Public Radio reported at the time, "Rashad Robinson, director of ColorofChange.org, a civil rights organization in the coalition, says they are trying to put ALEC's corporate members on the spot. 'They'll be making a choice, that they're going to stand with an organization that works to suppress the vote and supports shoot-first legislation, and they won't be able to do that in private.'"

Coke crumpled quickly, in early April publicly declaring that it would pull its donations to ALEC, pathetically explaining, "Our involvement with ALEC was focused on efforts to oppose dis-criminatory food and beverage taxes, not on issues that have no direct bearing on our businesses." Once Coke bailed, the lem-mings started jumping blindly.

By the end of the carnage, ALEC had lost as many as a hundred major companies, a significant portion of its mixed (small and large) five-hundred-company membership. It was a huge hit. Lib-eral outfits like the NAACP or Planned Parenthood or the Sierra Club (all 501(c)(3) groups themselves) have budgets that run to the tens of millions or hundreds of millions of dollars. ALEC, lean and mean, routinely operates at about $7 million. And it was at risk of losing it all.

CHAPTER 17

Driving Durbin

COMPANIES LEFT ALEC because they were under pressure, but they also left because ALEC itself was paralyzed. The organization had never experienced an assault like this, and its executive director, Ron Scheberle, struggled to find a response to end the drama. In April 2012, ALEC shut down its Public Safety and Elections Task Force, the unit focused on the policies now causing the group such headaches. It was a mixed result. One argument went that ALEC was better off without it, that it arguably should never have got sidetracked from its core, economic focus. The more powerful argument, however—at least at the time—was that the move made it look like ALEC, like the companies, was caving. "We suffered from the same loss of nerve as the companies. We did what they did," says one ALEC insider. "Had we at the time gone out and said, 'Go pound sand,' and got out in front of this, we might not have experienced such a shake-up. Giving in just inspired them to keep going."

ALEC limped through 2012, and by the end of that year the organization's board decided it needed some changes. A first move was a shake-up of the PR department. ALEC recruited Wilhelm "Bill" Meierling, a conservative who'd put in his time in the public relations trenches—at Edelman, as director of PR at United Way, and as a lecturer in crisis management. ALEC started to pivot. To undercut the "secrecy" line, it posted all its model policy and IRS documents online. Any citizen had already been able to go look up ALEC's IRS forms, but the move at least helped take away a few of the tired liberal talking points. The organization boldly began promoting its initiatives again and actively recruiting new companies.

Meierling couldn't have arrived at a more important time. A vast array of liberal organizations began to coordinate a national campaign against every aspect of the conservative group's work. Some of these attack groups were old, some new, some old-fashioned, some new media, some nearly fictitious. All were connected.

In one stovepipe are the usual characters that go after companies in proxy battles—the As You Sow network. Walden Asset Management. Trillium. The Center for Political Accountability. The floods of disclosure proxy resolutions these groups file routinely started containing demands that companies divulge their contributions to ALEC specifically. And the backroom pressure for "voluntary" disclosure is often aimed at extracting promises that companies won't make further donations to ALEC in particular.

In another stovepipe are the supposed watchdog groups such as the Center for Media and Democracy, designed to keep up a steady drumbeat of nasty headlines about ALEC and to feed them to receptive journalists at left-wing outlets such as the *Nation* or the *Daily Kos*. The watchers and the journalists are in some cases literally married. Liberal journalist John Nichols, the national affairs correspondent for the *Nation*, loves to bash ALEC. In 2011 he wrote a giant feature entitled "ALEC Exposed" in which he praised the work the Center for Media and Democracy had done to educate about the "procorporate strategy of this powerful right-wing group." Nichols is married to Mary Bottari, who is deputy director of the Center for Media and Democracy.

In yet another stovepipe are activist groups, among them Common Cause ("a nonpartisan citizen's lobbying organization promoting open, honest and accountable government"), Forecast the Facts and the Energy Action Coalition (two green groups

focused on climate change), Color of Change, MoveOn.org, and
the Citizen Engagement Lab ("a pioneer in using new media and
technology to advance meaningful social change"). They launch
online campaigns and social media events, as well as stage demonstrations and pressure campaigns against ALEC directly. They also
ally with liberal think tanks such as the Center on Budget and Policy Priorities and the Center for American Progress.

Another stovepipe is the unions. The SEIU. The AFL-CIO. The
American Federation of Teachers. AFSCME, the American Federation of State, County and Municipal Employees. They supply
people, manpower, and influence in Washington.

They may look disparate, but most of the groups are bonded
by the same political Gorilla Glue. Many are funded by George
Soros or by umbrella liberal financier groups like the Democracy
Alliance. Many shared the same professional PR organization,
FitzGibbon Media, a D.C. outfit that specialized in promoting liberal causes. (FitzGibbon shut down at the end of 2015.) Many
share or trade the same staff. The Citizen Engagement Lab was
cofounded by an activist who had also helped found Color of
Change and worked at MoveOn.org. Jay Riestenberg, a principal
agitator against ALEC, helped organize for Obama at his college
campus in 2008. He consulted for labor and progressive groups,
then went to the Center for Media and Democracy, and then to
Common Cause. Another top anti-ALEC agitator is Nick Surgey,
who moved in the opposite direction. He worked for a time as
staff counsel at Common Cause, but ultimately ended up at the
Center for Media and Democracy. There is a lot of job swapping,
but the same names are always targeting ALEC. And the groups
work in tandem. Walden will send a letter to a company about
ALEC. Common Cause will promote it. MoveOn.org will tweet
it. The unions will repeat it.

Many of the groups also front multiple entities, making them
look far more fearsome than they are. The Center for Media
and Democracy is a "national media group that conducts in-

depth investigations into corruption and the undue influence of corporations"—and spends much of its time bashing ALEC. It also runs PR Watch, an organization that reports on "spin and disinformation"—and spends much of its time bashing ALEC. It also runs SourceWatch, a wiki that "tracks corporations"—and spends much of its time bashing ALEC. It also runs ALEC Exposed, which is outright designed to bash ALEC. All these groups are run by the same handful of people out of Madison, Wisconsin. Yet get all the groups firing off press releases and reports against ALEC at the same time and it looks as if a veritable army of "watchdog" groups are all calling out the conservative organization. Which is the point.

ProgressNow—which promotes "progressive ideas and causes" (such as bashing ALEC)—employs a similar ruse. The group now boasts a number of state chapters—Progress Texas, Progress VA, Bold Nebraska. Many of theses entities are registered in D.C., and it is unclear just how much staff is on the ground in the states. Yet the "chapters" add an air of grassroots, making state legislators and companies think they are under local attack. Which is also the point.

Meierling's task was to start combating all the misinformation, but also to blow the whistle on the incestuous and insular nature of the supposed vast opposition. And he needed to get that message to another group that was under attack: state Democratic legislators. Liberals weren't just pressuring companies to resign. They were pressuring Democrats to quit the group.

The anti-ALEC coalition in fact used the flood of corporate resignations as additional evidence for why Democratic legislators should abandon the group. They issued press releases against them, targeted them on their websites, and threatened to mount and support primary challengers to Democratic ALEC members. And those members did start to leave.

"The goal was to try to reassure these Democrats that they weren't in fact under fire from their constituents; they were getting attacked by some twenty-three-year-old in his underpants in front of a computer, many states away," says Meierling. The ALEC team did start to make some progress—getting the message out that it was back in the game, reassuring members, recruiting new companies.

But it turns out Meierling had only just arrived in time for round two. Congress was joining the hunting pack.

ᪧᪧ

ALEC was holding its annual meeting in Chicago in August 2013 when the letter went public. Protestors thronged outside the Palmer House hotel. The unions came and shut down the streets. Then the anarchists came and got too violent for the unions, who left. The anarchists ultimately turned on the police who'd been sent to protect their free-speech rights, and the police lost patience and started arresting everyone in sight. It was wild.

The ALEC board was holed up, working through business, when one CEO's phone went off. "Beep, beep, beep, beep. I see the guy look at it, and then he shows me," says Meierling. "And I've barely got a glance when everybody's phone in the entire room all starts going off at the same time."

Illinois senator Dick Durbin, a member of the Democratic leadership, had just mailed out a letter to three hundred organizations across the United States that he suspected provided funding for ALEC. Durbin's letter began from the assumption that all "stand your ground" laws were a blight on society, and that ALEC was to blame. He mentioned Trayvon Martin's death, and complained that ALEC had yet to call for any of those laws to be repealed. The senator wanted to know where each group stood. Each organization, he said, needed to tell him: (a) whether it had "served as a member of ALEC or provided any funding to ALEC," and (b) whether it supported "the 'stand your ground' legislation that was adopted as a national model and promoted by ALEC."

He intended to make the results public at a hearing the following month.

The Durbin letter was half intimidation, half fishing expedition. The intimidation was obvious. Durbin had sent out an alert from the dais of one of the most powerful institutions in the country, explaining that any association with ALEC would earn companies and conservative groups congressional hearings, investigations, and public retribution. The simple sending of the letter was designed to scare any remaining companies away from the state group.

The fishing expedition was almost worse. As a 501(c)(3) organization, ALEC is entitled by law to keep its list of donors private. Some companies and organizations had chosen to make their relationship with ALEC public, and paid the price after the Martin incident. But the left had squeezed all it could out of that list and needed new targets. So Durbin and his staff sat down and dreamed up an inventory of any possible company or conservative organization that might give money to ALEC. They hoped the letter would coerce a few more companies into admitting a relationship. Then the proxy activists could gin up their shareholder resolution, Color of Change could rev up the board radio ads, MoveOn.org could mobilize protests, and ALEC would lose more support.

Durbin admitted in his letter that ALEC doesn't "maintain a public list" of donors and that his own list had been pulled from "public documents" that "indicate[d]" the organizations had "funded ALEC at some point" between 2005 and 2013. This Durbin roster in fact seemed to be little more than his team having put any name that had ever been mentioned in the same sentence as ALEC on a list, and adding a few more for good measure. Some of the targets were downright amusing. Some poor owner of a car dealership in Louisiana got a Durbin letter, simply because ALEC had once done an event on his lot.

Durbin, like all liberals, disliked ALEC—although the Illinois

Democrat had a particular, self-interested reason for trying to take the group down. More than most Senate Democrats, Durbin is a creation of the trial bar. Over his career, he has received more than $5 million from lawyers for his reelections, more than three times the amount of his next-biggest-donating industry (securities). ALEC over the years had been particularly successful at marching tort reform through dozens of states. Some fifteen had adopted reforms requiring more transparency or oversight in the state hiring of private attorneys. Another fourteen had reformed the method by which defendants pay interest on judgments. States had passed medical malpractice reform, class action reform, asbestos legal reform, and reforms on forum shopping and expert testimony and damages. Durbin's donors needed ALEC shut down, as did Durbin if he wanted to keep getting their money.

And so one of the most powerful men in the land sent a letter demanding that companies give him donor information to which he was in no way entitled and that was protected by law and the First Amendment. He also leveled the threat that those who did not comply would face Congress's wrath. If it hadn't been so serious, it might have been amusing that Durbin sent the letter from his seat as chairman of the Senate Subcommittee on the Constitution, Civil Rights, and Human Rights.

Up to now, ALEC had been on its hind feet. But Durbin miscalculated. He seemed unaware that ALEC had revamped its PR shop and moved into fight mode. Durbin had also sent his letter during ALEC's annual meeting, figuring it would cause internal disarray. It had the opposite effect. "Everyone that mattered was all in the same room; we were able to articulate a plan of action," says Meierling. "It galvanized us, because no one could believe he'd do such a thing."

Indeed, *no one* could believe Durbin would do such a thing. A bunch of liberal groups bashing ALEC and boycotting companies was one thing—the press had little interest. But a sitting U.S.

senator using his position to harass private organizations caught attention. Newspaper editorial boards across the country lambasted the Democrat—the *Wall Street Journal*, the *Orange County Register*, the *Washington Times*, *Investor's Business Daily*. Illinois's newspapers roundly slammed his letter. Durbin's own hometown *Chicago Tribune* published a blistering critique under the headline "Durbin's Enemies List." It scoffed at the senator's claim that he was looking into "stand your ground" laws: "If only thinly coded letters from senators with as much clout as Durbin were that benign. Because it would be more than wrong for a U.S. senator to use the power of his high federal office as a cudgel against his enemies."

Durbin also made the mistake of sending his letter to other conservative action groups and think tanks, which were themselves 501(c)(3) and 501(c)(4) organizations, and which were still outraged over the IRS. The Goldwater Institute publicly posted its response, flat-out refusing to list any group it funded. "In the wake of the IRS intimidation and harassment of conservatives organizations, your inquisition is an outrage," wrote Goldwater president Darcy Olsen in a letter publicly posted to Durbin.

Tiger Joyce, president of the American Tort Reform Association (ATRA), likewise refused to say what organizations his group gave money to. He instead wrote a skewering piece in *Forbes*, noting that "Durbin summons not-so-faint echoes of the late Senator Joseph McCarthy, who shamelessly purported to possess documents that somehow proved his targets' guilt by association. Such tactics, which went unchallenged for too long in the 1950s, today warrant vigorous criticism from Senators on both sides of the aisle."

Mr. Joyce also sent a letter to the *Wall Street Journal*, where he not-so-subtly gave Durbin a taste of his own medicine. "After all," wrote Joyce, "how would he feel if those of us he targets were to turn the tables by deciding collectively, if quietly, to conduct our many conventions, conferences and meetings in any state other than Illinois?" ATRA's head of communications, Darren McKinney—well known in D.C. circles for his witty go-rounds with the forces of the trial bar—went so far as to draw up a T-shirt design for attendees to Durbin's committee hearing. It pictured Durbin and Joseph McCarthy side by side, with the words "Have You No Sense of Decency, Sir?" printed in between.

Says Joyce, "I'm a lawyer, and I found this reprehensible. This was just really cheap intimidation. And utterly beneath the dignity of the office. I was counsel to a committee in the Senate once, and watching this offended me. The people I used to work for, they would have never considered doing something like this. And I'm talking about Republicans and Democrats." He adds, "But Senator Durbin did, and whether it's a senior member of the Senate, or a governor, or an attorney general, our response will always be the same: We will fight. In the ATRA playbook, page one, chapter one, our job is to build a strong coalition of different entities and interest organizations. If you allow for someone to fracture that, or peel it apart with intimidation, to in any way unduly limit our ability to advance our mission, we reject that. We push back with all we have."

Durbin also underestimated his corporate targets. Most of ALEC's weakest company links had fled the organization the year before. Those who remained were not only willing to see the organization through, but some were willing to take a public stand for corporate speech rights. One such profile in courage was AT&T's Jim Cicconi. Cicconi's from Texas—he still has the drawl—and he did time in both the Reagan and George H. W. Bush White Houses. These days, he's the head of the telecom giant's external and legislative affairs department. He's a big defender of the rights of debate and free speech, and unlike a lot of corporate execs, he has a complete spinal system. It helps that he had the full confidence and backing of his boss, AT&T CEO Randall Stephenson.

Cicconi was on August vacation when the Durbin letter hit. He was bothered enough to decide he'd write AT&T's response personally. "I figured I was likely to end up in a congressional hearing, and in any event would be held accountable for the response, so I decided I'd write and sign it myself—and say exactly what I wanted to say," remembers Cicconi.

His three-page letter back to Durbin was extremely polite, even as it was very direct. Cicconi noted that he found Durbin's request "unusual" because "we are not normally required by federal law to disclose contributions of this nature, and your letter makes clear that providing this information on a confidential basis is not an option." He then pointedly referenced the campaign against companies that support ALEC. It "seems to us inescapable that any response to your request will be used by those interests whose purpose is to pressure corporations to de-fund organizations and political speech with which they disagree." Translation: We know exactly what you are up to.

Cicconi informed Durbin that he was acknowledging that AT&T gave ALEC funding not because he had to, but because he wanted to. He said that AT&T contributes to groups "that span the political spectrum," since its goal is to "support healthy and respectful political dialogue and well-informed, well-debated public policies." He declared that just as ALEC's opponents are "certainly free to engage in such activity as part of their free speech rights, companies like AT&T must also be free to make our own decisions on such matters as part of our free speech rights." Where this balance of rights "breaks down," he wrote, "and where we must all be careful, is where one party seeks to enlist government in its pressure tactics."

ALEC itself turned around a letter signed by more than three hundred state legislators from thirty-nine states, protesting the Durbin assault. Its PR team stayed up for three straight days, rallying its troops, spreading the word, pushing back on the senator. ALEC's supporters lit up Twitter. ALEC's then–first vice chair and Iowa House majority leader Linda Upmeyer blasted back, "Members and donors to 501(c)(3) organizations are specifically protected by the Internal Revenue Service and the Supreme Court to shield them from the type of political intimidation found in Sen. Durbin's letter."

Meierling points out that the Durbin letter in fact became a big turning point for many on the right; it opened a lot of eyes. "It got people to realize there is a huge difference between secrecy and privacy. And that everyone has the right to associate freely, the right to debate free ideas."

Durbin had planned his hearing for September, though a shooting at the Washington Navy Yard pushed it back to October. By the time that hearing happened, it was a chastened Illinois Democrat who took the stage. Durbin barely mentioned ALEC, turning the hearing instead into a look at gun violence. He'd been called out.

In the coming months the left kept throwing things at ALEC, but they were things mostly dredged out of the archives and lacking any real-time relevance. It launched Stand Up to ALEC, a campaign designed to throw out a new attack every week and keep up the pressure. Responding to those attacks was time-consuming, Meierling admits, but ALEC's rapid response to them also meant that few of the attacks got any traction.

In late 2013, ALEC decided on a change. Ron Scheberle had been involved with the organization for decades as a board member, a consultant, and ultimately as executive director. He had spent his final years commuting back and forth from Texas. He wanted to go back to his family, and ALEC needed a shot in the arm. The board started recruiting.

It didn't take long for them to zero in on exactly who they wanted. A spunky dirty blonde who knew all about the left's intimidation tactics, and who had only recently left a top corporate job at Visa.

Lisa Nelson. She came just in time for round three.

CHAPTER 18

Climate Crusade

WASHINGTON HAS ITS SHARE of talented people, though especially prized are those with more than one talent. You can find legislators who are exceptionally astute about politics. You can find corporate lobbyists who are exceptionally astute about business priorities and concerns. You can find activists who are exceptionally astute about the grassroots. Finding someone who is exceptionally astute about all three is rare.

That's Nelson. The Californian cut her political teeth with an old pro. She was at Newt Gingrich's side as he ascended to Speaker of the House, serving as his public affairs liaison for three years. In the run-up to that job she'd worked under Gingrich as the executive director of GOPAC, the political group started in the 1970s by Delaware governor Pete du Pont as a training operation for Republicans looking to ascend to higher office. Gingrich had run his conservative revolution from within GOPAC, and Nelson had interacted with the wide conservative establishment, from the grassroots up. After Newt, she managed AOL Time Warner's shop of federal and state lobbyists for seven years. And then on to Visa, where she ran government relations not just in D.C. but for the financial company in Canada, Latin America, and Asia.

Nelson loved working with her CEO at Visa, and when he

retired she decided to leave too. "I was sitting on the shelf—retiring, getting my daughter off to college—when I got a call from an ALEC board member, saying, 'You should really think about taking this job on.'" Nelson turned that suggestion down, and about a month later turned it down again. But she'd been watching the ALEC struggles, and she understood just how important the organization was to the free-market fight. She'd also seen the struggles from the corporate side and watched the way the left had bullied companies into funding liberal priorities and backed them out of giving dollars or support to organizations that actually believed in business. The next time they called, she allowed her name to be put on a list. The next thing she knew, she was in charge.

ALEC was feeling good about its aggressive response to Durbin and to the Stand Up to ALEC campaign. It was starting to rebuild the organization, and Nelson, when she attended the group's annual meeting in Dallas in July 2014 (she still hadn't officially started), was impressed by its initiative to recruit new types of companies. That included a focus on pulling in tech firms. As onetime start-ups like eBay or Amazon had graduated to the economic big leagues, they'd fallen prey to the same troubles as the brick-and-mortar oldies. Federal and state government intruded more and more on their business models. ALEC was a new way for them to voice concerns and hammer out solutions at a state level.

What Nelson and ALEC didn't entirely realize, however, was the extent to which these companies were wimpy on environmental issues. It was 2014, and billionaire environmentalist Tom Steyer was ginning up a slow-rolling but growing campaign against the Keystone XL pipeline. Militant activists such as 350.org's Bill McKibben were redefining what it meant to be green. The McKibben view was that old-line groups like the Sierra Club and the Natural Resources Defense Council had gone soft, making too many compromises. McKibben's activists chained themselves to the White House; they demanded that all fossil fuels stay in the ground, starting immediately; they pressured pension funds to divest from all fossil-fuel companies, comparing their investments to the immorality of apartheid.

"I grew up in Palo Alto, I know the tech community pretty well, and there's a subtlety to how they operate that is very different from a Pepsi or a McDonald's," says Nelson. "These firms are more motivated by their employees, and it is part of the culture that the CEO has coffee with them on Friday to hear and address their concerns. And the progressives were targeting those tech employees with this message about climate and, it turns out, about us."

Fact: ALEC does not have a position or a model policy on climate change. Never has. Probably never will. What it does do very aggressively, however, is agitate against energy mandates. That includes things like renewable portfolios, which require states to generate a certain percentage of their electricity from renewable sources—requirements that distort markets and drive up prices. The group also promotes legislation to get rid of taxpayer subsidies for boondoggle state equivalents of Solyndra.

This hardly makes it a climate denier, but the left didn't care. It had its new issue, and it ran with it. And it was a particularly good wedge issue to run with. Polls show that few Republicans think climate change is a big concern, whereas close to 60 percent of Democrats do. So this is a debate that sends the right to sleep, even as it inspires the left. And a lot of tech employees in California sit on the left.

The slow-rolling campaign hit warp speed on September 22, 2014. (Nelson had only just started on September 11.) Google executive chairman Eric Schmidt was in Washington. His book *How Google Works* was out, and he went on the left-of-center *Diane Rehm Show* on National Public Radio to engage in a little self-promotion. Near the end of the hourlong interview, he fielded a

call from a woman in New York asking him about Google's financial support of ALEC, given its supposed climate denial.

Schmidt rolled out a perfectly scripted response, dropping
the bomb that Google would quit funding the group. He then
launched a broadside against the organization that had helped his
company out at the state level. Google "has a very strong view
that we should make decisions in politics based on facts—what a
shock," he said. "And the facts of climate change are not in question anymore. Everyone understands climate change is occurring.
And the people who oppose it are really hurting our children and
our grandchildren and making the world a much worse place.
And so we should not be aligned with such people. They're just
literally lying."

ALEC immediately believed it had been set up. Schmidt
seemed way too prepared, way too slick in his answer, to have
done it off the cuff. Most likely the question had been a plant,
much like the Lois Lerner question in the tax forum event. And
the full-scale backup Schmidt immediately received from all the
anti-ALEC forces suggested that more than a few people had been
in the know.

Schmidt's self-serving pablum was particularly frustrating to
free marketers, who know that Google is about as altruistic as
Gordon Gekko. The company publicly spins up its "Do No Evil"
motto even as privately it keeps a hardheaded focus on its bottom
line. It's no accident that at least one of Google's power-sucking
data centers is located in Iowa near extremely cheap coal-fired
electricity. Its Ivanpah, California, solar farm threatens tortoises
and incinerates close to forty thousand birds a year. That operation is meanwhile floated by a $1.6 billion federal taxpayer–
funded loan. Gmail may be free, but consumers pay for it dearly
elsewhere.

Nelson and the team went back into hyperdrive, putting out
a strong statement noting that it was "unfortunate" that Google
was succumbing to "public pressure from left-leaning individuals

and organizations who intentionally confuse free market policy perspectives for climate change denial." Yet ALEC's problem was that tech companies are the ultimate sheep. Google's departure sparked another (albeit far smaller) round of resignations. eBay. Yahoo. Facebook. "There is a strength-in-numbers question here for all companies," says Nelson. "Once one goes, they all go." This is the double whammy of disclosure. It doesn't just tee up one organization. It tees up lots of them.

Indeed, the left had been ready after the Schmidt defection with the usual tactics—sending threats to boards, revving up the netroots to send e-mails, issuing press releases, and hounding corporate donors. One tech CEO, who will remain unnamed, received twenty thousand e-mails protesting ALEC funding in just one day. Nelson notes that this is common; some companies have to regularly reconfigure CEO e-mail addresses just to spare them the spam effect.

The departures this time, however, were different. "The companies were incredibly apologetic," says Nelson. ALEC had done such a good job pushing back against Durbin that the corporate universe was now far more aware. "They understood what was going on." She remembers one company that as a result of public pressure announced it was getting out of ALEC. The next week, ostensibly in response to a piece of direct mail, the CEO of that company sent ALEC a personal check for the same amount the company had pulled. Coincidence? Not likely.

What frustrated ALEC too is that the left took credit for some strikeouts that weren't theirs. It kept claiming the climate issue had driven all the tech companies out of ALEC's orbit when in fact some had left for entirely different reasons. Microsoft, for instance, had ended its membership in July, well before Schmidt's interview. It ended it on the same day it had announced eighteen thousand layoffs as a result of its merger with Nokia. The company was tightening its belt, and presumably didn't feel it right to keep funding outside initiatives even as it was firing employees.

Yelp ended its membership even prior to that. It put out a friendly statement noting that it joined ALEC with the very specific purpose of developing model legislation that made it harder to bring frivolous lawsuits against individuals who share their opinions online. Yelp explained that its model bill passed ALEC unanimously, and that "given our very specific goal was achieved, we allowed our membership to expire." The anti-ALEC left nonetheless perpetuated the lie that it had driven these groups out of the conservative orbit.

The press believed it, and sometimes that's all that matters. Stories bubbled about the "flight" of corporations from ALEC. Durbin's letter—all the past outrage and bullying—was forgotten. ALEC was a "climate denier" and it deserved what it got.

∽

Nelson is a fighter, and she's spent the past two years rebuilding ALEC, donor by donor, member by member. She's gaining ground—recruiting new companies, honing ALEC's pushback, building back up political membership. And all the while she has been keeping true to ALEC's mission of developing model policy. What makes her progress a wonder is that she's doing it even as she does daily battle with the anti-ALEC forces.

Because the Durbin and Google episodes were just the big moments. Over the years, ALEC's foes had developed a roster of pressure tactics designed to hit the group daily, to grind it down, to make its hour-to-hour existence a headache. Make anything painful enough, goes the attackers' thinking, and maybe the other side will just give up.

One big tactic has been harassing ALEC for more disclosure. Nelson estimates that the Center for Media and Democracy has at this point filed more than twenty-five hundred sunshine requests for information against ALEC and its state-level chapters. Every state has its own sunshine law, and CMD leverages them to try to force ALEC to produce information about its work. These suits haven't produced much of any real ammunition for the left, but they do eat up hours and hours of compliance time, put in by legislative staff that is already lean and overstretched. "The point of these is to force us to keep our attention on these disclosure demands, thereby taking us away from our real work," says Nelson.

Another tactic is the daily drumbeat of press releases and news bombs, which requires ALEC staff to spend hours of their day refuting accusations and exposing lies. It's tedious work, but Nelson understands that her organization can't afford to let any misinformation permeate the ecosphere. A favorite liberal misrepresentation is that ALEC is a fully funded, secretive creature of Charles and David Koch, the billionaire libertarians who fund groups such as Americans for Prosperity. "I got hit with that one in a 2014 radio interview and we went back and looked. Turns out that, of our entire budget, about 1.5 percent is Koch money," says Nelson. "The fact that I had to look it up goes to show how diversified ALEC funding really is." What makes these accusations particularly rich is that they often come from groups that receive funding from billionaire George Soros.

The left has tried to string ALEC up for tax fraud. At least four different liberal groups, including Common Cause and the Center for Media and Democracy, filed complaints with the IRS, pushing the agency to revoke ALEC's 501(c)(3) charitable status. The IRS, reeling from its nonprofit escapades, has been wise enough not to take that bait—at least so far.

The congressional campaign continues. In April 2014, Arizona House Democrat Raúl Grijalva, among the left's worst intimidators, wrote to demand that the Interior Department inspector general "investigate the role of [ALEC] in efforts to pass bills at the state level" that undermine federal authority. It also asked the Interior IG to "liaise with the IRS to determine whether ALEC activities violate federal, state or local lobbying and disclosure regulations." Mr. Grijalva's letter was a repeat of Democratic demands for the IRS to attack Tea Party groups, and came less than a year after the agency admitted to doing so.

The pressure on Democratic legislators in ALEC has become even more wild and nasty. In 2012, the website for Bill Moyers, the liberal journalist, put up an interactive map to allow people to look up whether their local representative was a member of ALEC, an organization that Moyers's team described as existing to "dilute collective bargaining rights, make it harder for some Americans to vote and limit corporate liability for harm caused to consumers." ALEC doesn't disclose its legislators' names—because it turns out they get, uh, harassed. But groups like CMD created a wiki that lists who they "believe" to belong. Moyers based his tenuous map on that tenuous information, as well as putting out a call for his readers to help "complete" the map by calling their legislators and demanding to know if they were in ALEC.

The left uses this information to hassle legislators, even going so far as to employ it in campaigns against them. "This is the part that I hate the most," says Nelson. She acknowledges that some of the Democratic drop in ALEC membership is due to bigger forces. The Democratic Party has shifted to the left, and many of its pro-business Democrats were ousted in primaries, beaten by Republicans, or switched parties. "But those who are left are viewed and attacked as pariahs, just for deigning to work with the other side," says Nelson. "These activists don't want bipartisanship, they don't want solutions. They want anyone who doesn't agree with them shut down." Nelson has even struggled in recent years to get a Democrat to serve in the rotating top ALEC leadership position.

ALEC has even dealt with Democratic saboteurs. Chris Taylor, a lawyer and Democratic member of the Wisconsin State Assembly, took to attending ALEC meetings so that she could take videos to post and write diaries about her time in the "ALEC Otherworld." Anti-ALEC forces have also encouraged liberal-

leaning local news crews to plant hidden cameras to tape meetings of ALEC meetings outside of ALEC premises.

They've started using ALEC membership against the GOP,
too. That was a new theme in the 2014 election, when
Democrats smeared Republican Senate candidates for their ALEC
ties. Not long before election day the AFL-CIO blanketed Iowa
with flyers complaining that Senate Republican candidate Joni
Ernst had "accepted donations" from companies also supporting
ALEC, including a "tobacco company," "oil companies," and "billionaire industrialist Charles Koch." As a headline in the liberal
publication *Mother Jones* put it, "Labor's New Attack on Iowa
Senate Candidate Joni Ernst: She's an ALEC Shill."

And then of course there's the personal harassment. Folks
like Lisa Graves, the executive director of the Center for Media
and Democracy, essentially stalk Nelson and the ALEC team.
They monitor Nelson's Facebook and Twitter feeds, commenting
on her every action or thought. Nelson in early 2015 attended
a private gathering in D.C. at which Wisconsin governor (and
soon-to-be presidential candidate) Scott Walker attended. Nelson, purely for the fun of her Facebook friends, posted a picture
of herself with him. Within a few hours, Graves had grabbed the
photo and tweeted it out, suggesting that Nelson was plotting
with Walker over a right-to-work law in Wisconsin. "These people do this all day long. Their very existence is about coming up
with ways to track our movements and go after us," says Nelson.

Since 2012, ALEC has had to gear up every late February for
the anniversary of Trayvon Martin's death—where somebody,
somewhere, intends to make a scene. One anniversary, its headquarters in Crystal City, Virginia, right outside of Washington,
received a coffin draped in an American flag. ALEC is the only
nonmilitary establishment in the office complex it inhabits; it's
common to see men and women in uniform strolling about.
"That coffin," says Meierling, "didn't earn those protesters much
favor. It sent a bad message. These people. They have no class."

∿

ALEC, for all it has endured, is a hopeful tale. A lot of targets of intimidation succumb to the pressure. ALEC did for a bit, but then it started to fight back. It's learned a lot from the experience, and it has single-handedly started changing the dynamic.

In some ways, it hasn't yet fully recovered. Nelson notes that ALEC used to boast that it was a five-hundred-member organization. Now it pitches itself as a three-hundred-member organization. "That eighty to one hundred that left in 2012, that was a big blow," she says.

Then again, it is working more closely with those that remain. The exposure ALEC gave to the Durbin and Google events were teachable moments for the wider conservative and corporate worlds. Nelson believes a big part of her job today is education—coaching entire corporate teams about the new intimidation dynamic. "A lot of what we do now is trying to educate companies—and beyond just the state- or federal-government-relations people. We say, 'Look, this is the new normal. You are going to get hit all the time. You are going to get hit in all kinds of different ways. They are going to tell you that you can no longer take part in the debate. So you need to take a deep breath, understand what is happening, and be able to communicate it to your C-suite. You need to be able to explain that while this may feel like a threat, it is only a threat if you respond and give in. Pushing back is the best way to make them stop.'"

And she keeps pointing out the lessons ALEC itself has learned: "We are trying to explain to companies the benefit of saying, at the outset, 'Go away, because we're not going anywhere; we give to both sides, we engage in debate.' If they are definitive, the other side does go away. If they respond and tiptoe around, and say, 'Well, we might not renew in ALEC,' and hem and haw, well, that's the kiss of death, for them and for us. All they are doing is inviting more harassment."

Nelson feels lucky that she can highlight profiles in courage. And there have been many. Folks like AT&T. Or Pfizer. Or UPS. There have been nearly as many as the capitulators. Sometimes that courage comes down to an individual in the organization who resents the pressure and understands that the worst course is to give up. She's been grateful for some industrial sectors, which already understood the situation. "You look at the energy sector— they've been great. They've been under attack for years. Maybe not in the personal, ugly, direct way that has now come to dominate, but still, under attack. And they know from experience that giving in just makes it worse."

Worse is the operative word. Says Nelson, "The thing everyone in the corporate world has to understand is that these people don't have one ask. You can't negotiate. You can't deal. They want one victory, and then another, and it is all aimed at the end of you. They aren't going to be happy until you are gone." She refers to her continued mixed feelings on the organization ending its Public Safety and Elections Task Force. "It's gone, but now they are trying to disband our energy task force, and our health care task force. We gave them reason to hope they could."

She notes too that the ALEC campaign has spread to other nonprofit organizations. That includes the State Policy Network, an umbrella organization of conservative think tanks such as the Goldwater Institute, the Manhattan Institute, the Hudson Institute, and the Pacific Research Institute. The Center for Media and Democracy has now branched out from its ALEC campaign and runs what it calls Stinktanks.org, a website devoted to trashing the conservative innovation world, targeting it just like ALEC. "We got the first wave, but everyone is now realizing that they are targets too. We either all stand up to this or we are all a target," she says.

Nelson is also recruiting different, newer, braver types of backers. ALEC still cares about those big companies, but it has come to realize that a lot of the real fighters—those who still truly care about free-market principles—are smaller businesses that aren't in bed with government, that have a real stake in the state-level fights that ALEC wages. "The federal government has been a depressing place for limited-government advocates through the Obama years," she says. "The real power lately is in the states, and there are so many companies that are in the start-up model. They are young and aggressive and care about a smart business environment." As of the end of 2015, Nelson had recruited fifty-four new members.

Mostly what ALEC and Nelson have learned is that it's a brave, new, and very ugly world, one that requires a brave, new, and very determined mind-set. Nelson came of age in the riotous Gingrich years, and "back then, we thought we played tough." She laughs. Then she grows serious. "That's nothing. It's nothing compared to today, to the politics of personal and institutional destruction. We used to try to outdebate the other side. These people? They don't want debate. They don't want democracy. They want you gone. They play for keeps. And you'd better be ready."

CHAPTER 19

Raid Day

ERIC O'KEEFE was on a visit to Madison, Wisconsin, on October 3, 2013, when his phone buzzed. It was a cryptic text from an old friend and colleague, political consultant R. J. Johnson. He indicated that O'Keefe should go see his attorneys. They were in possession of something he needed to see.

O'Keefe is the director of the Wisconsin Club for Growth, a conservative outfit that pushes for lower taxes and smaller government. The club had only just finished playing a role in defeating the 2011 and 2012 union-led recall efforts against Governor Scott Walker and Republican legislators. Its headquarters is in Madison, and so a few hours later O'Keefe met there with club attorneys. The lawyers definitely did have something he needed to see. A subpoena.

A six-page subpoena, to be exact, which informed O'Keefe that he was the target of an investigation by Wisconsin prosecutors for supposedly breaking campaign finance laws. O'Keefe admits that the full force of the document didn't immediately hit him. But something did jump out.

The subpoena's sweeping demands included all of O'Keefe's correspondence going back to April 2009 with dozens of people—whose own names were listed on its first page. O'Keefe blinked at the length of time the document covered, but also at the list of names. Among several visible political figures were also listed lots of small vendors to, and fund-raisers for, the club. The government would have been hard pressed to know the club had such associations. "That's when I realized they had been spying on us for some time. There was no way they could have had those names otherwise," he says. He'd only later find out that prosecutors had already gone to all his Internet service providers and subpoenaed every conversation he'd ever had. They'd done the same to at least seventeen other people.

In addition to his correspondence, prosecutors wanted every document related to the club's work on campaigns, and every draft of related material. And they didn't just want documents related to Wisconsin. O'Keefe also works on national political issues; they wanted all that, too.

But the most sinister part of the subpoena was this: "This John Doe search warrant is issued subject to a secrecy order. By order of the court pursuant to a secrecy order that applies to this proceeding, you are hereby commanded and ordered not to disclose to anyone, other than your own attorney, the contents of the search warrant and or the fact that you have received this search warrant. Violation of the secrecy order is punishable as contempt of court."

It was almost Orwellian. Prosecutors were using speech laws to go after O'Keefe, while simultaneously telling him he couldn't speak to anyone about it. The conservative wasn't sure at this point how serious this was—"my head was whirring"—but he had little doubt about its motivation: It was a revenge attack for the success his side had had in defeating the recent recalls. The club had been extremely cautious in its election work, making sure to go nowhere near any lines. So nothing else made sense.

O'Keefe called his wife, Leslie Graves. In doing so, he was already breaking the law. He didn't care. O'Keefe has fought for the First Amendment his whole life, and in the time it had taken him to read the subpoena, he'd already decided that he'd never follow the gag order. Graves wasn't sure what to think of the sub-poena either, but suggested hopefully that it might just be some minor complaint—nothing to worry about.

O'Keefe departed for a Bible study group he attended in Madi-son. On the way, he put in another call, to an old and close mentor, a man in his seventies—a Vietnam veteran, and a hard-nosed political observer. O'Keefe never made it into the study group; he sat in the parking lot on the phone for an hour, working through his worries. His buddy was far less sanguine about the subpoena; it meant trouble. O'Keefe remembers that his friend then said what to this day remains "the biggest compliment I ever got through this whole ordeal. He said, 'I'm sorry this has hap-pened. But since it is happening, I'm glad you are the one in it.' And that helped to focus me."

∿

The subpoena hit on a Thursday. O'Keefe and Graves left the next morning for Chicago and then to a meeting in Kohler, Wisconsin, with other conservative activists. That's where they learned that O'Keefe wasn't alone in getting a subpoena. Thurs-day had witnessed a dragnet. Prosecutors had in one day de-livered them to twenty-nine separate conservative organizations across the state. O'Keefe also found out that those who'd re-ceived their subpoenas through their attorneys, like him, were the lucky ones. Other Wisconsin targets hadn't been treated so politely.

Johnson, the political consultant who'd first texted O'Keefe, had been in Atlanta with his wife, fund-raising for a charity. His sixteen-year-old son was alone in their rural Dodge County home. In the dark morning hours of that Thursday, a Milwaukee County investigator ushered a troop of armed law enforcement officers into the house. Johnson's son was not allowed to call his parents. He was not allowed to call his grandparents, who lived only a half mile away. The boy had the wits to ask to call a lawyer. He was told no. As Johnson would later sum up to the *Wall Street Journal*, "He was a minor and he was isolated by law enforcement." Armed deputies stood by him while investigators tossed the house, hauling off documents and technology. Johnson's son was told that the gag order applied to him. If he told anybody what had happened, he could go to jail. When he finally arrived at school, two hours late, he couldn't tell anybody why he was so upset.

Deborah Jordahl, Johnson's business partner, was still in bed at 6 a.m. when she heard noises and saw lights in the yard. An armed Dane County deputy sheriff rang her doorbell and presented her and her husband with a search warrant. Jordahl asked for permission to wake her children on her own, so they wouldn't be scared. Permission denied. The deputy sheriff accompanied her into each room. Jordahl would later find out that her son, upon waking and seeing a police officer, thought for several minutes that his father was dead.

The deputy herded them all into the family room and read the warrant, including the gag order. Jordahl's fifteen-year-old daughter sat on the sofa, weeping, as the deputy explained that the kids were also subject to consequences if they spoke. When the deputy was done, Jordahl got up to call her lawyer. The officer backed her onto the sofa and explained she wouldn't be calling anyone. And indeed, Jordahl would have been hard pressed to do so even later. After going through every closet and drawer and combing through the basement and the family vehicles, the police department left with her phone, her husband's phone, both their computers, the kids' computers, hard drives, iPods, an e-reader, a voice recorder, pocket calendars, and her files.

Jordahl later found out that most of this was unnecessary. It was simple harassment. Long before the raid, the police had already subpoenaed her e-mails, her text records, and her phone records. Police also raided the homes of former Walker aide Kelly Rindfleisch and Walker chief of staff Keith Gilkes.

When people hear the story of these predawn raids, they are appalled and outraged to think this happened in America, and over allegations of *campaign finance regulations*. O'Keefe and Johnson and Jordahl weren't accused of murder, or racketeering, or drug-running, or some elaborate white-collar crime. They were accused (falsely, as would be proven), and subpoenaed, and searched, for supposedly violating highly technical speech rules. About 95 percent of such cases are handled in civil proceedings. It is extremely rare for a campaign finance violation to trigger a criminal prosecution, and only then when it is clear that an actor deliberately and elaborately schemed to evade the law. Even then, it is unheard of for such an accusation to initiate police raids, isolation, and denial of legal counsel. It's like imposing solitary confinement on jaywalkers.

O'Keefe and Graves didn't find out about the Johnson and Jordahl raids until Monday morning, when they arrived back at Madison and ended up at the consultants' office. "They looked terrible. I don't know when they had last slept," remembers O'Keefe. Johnson was also under a gag order, yet he confided to O'Keefe that his home had been raided. "I don't care if I go to jail for telling you," O'Keefe remembers him saying, his voice pure exhaustion. The three targets spent an hour debriefing, and O'Keefe arranged for his Kansas City attorneys to be at his home the next day. That, too, was a long day.

O'Keefe was nervous, but had already decided he would fight it with everything he had. He remembers sending an e-mail almost immediately to one of his lawyers. It read, "Hey Eddie. I've already drafted a response to this subpoena. It's two words long, and the second word is 'you!' Think you can put that into legalese?"

∿

O'Keefe was right—it was revenge, and frustration. Wisconsin led the GOP progressive reform movement of the early twentieth century under Governor Robert M. La Follette, the first state to institute a workers' compensation law, and among the first to institute unemployment insurance and collective bargaining. That state identity shifted pretty seamlessly in the 1950s to life under Democrats. And Wisconsin stayed purple-blue right up to 2010, when, in backlash against its faltering fortunes and Obama policies, the Wisconsin electorate put in the governor's mansion a young and dynamic reformer by the name of Scott Walker.

Walker had been Milwaukee County executive, a powerful post, and his focus on reducing the size and scope of government had already earned him Democratic enemies. He brought the same fiscal conservatism to the governorship, and a new idea for implementing it. In 2011, he proposed a bill that limited collective bargaining for public employee unions. It was an innovative and overdue reform. Public-sector bargaining is a racket. Government unions pour money into electing Democratic politicians, who then hand unions generous pay and benefits, who then pour that money back into electing more Democrats. This unvirtuous circle is why even Democrats like FDR and Jimmy Carter opposed federal collective bargaining. Walker's reform was structural, and it held the potential to slash government spending, reform the state's bloated pension program, and bust up schoolteacher monopolies all in one go.

The left saw the threat for what it was in the state. But it also worried that Wisconsin might prove a model for other states. Walker's proposal therefore ignited a national firestorm. Unions and more than seventy thousand activists from around the country poured into the capital, protesting and thronging its halls. Obama weighed in, berating the measure. At one point, all fourteen of Wisconsin's Democratic state senators fled to Illinois, to thwart the necessary quorum to pass the bill. The governor didn't waver, and Republicans managed to push through the legislation.

Walker signed it, and a court fight ended with the state's highest judges upholding its provisions.

The right saw Walker's victory as epic. The left saw it as a calamity.

∿

In the calamity corner sat Milwaukee district attorney John Chisholm, an avowed Walker opponent. Chisholm was elected as a Democrat, and with widespread union support. His wife was a teachers' union shop steward. He was never shy about his political leanings. At least forty-three (possibly as many as seventy) employees in Chisholm's office also signed the recall petition against Walker. They were Democrats, and their fealty lay with the party. Chisholm's office—or rather his prosecutorial power—became a channel for the left's Walker rage.

Their vehicle was an investigation that had actually started in 2010, aimed at Walker's time as Milwaukee County executive. This wasn't just any old investigation. Chisholm had a particularly insidious legal tool in hand—Wisconsin's John Doe statute. It's a law unique to that state, with roots in the mid-1800s. It is designed to give law enforcement awesome powers to ascertain whether a crime has been committed, and, if so, by whom. Prosecutors in most states have to ask permission of a grand jury to issue subpoenas or force testimony. Not under John Doe. Prosecutors make the decisions on whom to harass and intimidate all on their own. And judges under John Doe have the power to keep everything secret with gag orders.

Chisholm's first John Doe was (in theory) aimed at investigating claims of theft from a veterans' fund while Walker was county executive. Chisholm would nonetheless enlarge the suit at least eighteen times over two and a half years, expanding it into a sprawling later look at Governor Walker and his campaign staff. Six people ultimately were criminally sentenced—

four of them on charges that had nothing to do with the probe's original intent.

Walker was never charged, but the left by mid-2012 had developed an insane desire to take him down. He'd beat them with his bargaining bill. But he'd also beat their first effort to make him pay for it. After the state's high court upheld his reform, the unions mobilized to make a national example out of him. They launched a recall drive, gathering the requisite number of petition signatures to force six state Republican senators into recall elections in the summer of 2011, and then to force Walker into a special election in June 2012.

It was only the third gubernatorial recall election in the history of the country. Tom Barrett, the well-known and well-funded Democratic mayor of Milwaukee, stood up for a repeat of his run against Walker in 2010. National unions and liberal groups poured money into the races, intent on using the recall to send a national message: Mess with our bargaining rights, and you will be sent packing.

The left's problem: The right also understood the stakes. They knew that if Walker and Republicans lost, no other governor would risk pushing similar reforms. Conservative organizations from around the country mobilized in unprecedented fashion. The fight over those state senate elections cost $30 million—and $25 million came from outside organizations on the right and left. The Club for Growth, the biggest player on the right, spent $12 million in 2011 alone.

Walker's own recall fight made that look like small potatoes. It was the most expensive election in Wisconsin history; candidates and outside groups spent more than $80 million. Unions spent a lot, but the broad Republican coalition—from the Republican Governors Association, to the state chapter of the Chamber of Commerce, to the NRA, to Americans for Prosperity, to Tea Party groups—spent more. And in the end, Republicans ultimately held the state senate, and Walker got 53 percent of the vote. Instead of making an example of him, the unions made him a national hero and set him up for a presidential run.

Here was the rich part: As recall day approached, as the unions realized that Walker looked likely to win, the left smoothly switched messages. They moved from talking about Walker's collective bargaining reform to talking about the election itself. Liberals decried the "dark" money flowing into the state. Newspapers obsessed on the spending, calling Wisconsin Exhibit A of the supposed horrors of *Citizens United*. Groups like Public Integrity and Common Cause held up the Club for Growth and Wisconsin Manufacturers and Commerce (the chamber's state chapter) as examples of corrupt influences that were "buying" elections. The unions had spent all they had in Wisconsin, and the left didn't mind that—they don't mind big money. They only mind when the right has more of it.

Walker won his race on June 5, 2012. By mid-August, Chisholm had convinced a judge, Neal Nettesheim, to roll all the information from his prior John Doe into a brand-new probe into allegations of Walker-related campaign finance violations. Nettesheim also agreed to transfer the "existing" secrecy order.

Not that the first John Doe had remained secret. Somebody had leaked its existence in early 2012, clearly hoping it would damage Walker in his recall fight. Chisholm never had found a thing on the former county executive, but the leaks nonetheless spread rumors that criminal charges might be filed before the June 5 vote. Barrett, Walker's recall opponent, had a field day with that smear, brazenly declaring just two days before the recall that his opponent was "the only governor in this country who has a legal defense fund." He still lost.

Walker still had to go through the normal reelection process in 2014. And the recall drive had given his opponents a new rationale for legally pursuing him: campaign finance "violations." The Milwaukee DA's office spent another year ramping up what became known as John Doe II. In August 2013—at just about the time Walker's reelection effort began in earnest—Chisholm's office moved to give itself some political cover for the abuse that was about to come. It named a special prosecutor to head the investigation, a nominal Republican and thirty-year federal attorney named Francis Schmitz. Schmitz's role was to serve as the supposed independent head of the probe, to provide insulation against inevitable claims of a political witch hunt.

Schmitz started getting ready for October 3: subpoena and raid day.

∿

Eric O'Keefe, now sixty, is one of those influential conservatives whom most Americans have never heard of. His interest in causes is a lot bigger than his ego. He's spent thirty years working behind the scenes—by choice. That's what made the John Doe situation, and the requirement that he go public, hard for him.

He grew up in Michigan, in a suburb just outside of Detroit. He hated high school and skipped college. But he'd spent his formative years watching Detroit plunge into decline, and became fascinated with public policy and politics. "I probably spent those years reading far more than all my buddies at college," O'Keefe remembers. His self-education led him, by self-description, into "pretty radical libertarianism," and he ended up serving as national director of the Libertarian Party in 1980, pushing the presidential ticket of Ed Clark and David Koch. That effort got less than 1 percent of the vote, and O'Keefe "learned the hard way that third parties are a waste of time." He went back to the books to figure out why. "That's the history of my life," he says with a laugh. "Charge, fight, lose, study." He met his wife, and they ended up moving into an old farmhouse of her grandfather's in Spring Green, Wisconsin. They started having kids, and O'Keefe, who kept reading, started moving toward the conservative side.

In the early 1990s he helped spearhead the national campaign for term limits. The fight gave O'Keefe an opportunity to be among the pioneers of broadcast "issue ads"—those in which groups promote or criticize a cause, rather than a candidate. They were new in the post-Watergate era, and O'Keefe and his colleagues helped clarify a lot of free-speech ground, in terms of what kind of groups could run them, and what they could say.

The experience turned the operative into an expert on finance laws. "There was a lot of caution in the post-*Buckley* era. But we had a blast doing those ads, and they were effective, and the methods started to spread," he remembers. He became convinced of the need to hold the parties—which were run by incumbents—more responsible and accountable to their voters, and became an activist for the rise of political organizations that are "controlled by donors" and engage heavily in primaries, elections, and policies. O'Keefe's view is that direct participation by these organizations—nonprofits, think tanks, 527s, the like—is the only way to keep politicians and government responsive.

He just as fervently believes that money is a foundational aspect of that. "It always bugs me, this obsession with political spending," he says. "Campaign spending as a percentage of the federal budget is a flat line—and it is all of 0.02 percent. The left, they act like there is too much money in politics. Really? The feds spend $10 billion a day. We have yet to have any election cycle—even counting every dollar by candidates and groups and unions and all the issue ads—that comes close to that.

"And yet think about the stakes. We are electing a person who will control a country for four years, electing senators who will sit for six years. They don't mind blowing $10 billion a day for federal spending, but they act like spending a fraction of that to debate the fundamental question of our governance is over the top."

O'Keefe cofounded the Campaign for Primary Accountability, which seeks to oust entrenched members of Congress. He's a founding board member of Citizens for Self-Governance, which seeks to elevate the grassroots. He's the chairman of the Health Care Compact Alliance, which seeks to shift more federal health dollars to states. He was the chairman and CEO of the Sam Adams Alliance, which promoted citizen activism. He's on the board of the Citizens in Charge Foundation. He sits on the board of the Center for Competitive Politics, which Brad Smith now runs, to help protect free speech. He definitely lives his philosophy.

O'Keefe had been active with the national Club for Growth since the mid-2000s, and briefly served on its board. He'd also agreed to sit on the Wisconsin state chapter board. That's where he met R. J. Johnson, and then Jordahl. He'd always been focused on national politics, but when the Walker fight erupted, his wife argued that a Wisconsin defeat would be a huge blow to the broader conservative reform effort. O'Keefe thought about it, then decided to go all-in politically in his home state.

He knew he'd lose his treasured privacy, so he threw up a fence around the farmhouse and installed an alarm. Then he shelved the national projects, cranked up the fund-raising machine, and took responsibility for the Wisconsin club. The organization would become a primary means of communicating to voters the merits of and stakes around Walker's reforms during the state senate recall fights. Notably, the Wisconsin club did not run any Walker-related ads during the governor's recall race.

The Senate races alone were enough to get Chisholm's attention.

∿

Schmitz's subpoena heyday threw the Wisconsin conservative movement into a state of panic. Which was undoubtedly one of the goals. The subpoenas demanded pretty much every document from twenty-nine groups involved in the 2011 and 2012 recalls. But they also seemed part fishing expedition, since they demanded records stretching back to 2009—from before Walker even took office. They'd gone out to the Club for Growth, to the League of American Voters, to Wisconsin Family Action, to Americans for Prosperity—Wisconsin, to American Crossroads, to the Republican Governors Association, to Friends of Scott Walker, and to the Republican Party of Wisconsin—to name a few. The subpoena to Wisconsin Manufacturers and Commerce was so enormous the group had to hire a forensic team to copy all the required information from computers.

O'Keefe remembers another (in retrospect) amusing aspect of the subpoena aftermath: the scramble for lawyers. "The John Doe forbade communications between parties, and everybody had a conflict of interest with somebody else, and meantime there are only about three campaign finance lawyers in the state. You can't imagine the bizarre conversations going on."

The subpoenas didn't spell out specific allegations, but there was little question what Schmitz and Chisholm were looking to prove. The argument was "illegal campaign coordination" by independent groups during the campaign. Campaign law barred candidates (in this case, Walker) from "coordinating" with independent groups engaged in express advocacy for the candidate.

But that's what made the John Doe investigation so bogus. That hadn't happened. The club hadn't run elect-Walker ads during the election. And the other groups hadn't run ads expressly calling for Walker's election, or calling for the defeat of Barrett. They had run "issue ads" that pointed out their own or the candidates' views on policies. Indeed, the prosecutors weren't claiming the standard definition of "illegal coordination." They were instead trying to stretch what counted as a crime. Their big beef was that Walker had asked donors to give money to independent groups in the course of the campaign.

Indeed he had. Just as Obama had when in February 2012 his official campaign committee blessed fund-raising for a liberal super PAC that was supporting him for reelection. Obama not only put out the call for donors to give money to that group, but his cabinet members spoke at its fund-raisers. And just as Harry Reid had when he sent a letter in 2011 to donors telling them about a new "group solely devoted to leveling the playing field and protecting the Democratic majority in the Senate: Majority PAC."

Obama and Reid hadn't got in trouble because this is legal by any standard definition. Outside groups are basically barred from turning over their dollars to a campaign. Beyond that, communication between groups and a campaign is kosher, as is coordination among outside players. It's not only kosher; it's protected by the First Amendment. The targets would later find out that prosecutors were also looking to redefine what counted as an "issue" ad, broadly claiming that any issue ad that was helpful somehow to a candidate was expressing advocacy on that person's behalf. They were looking at anything, hoping to make something stick.

∿

It was only later that the victims would find out something else. Something huge. The prosecutors weren't in this alone. They were working in secret with Wisconsin's Government Accountability Board.

Wisconsin's legislature created GAB in 2007, in the wake of an ethics scandal that involved politicians from both state parties. It technically oversees elections, campaign finance laws, ethics, and lobbying. Its board is made up of six former, nonpartisan judges, appointed by the governor. But they all tend to lean a certain way, and the staff leans even more a certain way, and GAB has in a short time racked up an infamous reputation for pushing aggressive regulation of speech. That tendency was aided (until recently) by a Wisconsin campaign finance law that was among the more outdated in the nation. GAB was primed to become another weapon in the left's arsenal against conservatives. And the John Doe investigation made it exactly that. Later documents would suggest that GAB was working hand in hand with the prosecutors.

The first tip that GAB was in on the Doe probe came via one of the search warrants, which revealed that they had been executed based on the request of Dean Nickel, who had worked as an investigator at GAB. Documents would later show that GAB's board had in fact voted to officially investigate "illegal coordination" among the groups in June 2013—just as Chisholm was gearing up to hire Schmitz and issue subpoenas. But e-mails would also show that GAB staff, including GAB director Kevin Kennedy, had been working for at least ten months prior with the DA's office to target and intimidate the twenty-nine conservative groups. To this day it is unclear if GAB's board knew about this earlier staff work or had given approval.

Schmitz and the GAB folk certainly seemed to feel a bond. There's an e-mail on November 27, 2013, from GAB staff counsel Shane Falk to special prosecutor Schmitz. This was about two months after the subpoenas came out, and just after news broke of them. Falk tells Schmitz to "stay strong" in his efforts to take down Walker allies. "Remember, in brief, this was a bastardization of politics and our state is being run by corporations and billionaires," he wrote. "That isn't democracy to say the least, but due to how they do this dark money, the populace never gets to know." This was a pretty good insight into how the average GAB bureaucrat thinks.

"The cynic in me says the sheeple would still follow the propaganda even if they knew, but at least it would all be out there so that the influences on our politicians is clearly known," continued Falk. By "the sheeple," Falk meant Wisconsin voters.

Documents show that GAB staff was almost fervent in its desire to bring down Walker allies, and at one point contemplated serving subpoenas or warrants on conservative TV and radio talk show hosts. Notes from a September 2013 meeting refer to a "discussion raised by David regarding media exemption and identifying what the standards are before Sykes/Hannity coordinate with [Friends of Scott Walker] and Walker." The "David" here appeared to be David Robles, an assistant DA in Chisholm's office. Sykes is a reference to influential Milwaukee radio host Charlie Sykes. Hannity is Fox News's well-known conservative host Sean Hannity. The conversation suggests that prosecutors were also suggesting some form of illegal "coordination" with the Walker campaign. The notes also includes "to-do" assignments for Robles and Schmitz and Falk—meaning that they, or representatives, were presumably all at the meeting.

Other documents showed that investigators were considering sending Sykes and Hannity subpoenas or warrants. The episode illustrated to what an extraordinary degree GAB and prosecutors had run off the rails. Some campaign finance laws are debatable. But few protections are stronger under the Constitution than the First Amendment's protection of a free press. And yet the Wisconsin speech police were thinking about hauling in Sean Hannity.

∿

GAB didn't just have friends in low places, like the Milwaukee DA's office; it had friends in very, very high places. Long after the Doe scandal tapered off, new e-mails showed that GAB's Kennedy was in frequent contact with none other than Lois Lerner.

The e-mails show that Kennedy and Lerner talked about all sorts of things, from the need for more donor disclosure to the recall election. In one July 2011 e-mail, Kennedy complains to Lerner, "The Legislature has killed our corporate disclosure rules." Sources also told the *Wall Street Journal* that in 2012 and 2013, Wisconsin investigators requested that the federal tax agency give it information about one of the conservative groups it was investigating. It is unclear if the IRS honored that request, but it is notable that prosecutors felt comfortable asking in the first place. Left-wing activist groups provided a further nexus between the two operations. In October 2014, the Center for Media and Democracy filed a complaint with the IRS against the Wisconsin Club for Growth, claiming it was violating its non-profit status. Its evidence was Doe-related material.

Kennedy and Lerner appeared to be personal friends as well as professional contacts. They even fit in face-to-face working sessions. One of those was in late January 2012, when Lerner suggested they work "two nights in a row." That was about a week or so before the IRS shipped off its enormous tranche of inter-rogatories to conservative groups around the country. It's also around the time when Wisconsin prosecutors were siphoning up information to prepare for the official opening of their second John Doe, in September of that year. Did Kennedy and Lerner work together on these topics? We still don't know.

GAB had also played a cameo role in the harassment of En-gelbrecht. The letter that Maryland Democratic representative Elijah Cummings sent to the Texas group cited GAB's criticisms of True the Vote. TTV had played a role in reviewing some of the petitions to recall Walker. GAB had been accused of a lackadaisi-cal approach to verifying signatures. Yet when outside groups attempted to do some verification, GAB thwarted them at every step. Obama counsel Bob Bauer praised GAB for taking "swift ac-tion in the aftermath of [True the Vote's] involvement in the June recall elections."

Obama, the IRS, GAB, Wisconsin prosecutors, CMD, Dick Durbin, Color of Change, the SEC, the FEC, Bruce Freed, Com-mon Cause, Media Matters. O'Keefe for his part says the ques-tion "isn't who else is in on such a large and coordinated cam-paign. The question is, who isn't?"

Chisholm's office undoubtedly hoped to get a conviction. But the John Doe investigation had more immediate partisan goals—all focused on the near-term Walker reelection.

One goal was (again) to obtain a list of donors. One subpoena revealingly contained a demand for "all records of income received, including fundraising information and the identity of persons contributing to the corporation." The prosecutors wanted donor names, even though these are protected by law. The left had already started donor harassment during the recall, with liberal groups publishing the names of Walker contributors and urging national boycotts. They wanted a larger roster.

The other goal was to help Mary Burke, Mr. Walker's opponent in the 2014 reelection. Burke just happened to announce her candidacy for the governorship a few days after the Schmitz subpoenas hit their targets. The documents inspired panic among independent groups, which in turn served to put the entire Wisconsin conservative ecosphere on ice. The groups' fund-raising plummeted, even as their legal bills piled up.

Not that anyone had an appetite for advertising and giving prosecutors more ammunition. "They had absolutely unlimited resources," Wisconsin Manufacturers and Commerce president Kurt Bauer would later tell the *Wall Street Journal*. "And I think part of the goal all along was to chill our fundraising and keep us off the airwaves. So the money and time we had to spend defending ourselves was money and time that we couldn't spend toward issue advocacy."

The separate gift to Burke was the public leak of the new probe, which happened only a few weeks after the subpoenas. Conservatives had been told they'd go to jail if they breathed word of the investigation. And yet word of the probe ended up in the column of a prominent *Milwaukee Journal Sentinel* reporter, known for his Democratic sources. Burke immediately made the probe part of her campaign against Walker.

That was a bit much for O'Keefe. The conservative had decided with that first call to his wife that he was going to violate the gag. "I think I violated it in some form every day," he remembers, somewhat proudly. But he hadn't gone public yet. His hesitation speaks to just how corrosive and corrupting to democracy a John Doe investigation is. O'Keefe was willing to go to jail over the gag. But there were twenty-eight other organizations that had varying responses to the subpoenas, and one big response was fear. A lot of them preferred to keep this quiet, not antagonize the prosecutors, hope it blew over. Some of those who didn't want publicity were named in O'Keefe's subpoena. If he outed himself, they'd be outed too, and they'd be unhappy. He was under pressure to stay quiet.

"But I wanted the fight now," says O'Keefe. "I wanted it on me, not wait to have my kids deal with the fallout one day." He talked it over with his children and wife, who asked if she could bail him out if he was arrested. The penalty for violating the gag was a $10,000 fine and a year in jail. He said no. And then, using the connections of a friend, he ended up sitting down with the *Wall Street Journal*.

O'Keefe told the *Journal*'s editorial page what had happened, and then he waited. He didn't know if the paper would take his story seriously—whether it would even bother writing anything. Two weeks later, the *Wall Street Journal* blew the lid off the story. It ran through the Doe, the subpoenas, the groups under fire—and it excoriated the whole exercise. It also quoted O'Keefe. He'd publicly and brazenly defied the gag. His phone started ringing off the hook.

CHAPTER 20

Fight Club

O'KEEFE DIDN'T JUST GO PUBLIC. He directed his attorneys to fight the subpoenas. The result was that he almost immediately proved just how political and out of bounds the investigation was. Within three months, a Wisconsin state judge had quashed several of the subpoenas as improper, bluntly writing that they "do not show probable cause that the moving parties committed any violations of the campaign finance laws."

The judge was Gregory A. Peterson, who had landed the duty of overseeing the second John Doe case. From the sound of his January 10 opinion, he wasn't impressed. He outright rejected the theory of "illegal coordination," explaining that there was simply no evidence that independent groups had expressly called for the election of Walker, or the defeat of his opponent. "Without political purposes, coordination is not a crime," he wrote.

O'Keefe also went on offense. He got in touch with conservative Washington powerhouse lawyer David Rivkin. Rivkin was born in the Soviet Union and emigrated to the United States in his teens. His time living under lawless communists gave him an additional love for the Constitution and the rule of law. "I don't have to guess at what might happen to this country if more things like Wisconsin happen," Rivkin told me. "I've already seen what that's like. I know."

The O'Keefe case was a new challenge. Rivkin's not a First Amendment lawyer. He made his name as an authority on separation of powers, with a special focus on national security and war powers. He defended former defense secretary Donald Rumsfeld in a case over the detention of José Padilla as an unlawful combatant. He was behind former House Speaker John Boehner's lawsuit against Obama for exceeding his constitutional powers with Obamacare revisions. But Rivkin was intrigued by what sounded like an extraordinary abuse of state authority. He met with O'Keefe, and took the case.

Five days after Peterson's opinion, Rivkin issued a press release explaining that he had a new client, and that he'd written to prosecutors to inform them that their secret, grand juryless investigation violated his client's rights. Cease and desist, warned his letter. Rivkin meant it. If the Wisconsin prosecutors kept it up, he had every intention of filing a civil rights lawsuit that charged prosecutors with violating O'Keefe's First Amendment rights to free speech and his Fourteenth Amendment right to due process. Unlike the Doe, this case would be out in the open, with documents available for public perusal. And under this case, the prosecutors themselves could be held personally liable for their abuse.

The prosecutors didn't desist, and Rivkin held true to his word. On February 11, the lawyer filed in federal court in Milwaukee on behalf of both the Club for Growth and O'Keefe. The complaint named four prosecutors, including Chisholm and Schmitz, and laid out how the group had spent more than four years using John Does to harass political opponents.

The lawsuit was a positive step. But there was no denying that the John Doe investigation was having its intended effects.

Some were deeply personal. O'Keefe lived with the knowledge that he might go to jail. After he went public, and after Peterson quashed the subpoenas, the prosecutors went back to the court to complain about his actions. Schmitz in a filing with the court argued that the conservative had "demonstrated contempt for the John Doe process, secrecy order, and Wisconsin legal system." The club director spent some sleepless nights wondering where that might go.

Some of it was professional. Johnson notes that after the probe went public, his business came under scrutiny. People weren't returning his calls, and he had to pass up opportunities for fear that he might prove a liability to clients. "Even if they hadn't heard about the Doe," he told the *Wall Street Journal*, "it would have been unethical for me to bring them in blind. So I had to turn down business on that account."

Deborah Jordahl would note how hard it was for her and Johnson to piece back their business after investigators absconded with all their equipment and their records. "You live under a cloud of suspicion," she said.

Some of it was very serious indeed. Kelly Rindfleisch was a deputy chief of staff to Walker when he was still Milwaukee County executive, and was a subsequent victim of the dawn raids. Rindfleisch had actually been a target of the first John Doe, and after years of combing through tens of thousands of e-mails and calls, prosecutors finally ginned up a charge. They found she'd used her county office for some outside campaign e-mails. In fact, all she'd done was sign in to a private e-mail account to answer a few e-mails related to a campaign (not even Walker's). If she'd walked just a few feet outside the building and answered them on her phone, no one would have blinked. She was nonetheless charged with a felony. Rindfleisch was terrified and panicked; she copped a plea.

She later appealed her conviction, and her reward was to have her e-mails made public. It was an exercise in public humiliation, broadcasting Rindfleisch's private conversations about her medication and her cats. The suit worked its way up, and even the state public defender's office filed a supporting brief on her behalf, arguing that prosecutors had set a dangerous precedent for digital searches. The state supreme court nonetheless declined to hear it. Rindfleisch served a six-month sentence with an ankle bracelet, for a crime that had nothing to do with the original John Doe proceeding. "The whole thing was a disgraceful operation," says O'Keefe. "All she's gotten for trying to protect her most basic rights is to have her e-mails blasted coast to coast. These people are sick."

∿

Rivkin had been right to warn the state prosecutors that their John Doe proceedings were a flagrant violation of the Constitution, and that no federal court would stand for it. They should have listened to him. On May 6, 2014, federal Judge Rudolph Randa shut the whole sordid operation down, issuing a preliminary injunction against the probe.

It's no easy thing to get a judge to issue an injunction; a defendant has to prove he has a high likelihood of succeeding on the merits. Randa didn't take much convincing. His opinion wasn't so much a legal reading as a legal reproach.

The Doe suit, he said, was based on a mistaken reading of campaign finance law that infringed on O'Keefe's free-speech rights. He reminded everyone that the intent of campaign finance law is to prevent corruption, but that it was hardly corrupt for candidates and outside groups to believe in similar things. He noted that "the larger danger is giving government an expanded role in uprooting all forms of perceived corruption which may result in corruption of the First Amendment itself."

The Wisconsin prosecutors immediately appealed to the Seventh Circuit Court of Appeals, demanding a stay of the judge's order. They ultimately got it, on a technicality. Rivkin notes that the panel of judges expressed real concern about the gag orders and other aspects of the case. But they felt this was properly a state issue, to be heard in state court. So the Doe proceeded.

Rivkin says the case gave him a new wariness of power. "Given my background on national security issues, I generally have held the view that the executive is right, cops are good people, prosecutors are honorable. So it was an unbelievable stunner to learn about the levels of chicanery by the Milwaukee DA, by other DAs, by judges, by the GAB," he says. "Power corrupts, and government power corrupts very robustly, and we have very little oversight. I look at prosecutors in a very different light now. A lot of them are bums."

The Walker case made a lot of people think differently—including about Walker. In the late spring of 2014, the *Wall Street Journal* broke the news that Steven Biskupic, representing Walker's campaign committee, Friends of Scott Walker, was negotiating a settlement with Schmitz. It looked as if Walker wanted to save his own skin—to get the Doe out of the way in a reelection year—while hanging everybody else out to dry.

The news frustrated conservatives, who were otherwise winning in court. And some worried that a settlement might give credence to the prosecutors' nonsensical theories. The *Journal* news caused an uproar, and not long afterward, Walker backed away from the whole thing: "I'm an economic and fiscal conservative. Obviously the last few years I've shown it, that I've committed to those principles even in the face of extreme outside pressure. And it just surprises me that anyone would think that in any way I would undermine anyone who shared those same principles. Clearly, I would not," he said in a Wisconsin interview.

∿

The prosecutors were losing in court, so they decided to try to win with the public. A main point of the John Doe was to smear Walker and the groups and get them out of politics. They'd done that a bit, through selective leaks. Now they asked an appeals court both to block Randa's ruling and to unseal all their documents, to give the public a taste of what they'd been digging up.

Randa knew what was up. When the appeals court made the decision to dump more than 250 pages of Doe documents on the public, the judge had harsh words for the prosecutors, who "by their position appear to seek refuge in the Court of Public Opinion, having lost in this Court on the law," he wrote. Their position in favor of unsealing is "at odds with their duty as prosecutors, which is to see that in any John Doe proceeding the rights of the innocent are protected in pursuit of a criminal investigation."

The document download nonetheless had the prosecutors' intended effect. The national media, which had paid no attention whatsoever to the Doe case and its abuses up to now, suddenly seized on the papers, presenting as fact all the prosecutors' accusations. Walker, the stories ran, had been part of a "criminal scheme." There was little or no mention in the newspapers that these were nothing more than theories, and that two judges had already ruled them wrong.

The appeals court released yet more documents in August, inspiring another round of breathless reporting, this bout focused on the supposedly shocking news that Walker had (like Obama, like Reid) encouraged donors to give money to allied groups.

Mary Burke had a field day with all the revelations, running one campaign ad calling Mr. Walker's time in office "four years of political fistfights, criminal convictions, and secret donations." The new Milwaukee County executive, Chris Abele, unveiled another sixteen thousand e-mails—these from the first probe, when Walker had served in that seat. Abele had been in possession of those documents since May, but only got around to releasing them two weeks before the election.

Abele and his wife had each donated $10,000 to Mary Burke's candidacy. Abele's campaign handed over another $43,000 toward her effort. Abele had in past given more than a quarter of a million dollars to a union-connected nonprofit called the Greater Wisconsin Committee. And of course he'd donated to Chisholm.

Walker won reelection despite the smears, despite the coordinated Democratic effort to use the tools of the state against him. And yet even then—even then—prosecutors and GAB weren't ready to give up.

The election came and went, and the Wisconsin Supreme Court decided to take on the John Doe question. GAB looked at its court track record to date and decided to try to better stack the deck in its favor—by getting rid of judges who might not like its case.

~~~

Francis Schmitz was always an intriguing character in this drama. He's ostensibly a Republican, but one who allowed himself to be brought in to give cover to a Democratic campaign. He was technically appointed by a judge, though documents show that the prosecutors put forward his name and were quite insistent he got the position.

Maybe that had something to do with his views on finance laws. It turns out that prior to his appointment, Schmitz was on the GAB payroll as an investigator. O'Keefe's guess is that Schmitz, as a former federal attorney who worked terror cases, was one of those men who focused only on the dollars—not on the free-speech rights. "The prosecutors just threw a bunch of our stuff in front of him, and he looks and he sees all the money shuffling about, and it reminds him of how he used to track terror money. And so they tell him it's illegal and he just buys it—never stops to think that unions do it, that the law allows it," says O'Keefe.

Whatever his opening into the case, Schmitz became the public face of it. And he bought into, and built on, increasingly rough tactics. One was an extraordinary and early effort to target the state supreme court's justices, who are elected by the public to

ten-year terms. Prosecutors went searching for connections that
would force the conservative justices to have to recuse themselves
from the Doe case. One e-mail from the GAB's Falk to the district attorney's office in February 2013 noted that the Wisconsin
Club for Growth had run issue ads favorable to one of the conservative justices.

The strategy was to accuse the justice of a conflict, to force recusal. But note the timing: Schmitz had yet to even be appointed
or send out subpoenas. The Doe victims had yet to know they
were targets. Already, in the earliest days of this second Doe investigation, the GAB and prosecutors knew that their case was
legally problematic—so much so that they might have to kneecap
some Wisconsin Supreme Court justices to make it fly. E-mails
would later show that the GAB investigators even trolled through
the material they had subpoenaed from the *independent groups* to
try to find more details that would allow them to disqualify more
justices.

Collin Levy, a member of the *Wall Street Journal*'s editorial
board, who has written her fair share about the IRS, was struck
by how Wisconsin resembled that Washington scandal—only
with a twist. In her mind, it was a hyperconcentrated version.
"It was a smaller set of individuals, in a smaller political market. It was clear they'd watched and taken in all the liberal
points—dark money, disclosure, lists, the Kochs, conservative
conspiracies—and then had completely soaked it in, completely
absorbed it into their mentality. Then add that they had, in a
way not possible at the national level, complete and unfettered
freedom to do what they wanted. So they applied it, and the
level of poison was insane."

∿

The justices and the victims and the victims' lawyers wouldn't
find out until much later about these slimy efforts to rig the court

hearing. All they knew was that in February 2015, Schmitz filed a motion with the supreme court pushing judges to bow out. Schmitz wanted at least one, and as many as four, of the conservatives to step down on the grounds that they had benefited in their judicial races from issue ads from some of the groups now victims of the Doe.

Wisconsin's code of judicial conduct made for no such allowances. It clearly stated that recusal couldn't be "based solely on the sponsorship of an independent expenditure or issue advocacy communication." And that's the only type of support the conservative justices had ever received from the groups in question. Schmitz tried to argue that a separate, U.S. Supreme Court ruling ought to hold sway, but the circumstances were entirely different.

In July, it became clear why Schmitz had been so eager to knock off any free-speech court voices. In a definitive 4–2 decision on July 17, 2015, the state's highest court unceremoniously shut down the Doe, slapping the prosecutors six ways from Sunday. "It is utterly clear that the special prosecutor has employed theories of law that do not exist in order to investigate citizens who were wholly innocent of any wrongdoing," said the court, in an opinion written by Justice Michael Gableman. "In other words, the special prosecutor was the instigator of a 'perfect storm' of wrongs that was visited upon the innocent [targets] and those who dared to associate with them."

Walker was among the first to offer a reaction to the decision, and it caused some eye-rolling. He was already running for president, on a campaign stop in New Hampshire. He explained that he'd felt "all along" that the courts would rule on the right side. (There was no mention of his settlement talks.) "As folks in Wisconsin will tell, I've gone through these battles so many times I don't get too up or too down. I'm pretty even-keeled in all this."

But his state Republicans were energized, at last, and determined to finally do something to rein in both the John Doe statute and the renegade GAB. Some called for an investigation into the body. Some called for a reckoning for the prosecutors who had abused their powers.

Democrats denied that they'd done anything wrong, even as they rejected the decision. Schmitz's request for recusal had allowed the left to claim that the decision was partisan and biased. Common Cause moaned that a "highly compromised" court had just ruled for "unlimited money" in Wisconsin. Democratic legislators refused to acknowledge that the state's finance law was unconscionably vague and that prosecutors had used that to drive a Mack truck through constitutional rights. They instead insisted the court had rewritten the law—a position echoed by GAB. In a sour statement, it claimed that the court's decision "reverses a longstanding interpretation and application of campaign finance law."

The victims were exultant. O'Keefe's attorneys, Graves Garrett out of Kansas City, noted that Chisholm and the GAB had "violated about one third of our nation's Bill of Rights" with their raids and subpoenas and seizure of material and secrecy and muzzling. Some, like Wisconsin Manufacturers and Commerce, demanded an apology from the prosecutors and GAB regulators. They never got it.

All they did get from Schmitz was the crazy sight, a month later, of his refusal to accept that the court really meant what it said. In a motion in August, the prosecutor demanded a stay of the decision, pending a possible appeal to the U.S. Supreme Court. That appeal is a long shot, since the Wisconsin court decided the case on the basis of state law—an area the Supremes don't usually mess with.

Schmitz surely knew this, and that instantly made victims wonder what he was up to. The answer looked to rest in his accompanying request that the Wisconsin high court also stay its order that prosecutors destroy any evidence collected in the course of its subpoenas—bank records, e-mails, donor names. Schmitz and his team seem to want to hold on to those goods indefinitely. They had after all been very useful up to now.

∿

The John Doe got shut down, but not before the left accomplished many of its goals. It harassed and put in suspended animation most of Wisconsin's conservative movement during a crucial election period. It disclosed donors and pertinent information that could be used to attack and silence the right. It required its victims to spend, collectively, millions of dollars on legal defense—money diverted from advocacy. It subjected individuals to the terror of personal prosecution, wreaking havoc on their livelihoods, their families, their ability to sleep at night. It made them think twice about taking part in the electoral system. This is what intimidation is all about.

The outrage over the tactics, and public concern over government abuse, did at least give Republicans an opening to right a few wrongs. In October 2015, Walker signed a bill gutting the John Doe as a tool for political persecution. The new law outlaws John Doe investigations for allegations of political misconduct. Prosecutors can henceforth only use them for grave and specific lawbreaking—namely violent felonies and some drug crimes—and also must obtain permission from a majority of the state's chief judges to extend probes beyond six months. Secrecy orders now only apply to prosecutors, court officials, judges, and investigators. There are no more gags on suspects or witnesses.

Every Democrat in the Wisconsin Assembly and Senate voted against the measure. Which is another way of saying that Wisconsin liberals went on record in favor of gag orders, predawn raids, limitless warrants into e-mail, phone, and bank records, and the targeting of Americans for their ideology.

The legislature also steamed ahead on campaign finance reform and an overhaul of the GAB. The board's response to the reform only highlighted why it was necessary in the first place. New GAB chair Gerald Nichol accused the state high court of having a "problem with [its] integrity," claiming all four Republican justices should have recused themselves from the Doe case. The bureaucrat also slammed the court's ruling as a "very poorly written decision."

Rivkin echoes a point of Don McGahn's: Organizations like the FEC and GAB have their share of partisans. But what creates an environment that allows those partisans to act is a righteous regulatory mind-set. "People wonder what causes a place like GAB: politics or ideology?" he says. "But there's no tension between those two; there's synergy. You have the sheer institutional dynamics. You've got career people that honestly don't care about politics, but do believe everybody cheats and it's their job to make them follow the rules, and to bring even more people under their system of rules. You've also got self-interest and job security thrown in there.

"Then you've got people animated by their ideology, and the reality is that people who are drawn to work for government are disproportionately liberal and have that worldview. They hate money, they hate speech. They may not be partisans themselves, but they create a perfect environment for liberal partisans to do their own thing."

On December 16, 2015, Walker signed a law getting rid of GAB and replacing it with two commissions—one in charge of ethics, the other in charge of elections. The new bodies are evenly split between parties, and subject to new rules governing due process in complaint and investigation procedures. They are barred from secret investigations with unlimited budgets.

O'Keefe sees parallels with the IRS, and more evidence of the need for strict rules for bureaucracies. "Obama didn't call the IRS up and order it to do anything. He talked, and government employees heard it, and felt compelled to act. And that's what I've discovered here, too. Debate matters, and it formed opinions in the heads of these GAB people, and in the heads of midlevel law enforcement, and they ran with it."

~~~

Prosecutors are among the most powerful agents of government in this country. The Wisconsin district attorneys had a particularly scary law with which to target their enemies on the right. But prosecutors don't need a John Doe law to harass the conservative movement.

The latest officials to join this party have a broader aim. They are liberal state attorneys general, who aren't bothering to concoct some argument that conservatives broke the law or hoodwinked shareholders. They are instead imposing sweeping new disclosure requirements, on the simple grounds that that's what they want. Which they can do as prosecutors. They aren't even hiding what they are attempting to do.

The ringleaders are the attorneys general of two of the country's most liberal states: New York and California. The Empire State's new king of enforced disclosure is Eric Schneiderman, elected to that state's top law enforcement post in 2010. Schneiderman was on board with a thumping IRS campaign against conservative nonprofits. He launched his own inquiry into what the *New York Times* termed the "darkest corner of the campaign world"—nonprofits. By August 2012, Schneiderman had sent requests to dozens of tax-exempt groups demanding they turn over their tax returns and other financial documents. He aimed his probe at conservative organizations like Crossroads and the American Action Network and the American Future Fund, though he made sure to toss in a few liberal outfits to make it look kosher. "The requests appear to be an early but aggressive step by Mr. Schneiderman's office to curtail the intense secrecy enveloping these groups," wrote the *Times*.

The aggressive aspect of Schneiderman's probe was that he had no pretext—he wasn't making a case that the groups had broken regulations or violated state campaign finance laws. Under New York law, nonprofits that raise money in the state already have to file their federal tax returns and audit reports with the AG's office. This was an exercise in snooping—Schneiderman wanted his own list. And New York was a good place to put one together. Nonprofits are allowed to collect money from around the country, and New York, with its Wall Street millionaires, is a popular place from which to solicit. His letters requested the information, but menacingly reminded recipients that he had subpoena power.

In less than a year, Schneiderman had used his probe to finalize a new regulation requiring nonprofits registered in his state to include in their annual filings their federal IRS Schedule B—a list of names and addresses of their larger donors. Schneiderman based his rule on a reinterpretation of a 2006 New York law, and the claim that he was protecting the New York citizenry from being preyed upon by charities—an argument that had been knocked down in prior Supreme Court cases. The average New York hedge fund manager negotiating a donation to Crossroads is hardly confused about what is happening. Schneiderman also didn't bother to go through the usual process for a regulation, which would require public comment. He imposed it by fiat.

In his press release, the AG bragged that the "'Dark Money' Groups That Proliferated Since Citizens United Will Be Brought into the Light." "There is only one reason to funnel political spending through a 501(c)(4), and that is to hide who has bankrolled the effort," declared Schneiderman. The AG predicted that "New York will serve as a model for other states." And he proudly boasted that the "disclosures" would be available to "the public." He graciously suggested that if groups could demonstrate their donors might suffer harm, they could ask for a "waiver" from donor disclosure.

Schneiderman's announcement corresponded almost precisely with the Lerner revelations and a growing conservative awareness that they were under attack. By May 2014, Citizens United—the same group that had inspired the Supreme Court case—had sued Schneiderman in federal court, arguing his regulation infringed on the group's First Amendment rights, and that federal law protecting donor privacy trumped his interpretation. Citizens hired Don McGahn, now at the Jones Day law firm, to represent it. A few months later, the first federal judge to hear the case rejected Citizens' request for a preliminary injunction—but the trial is ongoing.

∿

It's getting a close watch by Kamala Harris, Schneiderman's counterpart in California. The Golden State AG is a Democratic up-and-comer, who is already running for retiring California senator Barbara Boxer's seat in 2016. Harris likes hot-button issues that keep her name in the headlines, and she's made one of them a takedown of conservative nonprofits.

In early 2014, those nonprofits started receiving letters from Harris's office. Nonprofits that operate in California are required to annually file their public IRS 990 tax forms with the AG. In keeping with protections under federal law, most groups file the report but scrub the Schedule B attachment that lists their larger contributor names and addresses. Harris's letter changed the rules of the game. She claimed that these groups' filings with the state were "incomplete" because they didn't include the full donor attachment. She gave them thirty days to cough up the form. Harris claimed that the names would only be subject to scrutiny from within her office, and would not be publicly released.

Brad Smith's organization, the Center for Competitive Politics (CCP), which has operated in the state since 2008, sued Harris's office, arguing that federal law protected those names. It ran through the roster of Supreme Court cases protecting anonymity—*NAACP v. Alabama* and the like. In December, the Americans for Prosperity Foundation filed its own suit, claiming that her demand violated its First Amendment rights and put its donors at risk of ugly retribution. The foundation noted that it had been registered in California since 2001 and had never been forced to give its donors before. Harris, "for reasons known only to her, is nonetheless trying to compel disclosure of the confidential Schedule B by nonprofits around the state," read the filing.

Harris's office issued a laughable response, claiming the law had always meant what she said, and that Americans for Prosperity had in fact been "out of compliance with the law for a number of years." The only reason no AG had ever done anything about the "backlog of delinquent charities" was that the department had been "chronically underfunded." They were now receiving "delayed enforcement notifications."

If Harris gets her way, groups like CCP won't just have to hand over their details about California donors; they will have to release the details of their donor network nationwide. And nobody thinks that information will ever stay secret. Leaks aside, California has sweeping sunshine laws. How long before Harris's liberal buddies petition the government to hand over the donor details? How likely is it that Harris would do anything to stop that process?

Rivkin believes the behind-the-scenes state coordination is vast, and worrisome. "It's like a hydra; you can try to cut off one head, and just get more," he says. And Harris is betting nobody will stop her. In addition to her AG powers, she has one other advantage: California. Even the federal judges in the state lean left, and the appeals court that oversees those judges, the Ninth Circuit, is infamous for its indulgence of liberal legal theories.

Sure enough, the first judge overseeing the CCP's case ruled for Harris, and in spring of 2015 a panel of Ninth Circuit appeals judges upheld that decision. The judges in both the CCP and

Americans for Prosperity cases have at least allowed the groups to keep their donor names to themselves until the legal question is solved.

In September 2015, fifty-eight organizations filed a friend-of-the-court brief to the U.S. Supreme Court, asking it to hear the CCP case. In November, the Supremes declined.

∿

The lawsuit against O'Keefe is done, but O'Keefe isn't done with his lawsuit. He's continuing with his own litigation against the GAB, prying out documents, so that the public can see just how this travesty came to be. In October 2015, a new editorial in the *Wall Street Journal* revealed that Wisconsin investigators trawled through the files they'd taken from Wisconsin targets and put together a spreadsheet dossier that included the names and e-mail addresses of national conservatives—Jeb Bush, House Speaker Paul Ryan, RNC chairman Reince Priebus, former House Speaker Newt Gingrich, *Wall Street Journal* contributor Karl Rove. Documents also show that investigators used "search words" to attempt to turn up damning information—including "big union bosses" and "big government." This is exactly what the IRS did to isolate and then smear conservative groups.

One other revelation in the GAB litigation is noteworthy: The agency's staff ran a lot of their John Doe communication through Gmail accounts. Which raises the question of whether O'Keefe will ever obtain all their correspondence. The prosecutors went directly to O'Keefe's ISPs to sweep up all his e-mail. Yet they appear to have gone to great lengths to try to hide their own from the public. And unlike Wisconsin prosecutors, O'Keefe doesn't have warrant power.

On October 3, 2015—two years to the day after receiving his subpoena—O'Keefe and his wife held a party on a Wisconsin lake, hosting more than ninety people, many of whom had been subject to the prosecutorial abuse. "The idea," he says, "was to re-define that day, October 3. To redefine the memory, away from being victims." Guests spoke about their experiences and cele-brated their victories. "It was a happy evening," says O'Keefe.

Litigation discovery aside, O'Keefe has learned a few bigger things over the past three years. He's realized that the free-speech movement has a new job, to clean up fuzzy campaign finance laws. "If we are going to live with rules about speech, they have to be clear," he says. "Because that's how they went after us in Wis-consin. They used the looseness in the law to subjectively attack. That's a dangerous situation for citizens."

He's learned something about the left. "This is a party that used to embrace freedom. But they've now abandoned the principles of Thomas Jefferson and adopted the tactics of Joseph Stalin," he says. And he notes that those tactics are aimed even at fellow Democrats who don't fall in line. "I talk to Democrats at the state capitol. A lot of them, they didn't like these raids, or the sweep-ing warrants. But they are afraid of their own side, of getting ostracized or attacked themselves. And so when the legislature moves to reform the Doe law, something that everybody under-stands is good for the cause of liberty, every one of them votes against it."

He's also learned that the country is at a tipping point. "What the Founders understood is that you can't have tyranny in a coun-try if you have free speech," he says. "So ask yourself: Why does the left want to get rid of free speech?"

CHAPTER 21

The President Has a List

FRANK VANDERSLOOT woke up on April 21, 2012, from both a nightmare and a dream.

The nightmare had started the day before. VanderSloot, then sixty-three, arrived at work at 7:30, just like he did every day of the week. The morning was as usual, right up until one of VanderSloot's employees came in with some odd news. A blog post had just gone up, and it contained an ugly smear against the boss. This wasn't in itself a surprise; VanderSloot had in recent months received some negative attention. The surprise was who had delivered the latest broadside. It had come from the most powerful man on the planet: Barack Obama.

It was an election year, and Obama was already going in heavy against the presumptive Republican nominee, Mitt Romney. The president's reelection campaign erected a website, called "Keeping GOP Honest," and had been using it to "truth check" Republican statements. But on that April 20, it broke new territory. In a post entitled "Behind the curtain: a brief history of Romney's donors," the president's team publicly named eight private citizens who had given money to the Republican, accusing them all of being "wealthy individuals with less-than-reputable records."

The site bluntly claimed that all eight men were "betting against America." They were then each singled out, subjected to slurs and allegations. Investors Paul Schorr and Sam and Jeffrey Fox were attacked for having "outsourced" jobs. T. Martin Fiorentino was demeaned for his work for a firm that forecloses on homes. Louis Bacon (a hedge fund manager), Kent Burton (a "lobbyist"), and Thomas O'Malley (an energy CEO) were denigrated as oil profiteers. Most astonishing, the site outright accused "quite a few" of the men as having been "on the wrong side of the law" and succeeding at "the expense of so many Americans."

Nixon's private "enemies list" was bad. Barack Obama's public "enemies list" was arguably worse. Obama had used 2010 to alert and sic the IRS on Tea Party groups. But by calling out private citizens by name on his website, he was alerting and siccing every part of his government on Republican donors. The message from the man who controls the Justice Department (which can indict people), the SEC (which can fine people), and the IRS (which can audit people) was clear: Donate money to Romney, and you are fair government game. The posting was also an APB to every liberal group and activist in the country to target those donors.

VanderSloot had for twenty-six years run a successful wellness-products company called Melaleuca out of Idaho Falls. He'd been involved in Idaho politics, but had only recently gained an interest in the national scene. He'd met Romney in the mid-2000s, when the former governor spoke at an Idaho Republican convention, and VanderSloot liked him. So when the presidential aspirant later reached out to the Idaho businessman for help with his 2008 campaign in the Gem State, VanderSloot agreed and gave money to a Romney group. He signed up for the second run, too, and in August 2011 made a $1 million donation to a Romney super PAC. Such political organizations must disclose their donors. Obama's team clearly lifted the eight men out of those public files.

VanderSloot made the Obama list. And the entry against him was particularly vile. It accused the CEO of being "litigious, combative and a bitter foe of the gay rights movement." The other donors were merely slammed as profiteers. VanderSloot was accused of being a profiteer, a bully, and a gay basher. Obama had only a few months earlier given a national address, in the wake of the shooting of Representative Gabby Giffords, on the need for more "civility" in politics.

Melaleuca is a company that depends heavily on its good reputation. It sells nutrition and cleaning and personal care products that are marketed as having natural ingredients and being environmentally friendly. Hundreds of thousands of customers order direct from the company, and Melaleuca encourages those orders by paying commissions to home-based operators who refer the products. (Melaleuca is neither a pyramid scheme nor a multi-level marketer, contrary to liberal spin.) Those thousands upon thousands of operators and customers had just been told Melaleuca's owner was an intolerant thug.

"And we just got hit. Just blasted," VanderSloot remembers. "The phones are ringing off the hook in the office, customers calling, so angry, canceling orders. And I was having to answer questions inside our own office, too, from my people saying, 'Look what you've done.'"

VanderSloot spent a feverish day trying to put out the fires. He was so overwhelmed by the blowback that by the end of the day he'd called his staff together and abjectly apologized for getting involved in the election. "I ate a whole humble pie," he says. "I said, 'I'm really sorry I've done this to us, to our company, to all of you—to bring this much pain to everybody and to cause all this ruckus, and I'm just . . . sorry.'"

The dream came that night, after VanderSloot had ended that harrowing day. "At least I think it was a dream," he says. "I just remember waking up, and very clear in my mind was the Declaration of Independence, and those guys who signed. I'd been feeling guilty for the pain to my family, but then I got to thinking.

"Those guys didn't sign on the spur of the moment. They went home, and they told their wives, 'I'm gonna sign this thing, honey.' And their wives said, 'Don't you dare! They'll come after us; they'll deem us traitors; they'll kill us.' And these guys heard their family out, and then they signed anyway.

"Because this is America. That was my thought, laying in bed: This is America. And whatever might happen to me is nothing compared to those guys. So I'm not going to run and cower. I'm going to stand up for what I believe in."

It was a good thing VanderSloot woke up with that resolve. Because things were about to get a whole lot worse.

ᴧᴧ

Frank VanderSloot was born in Billings, Montana, but grew up in the Idaho Panhandle. His dad worked hard as a railroad man and small-time rancher, though he never earned much. VanderSloot isn't sorry about that upbringing or the values it instilled, and he has an abiding love for the idea of the little guy. His dad was a little guy, and so are thousands of his home-based operators. He still sees himself as one, despite his financial success.

VanderSloot is not too tall. He has neatly clipped white hair, a round face, and an easy smile. He has a soft voice, which is often heard emitting old-fashioned phrases like "golly" and "darn it." We've talked numerous times since he was targeted, and I've never once heard him brag, or raise his voice, or even use a bad word against someone. He's a straight-arrow type.

His employees love him. They like to talk about how he really believes in his company, and how he champions lots of "little guys." The *Idaho Statesman* in 2011 told the story of Debra Lish, who at the time made about $150,000 a year marketing for Melaleuca, and who won a contest for a trip to Las Vegas. She was allowed to take a spouse, but as she wasn't married, she asked to take a friend. A Melaleuca executive said no, so Lish chose not to go. She later told VanderSloot. "This will be changed as soon as we're off the phone," he told her. He paid for her, her two daughters, and her mother to go to Las Vegas. There are a lot of stories like this about VanderSloot.

That being said, he's hardly a pushover. The same *Statesman* story recounted how VanderSloot once took away his daughter's car. He'd told her she needed a 3.0 in her first semester of college to keep it. She got a 2.98. "VanderSloot doesn't round up," reported the newspaper. He doesn't round up in business, either, which is how he got a reputation for being "litigious." Melaleuca's entire business model rests on proprietary products and marketing, and the company is serious about enforcing nonsolicitation and separation agreements with its marketers and executives. It also goes after libelers, to protect its reputation. VanderSloot makes no apology for any of this, believing this zero-tolerance approach—through the courts, if necessary—is fundamental to protecting his workforce.

VanderSloot became a Mormon when he was sixteen, and graduated from Brigham Young University. He paid for college in part by working and living in a laundromat. Post-degree he spent a decade at Automatic Data Processing and then a few more years at Cox Communications. In 1985, he left to help a brother-in-law start a business. It was a bust, and six months later VanderSloot built Melaleuca out of its ashes. Today, it has more than 1.2 million customers each month, and 200,000 "independent marketing executives." VanderSloot calculates that over the years the company has paid out $4.2 billion to those home-based marketers. It sells 450 products across a network that spans 16 countries and pulls in $1.3 billion a year. It's a big employer in Idaho Falls, with some 2,000 workers.

VanderSloot is today, by self-description, a "young sixty-seven." He loves the West, and he and his wife live on a working ranch outside of Idaho Falls that runs 5,000 head of cattle. He has six children and his wife has eight, and the number of grandchildren may soon outnumber the cattle. He still goes to work every day at his office in Idaho Falls, and still puts in eleven hours.

∿

VanderSloot can't peg exactly when he got interested in politics, but he remembers he was inspired to it by a desire to defend free enterprise. "It's what made this country great—the ability to go and build businesses and create jobs. It's what made America the most prosperous nation in history. That's the paradigm I've always thought we have to protect if we want to keep America great," he says.

VanderSloot got active early on with the U.S. Chamber of Commerce, and by 2004 was on its executive board. Chamber CEO Tom Donohue tried recruiting him as chairman of the group. The Idahoan declined, telling Donohue he needed to remain committed to his business and employees.

He remembers meeting Romney around 2006, which is also about the time he got active in Idaho politics. VanderSloot over the years has backed conservative candidates in state judicial elections, backed state ballot initiatives for school reform, and supported Republicans for Idaho's attorney general and governor's slots. But what ended up getting him slammed on Obama's list was his even earlier involvement in the state's fight over traditional marriage.

VanderSloot's position on that issue was neither outrageous nor even uncommon. This was the 1990s, when the vast majority of America was still opposed to gay marriage, and far less comfortable with gay issues than it is today. In 1999, VanderSloot discovered that PBS was intending to air a program called *It's Elementary* about how schools dealt with homosexuality in the classroom, and that suggested addressing the issue with even first and second graders. PBS intended to air the program in Idaho at peak kid watching hours. VanderSloot objected, and he was hardly alone. The documentary provoked a debate across the country, and dozens of public TV stations refused to air it. VanderSloot in particular opposed using public tax dollars to air a show at prime kid time that promoted concepts many parents might disagree with. He helped fund billboards asking, "Should public television promote the homosexual lifestyle to your children? Think about it." His main goal was to get PBS to broadcast the show at a later, adult viewing time. Which is exactly what ended up happening. It aired in Idaho, just at a different time.

A year later, he donated money to a PAC that opposed the re-election of a liberal state supreme court justice, and that warned that the justice might use her power to impose gay marriage on the state. And in 2006 he ran full-page newspaper ads asking critical questions about a newspaper series by local journalist Peter Zuckerman. The series focused on several pedophiles who had been exposed in local Boy Scout troops. The articles implicated the Mormon church and Scout leaders, serious charges that VanderSloot felt lacked evidence. The ads questioned some of the facts, but also responded to some of the community's speculation that Zuckerman's sexual orientation (he is gay) may have prompted him to attack the Scouts and the Latter-day Saints. The ad defended him against the charge, saying it would be "very unfair" to "conclude that is what is behind Zuckerman's motive."

Zuckerman and the left would later claim that VanderSloot had "outed" the reporter. This is untrue. Zuckerman had previously written openly about being gay. And the ad's mention of speculation was in reference to a radio show that had spent at least twelve hours of airtime accusing Zuckerman of bias because of his sexual orientation. The advertisement, if anything, was defending him against that allegation. Zuckerman would later under oath admit that many of the accusations he had in turn leveled against VanderSloot (including the charge that the ads had caused his boyfriend to be fired) weren't true.

While this provoked some local debate (which is, after all, the point of free speech), it didn't cause drama. VanderSloot carried on with his life, and in August 2011 made his donation to the Romney super PAC. In January 2012, that money became public under disclosure laws. And the left, now in full intimidation swing, started a brutal campaign.

∿

Suddenly, VanderSloot was the focus of every left-wing journalist in America, who went back to those episodes to smear the Romney donor. In early February, the liberal *Mother Jones* posted an article under the headline "Pyramid-Like Company Ponies Up $1 Million for Mitt Romney." It railed that the donation was what *Citizens United* had wrought. It bashed Melaleuca's business model, and trashed VanderSloot on the gay issue.

The then and now infamous Glenn Greenwald subsequently wrote a hit piece in *Salon*, in which he variously talked about "Melaleuca's get-rich pitches" and derided VanderSloot as "bullying," "a litigious billionaire," and guilty of "virulent anti-gay activism." MSNBC's Rachel Maddow went on air to repeat Greenwald's claims. In March, the Human Rights Campaign started its own online "action," calling on supporters to sign a letter demanding that Romney fire VanderSloot from his finance committee. They labeled VanderSloot "viciously anti-LGBT." Bloggers started harassing his children, stalking their social media accounts.

VanderSloot was stunned, and attempted to set things straight. He put out a long statement in February addressing many of the claims about his business and the history of the newspaper series. He publicly stated that he had "many gay friends whom I love and respect. And I believe they love and respect me. I am very close to some of these very good people. Our company has thousands of gay customers, independent marketing executives and employees. I believe they feel welcomed and valued. I believe that people deserve freedom, respect, and privacy in their own lives." He added, "At the same time, I believe there are both appropriate and inappropriate ways to address the concerns of the gay community," and listed his opposition to using public tax dollars to air the PBS documentary at a "time when it would attract the most children."

VanderSloot flew to San Francisco to meet with the editor of

Mother Jones and the reporter who wrote the piece. He wanted them to understand what had really happened. They refused to retract the attacks on his and his company's reputation. VanderSloot ultimately decided to litigate.

One of VanderSloot's gay friends meanwhile set up a meeting between the CEO and the Human Rights Campaign, so that he could mend fences. He and that friend flew to New York and spent a long time explaining to the HRC that while he'd taken a position on gay marriage, he'd never taken one against gay people. The HRC never retracted its comments, but it did let its online action die off.

VanderSloot meanwhile spent a lot of time back in Idaho Falls on conference calls, reassuring employees and customers. "We lost business at that time," he says. "It was tough. But we were putting a lot of time into it, and we were able to manage it."

On April 20, Barack Obama's campaign swept up every innuendo, insult, stain, and insinuation against VanderSloot and threw it up on the website.

That proved far less manageable.

∿

I was on the phone with a source a few days after the Obama post came out. He was complaining about the audacity of the president, and randomly mentioned the website, and that Obama had taken to smearing private donors. I hadn't seen it, but I went to look.

A few liberal bloggers were busy recirculating the smears. But while there was no question that the mainstream media was monitoring Obama websites, nobody had really written about the post. Few in the press corps seemed remotely bothered that the leader of the free world had named names.

I wrote a column called "The President Has a List." It went through the blog entry, and the president's history of smearing other political "enemies." It pointed out that, unlike senators or congressmen, presidents alone represent all Americans. Their powers—to jail, to fine, to bankrupt—are so vast as to require restraint. It noted that any president who targets a private citizen for his politics is de facto engaged in government intimidation and threats—which is why presidents since Nixon had carefully avoided the practice.

It also noted that while the men listed were wealthy individuals, they were private citizens nonetheless. Not one held elected office. Not one was a criminal. Not one had the barest fraction of the power of the president who was attacking them. And I quoted Ted Olson, the former solicitor general. "We don't tolerate presidents or people of high power to do these things. When you have the power of the presidency—the power of the IRS, the INS, the Justice Department, the DEA, the SEC—what you have effectively done is put these guys' names up on 'Wanted' posters in government offices."

The article noted that the men's only real crime, as the site tacitly acknowledged, was that they'd had the presumption to give money to Mr. Obama's opponent. The White House had spent two years claiming it was simply interested in outing dark money. But these donors had acknowledged their giving, and here was an example of what Obama was really after—names, for retribution. And the campaign's argument that its website was about holding "the eventual Republican nominee accountable" was silly. What did VanderSloot's billboard of fifteen years earlier have to do with Romney? To this day it remains the most-read column I've ever written—a testament to Americans' abiding interest in free speech.

A few weeks later, I got a call from Frank VanderSloot. I recognized the name from the blog post. By this point, the CEO was a bit media shy. He'd been through the liberal wringer, and he was nervous on the phone. I didn't blame him. He'd seen my piece and was hopeful I was open-minded. Because he had a tale to tell—about what had followed the president's blog post. It turns out that when the president singles you out, bad things really do happen.

Twelve days after VanderSloot ended up on the list, he got a tip from someone he knows in Idaho Falls. A man named Michael Wolf had just contacted the Bonneville County Court in that city, in search of court records about VanderSloot. Specifically, Wolf wanted all the documents dealing with VanderSloot's divorce records, as well as a case involving a dispute with a former Melaleuca employee.

Wolf sent a fax to the clerk's office—which I obtained—listing four cases he was after. He would later send a second fax, asking for three further court cases dealing with either Melaleuca or VanderSloot. He listed only his name and a private cell phone number.

This is what VanderSloot told me. When I started reporting, I found out that Wolf until a few months prior had been a lawyer on the Democratic side of the Senate Permanent Subcommittee on Investigations. But he'd found new, shadier work. The ID written out at the top of his faxes identified them as coming from "Glenn Simpson." That's the name of a former *Wall Street Journal* reporter who in 2009 founded a D.C. company that performs private investigative work.

The website for that company, Fusion GPS, describes itself as providing "strategic intelligence," with expertise in areas like "politics." That's a polite way of saying "opposition research."

When I called Fusion's main number and asked to speak to Michael Wolf, a man said Wolf wasn't in the office that day but he'd be back the next week. When I reached Wolf on his private cell, he confirmed that he had until recently worked at the Senate.

When I asked what his interest was in VanderSloot's divorce records, he hesitated, then said he didn't want to talk about that. When I asked what his relationship was with Fusion, he hesitated again and said he had "no comment." "It's a legal thing," he added.

Fusion dodged my calls, so I never was able to ask who was paying it to troll through VanderSloot's divorce records. As my column on this was about to go live, Simpson finally sent an e-mail stating, "Frank VanderSloot is a figure of interest in the debate over civil rights for gay Americans. As his own record on gay issues amply demonstrates, he is a legitimate subject of public records research into his lengthy history of legal disputes."

A look through Federal Election Commission records did not show any payments to Fusion or Wolf from political players, such as the Democratic National Committee, the Obama campaign, or liberal super PACs. Then again, when political groups want to hire researchers, it is not uncommon to hire a less controversial third party, which then hires the researchers. VanderSloot would later do some of his own research, but couldn't find out who Simpson's client was. It isn't too hard to guess.

Fusion, interestingly, surfaced again in 2015. It turned out to be the creator of a "forensic report"—commissioned by Planned Parenthood—that sought to claim that videos showing the group discussing the harvesting of fetal organs were "manipulated." Planned Parenthood never mentioned that Simpson's Fusion GPS is a for-hire hit group.

The column about VanderSloot's travails caused quite a stir, and he ended up going on a lot of TV shows. One was Bill O'Reilly's Fox News show. On the show, the CEO worried out loud about who was "supposed to receive the message? Is it only the liberal press that's supposed to go after these folks? Or is it also the agencies that he runs . . . that he's in charge of and who report to him and want to please him? The FTC, the FDA, the USDA?"

Turns out that was a very legitimate worry. In a letter dated June 21, he'd been informed that his tax records had been "selected for examination" by the Internal Revenue Service. The audit also encompassed VanderSloot's wife, and not one but two years of past filings (2008 and 2009).

VanderSloot had been working since his teens, and neither he nor his accountants could recall his ever being subject to a federal tax audit before. He was once required to send documents on a line item inquiry into his charitable donations, which resulted in no changes to his taxes. But nothing more—that is, until after he'd written a big check to a Romney-supporting super PAC.

Two weeks after receiving the IRS letter, VanderSloot received another, this one from the Department of Labor. He was informed it would be doing an audit of workers he employed on his cattle ranch under the federal visa program for temporary agriculture workers.

The H-2A program allows tens of thousands of temporary workers in the United States; VanderSloot employed precisely three. All are from Mexico and have worked on the VanderSloot ranch—which employs about twenty people—for five years. Two are brothers. Mr. VanderSloot had never been audited for this, though two years prior his workers' ranch homes were inspected. (The cattle ranch was fined $8,400, mainly for too many "flies" and for "grease build-up" on the stove.)

This letter requested an array of documents to ascertain whether VanderSloot's "foreign workers are provided the full scope of protections" under the visa program: information on the hours they'd worked each day and their rate of pay, an explanation of their deductions, copies of contracts. And on and on.

In September, the IRS informed him of a second audit, of one of his businesses. The CEO, never audited before, had suddenly been subjected to three in the four months after Mr. Obama teed him up for such scrutiny. And he was audited by the Labor Department again. The last of his IRS audits didn't conclude until May 2013. Not one resulted in a fine or penalty. But VanderSloot had by then been waiting more than twenty months for a sizable refund. And his legal bills came in at around $80,000. That figure didn't account for what the president's vilification had done to his business and reputation.

It's a testament to VanderSloot's integrity that there was yet more that he never told me about. When I called him in October 2015 to do a follow-up interview for this book, he acknowledged he'd also been subject to an audit by the Food and Drug Administration. When I asked why he'd left that out, he simply said, "Well. You know. The FDA does these audits from time to time. And I just didn't think it was fair for me to say it was deliberate. Maybe it would have happened regardless of everything else."

VanderSloot had known all the way back when the post came out that what Obama had done was like "taping a target on my back." And, again, Obama hadn't had to pick up the phone to order an attack. All he'd had to do was put out the web post. Moreover, he'd left a man with no recourse. To what authority was VanderSloot to appeal if he believed this was politically motivated? The Obama Justice Department? The same Justice Department that by that time was running its Lerner non-investigation?

Here's the truly sad part of the VanderSloot story. He was largely alone. The Obama website listed eight donors. After VanderSloot got in touch, I tried calling all seven others. One, investor and conservationist Louis Bacon, called me back with a quote for a column: "It is un-American and irresponsible for a president to target individual, law-abiding citizens for political retribution, and it is inconceivable that any U.S. agency would stoop to do the bidding for this campaign's silliness."

The others either didn't return calls, or didn't want to go on the record. And VanderSloot's experience was the same. Following his targeting, he reached out to the other seven as well, with an idea. He suggested they go public, make a campaign of it, with T-shirts and numbers. "I'm No. 227 on the Enemies List, I'm No. 228—that sort of thing," he says. Four were open to the idea, and were willing even to get a picture taken together. The other four went underground. "We don't want to talk, this has been horrible on my life and family and my business, so please, no more," they told VanderSloot.

He didn't blame them. "It isn't much different than the Middle

Ages, really," he says. "They had the stocks, or a beheading. It's done in public. They put you out there, so that everyone can see what happens when you do something they don't like. The public watches and they think, 'Well, he did X, and I'm never going to do X—because look at that. They still do this in third-world countries. And I guess we do it here."

Public humiliation only works if you let it. VanderSloot had his dream. And from that moment, he didn't waver. He called me. He went on O'Reilly. While he was on that show—even before all the audits and abuse—he publicly announced that he was writing a check for another $100,000 to the Romney campaign. That was his response to the intimidation.

VanderSloot went on a slew of other TV and radio shows— Greta Van Susteren, Neil Cavuto, Megyn Kelly, Rush Limbaugh, Glenn Beck—to tell his story. And the phones went wild again. Americans were appalled by his tale, and they wanted to show support. "'What does Melaleuca sell? We want to buy some,'" was the new message, VanderSloot remembers. The episode sparked a tremendous resurgence in Melaleuca's sales, a boom that hasn't let up. The company's revenues have increased by $400 million annually. And 2015 was its best year ever. VanderSloot sees it as more inspiring evidence that it is always worth speaking out.

He's now embraced a national role. Obama didn't shut him out of politics; he created a new national player. He's fully committed in 2016, with money and support. In the Republican primary election season of 2015, he had national candidates flying out to see him to try to get his blessing. "We've been getting three or four media calls every week—asking, 'Who are you supporting, who are you going to back?'" says VanderSloot. "Because we will back someone."

He finishes, "My bottom line is this. I decided I could not run and cower from this, that I'd be setting a bad example. And I feel my voice—for whatever that voice is worth—is maybe worth a little bit more. Because I didn't run away."

CHAPTER 22

A Koch and a Smile

MARK HOLDEN has one of the coolest yet hardest jobs in the world. It's cool, because he's general counsel for Koch Industries, one of the biggest companies in the country. Koch does manufacturing, refining, ranching, fertilizers, paper, finance, and things you didn't even know existed. It has more than one hundred thousand employees worldwide, and brings in more than $100 billion a year. Holden is the top lawyer for all that. Which is pretty cool.

It's hard, because Holden works for Charles and David Koch. And Charles and David Koch have over the past five years been turned by the left into the most publicly reviled people in America, possibly the world. Dealing with that—which is one of Holden's jobs—is a pain in the ass. And hard.

Five years ago, most people had never heard the name Koch. If they had, they assumed it was something you bought at McDonald's, with a smile. Koch is big, but it is also a private company, and it is based in Wichita, and its core businesses aren't the sort of stuff the average consumer interacts with. Five years ago, Koch was pretty much as big as it is today. Five years ago, the Koch brothers were well into a lifetime of putting money into politics. Nobody had made that an issue up to then. So what changed?

Citizens United, of course. Holden traces a more precise beginning to that Jane Mayer article in the *New Yorker* in August 2010, the one she titled "Covert Operations," the one in which she managed to pound out ten thousand words about an organization she claimed nobody knew a single thing about. The left loves to label things "secret." It sounds really shady. And it uses the word "secret" a lot when describing the Kochs.

The Kochs aren't secret at all—or at least no more than most Americans. Charles and David Koch are some of the biggest philanthropists in the country; they individually and through their business underwrite universities, cancer research centers, arts centers. Their corporate structure is known, and subject to the same regulation as any other firm. David Koch once ran for the presidency, and a lot is known about the brothers' free-market political philosophy and the organizations they run. There is a nonprofit group called Freedom Partners, which is structured like a trade association. They started Americans for Prosperity, a 501(c)(4) that maintains a grassroots network with 2.3 million average Americans as members. There is KochPAC, which is the official political action committee for Koch Industries. And others.

The Kochs just aren't easy to attack in the usual ways. Post–*Citizens United*, the left wanted to take down and intimidate anyone supporting Republicans or challenging the establishment, be they conservative or liberal. But the Kochs are tough. Their business is private—not subject to shareholder proxies. And it is hard to boycott. Charles and David Koch also choose to put some money into think tanks and nonprofits that have a greater degree of protection from disclosure. It also happens that those organizations are very effective. All this drives the left nuts.

As a result, its attack on the Kochs represented a bit of a twist. Mayer and crew knew that the two brothers, who are as stalwart as they come, would never give in to intimidation. So the Koch attack had other aims. One was to use the Kochs—as the left was doing with the Chamber of Commerce—as an example of the supposed evils of *Citizens United* and "dark money," and to further their calls for disclosure. Another was to delegitimize the Kochs and any political work they did. Yet another was to throw up roadblocks—to slow down Koch work with harassing FOIA requests and IRS complaints. A final one was to make an example of the brothers, and make other donors fear they might face the same public defamation.

Holden thinks the first real hit came via Lee Fang, the same *ThinkProgress* employee who had made the spurious claim that the chamber was funded with foreign money. In a December 2009 piece in the *Boston Globe*, Fang recounted a Tea Party demonstration against Obamacare, noting that "few of the protestors were aware that a right-wing billionaire had paid" for the event, via its highly successful organization, Americans for Prosperity. The piece offered a misleading potted history of the Koch family fortune, but its key point was this: The Kochs' "hidden presence in the health care debate illustrates the extent to which the Old Right is creating—and then hiding behind—the grassroots fervor of middle-class opponents of health reform."

"That was their first argument," recalls Holden. "That the grassroots wasn't 'real,' that it was 'astroturf,' that citizens were being controlled by powerful forces. Because, gee, what average person would be upset by the greatest collapse of the economy since the Great Depression? Why would anybody be upset about universal health care, or bailing out banks and automakers, or all that spending? Why would they care? Obviously, somebody had to be controlling their minds." (Holden can be a really sarcastic guy.)

The article also happened to be wrong. AFP, a 501(c)(4), is the ultimate grassroots organization. It has chapters in thirty-six states, and as of 2015 it had millions of members and volunteers. A lot of them give their time to the organization—attending rallies, pushing for legislative reforms, signing up new voters, getting out the vote. But a lot of them also give money, and that's a big source of the group's finances. Wealthier Americans also give, but the heart and soul of the group is a mass of ordinary impassioned Americans.

Holden found the piece ridiculous, and didn't worry too much. But the Mayer article, which ran in August 2010, was a wake-up call. The entire corporate team understood that the left was getting ready to paint the company as *Citizens United* gone wrong, and a menacing force in American politics.

That's one reason why Holden today finds himself spending a lot of time setting the record straight. The fifty-two-year-old grew up in Worcester, and still has a sharp Massachusetts accent. He's been general counsel of Koch Industries since 2004, but as the attacks grew he stepped up his involvement with the corporate defense team—working with the company's public affairs and communications teams. The tall, angular Irish Catholic is perfectly suited for the job. He gets the politics. He gets the law. He's sharp, quick, and aggressive. But mostly, he knows better than to wind himself into an angry pretzel over every attack. He has a sort of wry, sarcastic, even humorous approach to a lot of what goes on. And that's good for the Koch enterprise. Holden is a very normal and human kind of guy. (The mainstream media is constantly surprised that people who work for the Kochs are normal and human.)

At almost precisely the moment the Mayer article hit, Obama began his "shadowy group" stump speeches. The president often talked in generalities about conservative front groups, but he made an exception for the Kochs. He called their flagship group out by name. He did it for the first time on August 9, 2010, when he called groups with "harmless-sounding names like Americans for Prosperity," and suggested it might be a "foreign-controlled corporation." It was disingenuous to suggest that AFP was funded by foreign money (which is illegal). It was more disingenuous given that Obama knew it was backed by the Kochs. Which is why he was saying its name in the first place.

Because the administration was obsessed with the Kochs, as

became clear in an incident at the end of August. White House economist Austan Goolsbee was providing a background briefing to reporters on tax policy—specifically reform of the corporate tax code and the White House's complaints about tax avoidance. Goolsbee in the course of it almost casually claimed that Koch Industries didn't pay any taxes. "So in this country we have...a series of entities that do not pay corporate income tax. Some of which are really giant firms, you know Koch Industries is a multibillion-dollar business." Out of the millions of companies in the United States to use as an example, Goolsbee had chosen one that most people have never heard of. And coincidence or not, it was the same day that Maryland representative Chris Van Hollen (still smarting from his DISCLOSE Act defeat) filed a complaint with the Federal Election Commission against AFP, challenging its status as a nonprofit.

The scandal wasn't so much that Goolsbee had chosen Koch; it was how he'd have known to choose it. Koch is a private company. Its taxes are confidential. Goolsbee and other White House officials are barred by law from looking at confidential taxpayer information. (It's also a felony to release confidential taxpayer information.) Either Goolsbee had illegally accessed information, or he had made the accusation up. Neither of which is good behavior by a senior official in the U.S. government.

No one in the press reported on the reference. But in the days that followed, Holden and the company heard from several sources about the mention. One participant had taken careful notes. The *Weekly Standard* revealed the Goolsbee reference on September 20, and it caused an instant controversy.

The White House's first response was to have an anonymous official provide *Politico* with a series of justifications for how it had Koch information. It started off with a slippery statement: "No senior administration officials have any access to anyone's tax returns." (Did a junior one?) The anonymous official went on to say the information had come from public testimony to the

President's Economic Recovery Advisory Board (PERAB) (which Goolsbee had directed) as well as publicly available websites, including *Forbes* and the Koch Industries site. Holden instantly threw up a red flag, noting that there was no information about Koch's taxes on its or *Forbes*'s websites. There was also nothing in the PERAB testimony about the company's tax status. "My primary concern is, Why does our name keep coming up, why do they single us out?" he told the *Weekly Standard*.

California Republican representative Devin Nunes sent a letter to the House Ways and Means Committee asking for it to probe whether the White House had misused tax information. And Iowa Republican senator Chuck Grassley went straight to J. Russell George, the Treasury inspector general, asking for an investigation. George agreed to start one. The White House then tried a new way to calm the storm, this time saying that Goolsbee had been "mistaken." It promised not to use the example again.

The story got even weirder three years later when, in the wake of the IRS revelations, the press began to look at Goolsbee's comment with fresh eyes. The IRS had been helping out the president with conservative groups; had it been giving the White House information on companies too? Goolsbee on May 14—just a few days after the Lerner revelations—posted a bizarre tweet, in which he said "there was no secret info on koch bros." and went on to claim he'd got the information from a news article. But, as Goolsbee later admitted, the article was from 2003, and it was about an entirely different Koch brother (there are four of them), and about how he didn't pay corporate taxes in the state of Florida. A few days after that, Goolsbee deleted the tweet.

Thanks to continued administration obstruction, we still don't know whether the White House accessed confidential information. In October 2011, more than a year after the event, TIGTA sent a letter to Grassley saying his investigation was complete. He also added that Grassley couldn't see it. Why? Because the report was about confidential taxpayer information, and that meant it was confidential, even for congressional overseers. Amazingly, the White House was getting to hide behind the very law it was accused of breaking.

The government wouldn't even release the information to the Kochs, even though it was their confidential taxpayer information at issue. Holden was hopeful for a while. A TIGTA agent had alerted him when the report was finished, and advised him that he could file a Freedom of Information Act request to obtain it. Holden did, and was denied by both Treasury and the IRS. The IRS told him to submit again. He did. Denied again. Holden had plenty else to be getting on with at the end of 2011, so he dropped the issue.

But an outside organization known as Cause of Action didn't. At first it filed a FOIA asking about any White House requests for information from the IRS. After it got the runaround, it filed a FOIA lawsuit in fall of 2012 requesting documents showing "any communication by or from anyone in the Executive Office of the President constituting requests for taxpayer or return information." Astonishingly, the IRS refused, again claiming that it did not have to turn over potentially illegal communication, because that potentially illegal communication dealt with "confidential" taxpayer information.

Even an Obama-appointed judge found this ludicrous. In August 2015, federal judge Amy Berman Jackson ordered the IRS to hand over any White House requests for taxpayer information. She wrote, "The Court is unwilling to stretch the statute so far, and it cannot conclude that [the confidentiality provision] may be used to shield the very misconduct it was enacted to prohibit."

Yet to this day, the IRS has continued to resist that judicial ruling. The issue is likely destined for the full D.C. Circuit Court of Appeals, which Democrats packed with liberal judges in their waning days of Senate power, after unilaterally changing the Senate's long-standing filibuster rules in November 2013. Which means we may never know about any White House taxpayer snooping.

~~~

The 2012 election started with a bang. Obama was running as the incumbent, which meant he could start his campaign early while the Republicans warred over a nominee. His organization didn't waste any time. It ran its first national broadcast ad of his presidential reelection campaign on January 19, 2012. It was about Charles and David Koch.

Specifically, it was about Americans for Prosperity, which had just announced its own $6 million ad campaign, in which it intended to highlight the administration's failures. AFP's first ad, which ran in mid-January, focused on the politics behind Solyndra, the solar power company that went bankrupt in 2011. Investors behind Solyndra had helped fund Obama's campaign, and the administration had later loaned hundreds of millions of dollars to the firm, which then collapsed. Obama's ad was testament to just how sensitive he was to the issue and to those making it a voter topic.

The Obama ad predictably complained about "secretive oil billionaires" whose accusations weren't "tethered to the facts." It then pivoted to a brag about the administration's economic and energy and ethics record. Nobody in Washington or the press could have any doubt who the "secretive oil billionaires" were.

In February 2012, Obama campaign manager Jim Messina blasted out a fund-raising e-mail to the president's supporters entitled "They're obsessed." It slammed AFP as a "front group founded and funded by the Koch brothers." It then went on to make the absurd claim that "those are the same Koch brothers whose business model is to make millions by jacking up prices at the pump." He also claimed the company had committed $200 million to "try to destroy President Obama."

Saudi Arabia has some control over oil prices. Koch Industries, which buys crude oil at world prices, refines it, and sells it back into a competitive market, does not. Koch doesn't even own gas stations. And this was the *president's team*—singling out people by name and spouting untrue facts.

Koch's president for government and public affairs felt compelled to write to Messina and object to the scurrilous accusations. He pointed out the realities of refining. He noted that Koch had for months denied the $200 million rumor, which had been ginned up by the press. "It is an abuse of the president's position and does a disservice to our nation for the president and his campaign to criticize private citizens simply for the act of engaging in their constitutional right of free speech about important matters of public policy."

Messina seemed to take near glee in writing a return letter, claiming it was "cynical" to suggest that AFP was about average citizens "furthering democracy." He then dared Koch to "verify" the point: "Disclose those donors," he demanded, so that the public could make "that judgment."

And right there was the strategy. Messina and the White House were trying to get another list of names. They knew that more than just the Koch brothers gave money to AFP. They wanted a list of all the donors, so that they could do to them what they were currently doing to the Kochs.

Obama followed up, tweeting the same demand from his personal account: "@Messina2012 challenges the Koch brothers to disclose the donors funding their attack ads." A few minutes later, the president added, "Add your name to demand that the Koch brothers make their donors public." The tweet contained a link to an Obama website with an online petition that read, "Americans for Prosperity, the special-interest front group run by the oil billionaire Koch brothers, is claiming that its donors are 'tens of thousands' of folks 'from all walks of life.' We're asking them to prove it by disclosing their donors to the public." Try to imagine George W. Bush conducting a campaign like this against Michael Bloomberg (who funds a nonprofit gun control group) or Tom Steyer (the pro–green energy, anti–Keystone pipeline activist who made a fortune in fossil-fuel deals overseas). The press would have had a meltdown over such hardball tactics.

The campaign rolled on this way through 2012, turning the Kochs into an ever-bigger bogeyman. "And gee, what happened in the end?" says Holden, back in sarcasm mode. "They complained the entire campaign—about the Kochs, and AFP, and Karl Rove and the like, and about how the entire electoral process had been taken over by sinister influences and dark money. And guess who won? Guess who outraised and outspent Mitt Romney? Barack Obama. Guess we didn't do that good of a job, did we?"

Holden admits that this was in fact the feeling within the operation, that it had done a poor job on the electoral side of things. It had poured a lot of money and time into the election, and yet had failed to elect candidates to change the balance of power in the Senate (in a year favorable to Republicans) and failed to win the White House (against a president with a lot of political liabilities). "We'd had an irrational exuberance," says Holden. "And too many in our camp fell into that thinking and we paid a heavy price. If this were a business, everybody would have been looking for a new job. So we decided to retool and rebuild."

Retool they did, an effort that resulted in the most sustained and direct attack against the Kochs yet. The president had made a point of singling out AFP during 2010, and the Obama reelect had used the Kochs as a foil during 2012. But this would prove nothing compared to the belligerent assault in 2014 of yet another powerful Democrat: Senate majority leader Harry Reid.

∿

Reid had over the 2012 campaign talked about the Kochs here and there, joining the left in the usual bashing parade. But his approach took a lurch toward the hostile around March 2014. A revamped AFP had entered the midterm cycle with a new strategy of running "accountability" ads against a number of particularly vulnerable Senate Democrats—those in states where Romney had performed well in 2012. Most of the ads focused on health care, which had become a nightmare liability for congressional Democrats. Obama's Healthcare.gov launch in 2013 had proved an epic failure. Americans couldn't sign up; they were losing their doctors and insurance plans; prices were skyrocketing.

The AFP ads reminded voters of the history. A typical one, which ran against North Carolina senator Kay Hagan, featured a local woman who recounted, "Kay Hagan told us if you like your insurance plans and your doctors, you can keep them." The woman went on to detail her own health insurance travails and steep new costs. Other ads featured Americans telling their life stories. One showed Julie Boonstra, a Michigan woman who'd been battling leukemia for five years and who explained how her insurance was canceled and her out-of-pocket costs had become "unaffordable." The ad inspired liberal activists groups to team up to attack a leukemia patient. The mainstream press jumped in, quibbling over the definition of "unaffordable." Democratic representative Gary Peters, running for the Michigan Senate, demanded that Michigan broadcasters pull the ad.

What worried Reid, however, was that the AFP broadcasts, which first started in the fall of 2013, were in fact proving highly effective. They were softening up the incumbents. The disapproval numbers for more than a half dozen Democratic senators started to rise.

This was a direct threat to Reid himself. If he lost the majority, he lost the majority leader's office. In March, he took the highly unusual (and unseemly) move of going to the Senate floor itself to attack Boonstra and the Kochs. "Despite all that good news, there's plenty of horror stories being told. All of them untrue, but they're being told all over America. The leukemia patient whose insurance policy was canceled, who would die without her medication. Mr. President, that's an ad being paid for by two billionaire brothers. It's absolutely false," he said.

He was now unleashed. He started going to the Senate floor to decry the Kochs by name, in increasingly bellicose language. They were un-American. They were dishonest. They were power-drunk billionaires.

By September, Reid had attacked the Kochs from the Senate floor more than twenty-two times. And it didn't escape some conservative lawyers' attention that he reserved his most obnoxious accusations against the Kochs for the Senate well. Why? Because Article 1, Section 6 of the Constitution contains what's known as the "Speech or Debate" clause. The Founders wanted to protect elected representatives from tyrannical executives, and so the clause says that lawmakers can carry out their duties without fear of arrest or jailing. In short, it means that Mr. Reid can say whatever he wants on the floor of the Senate in complete knowledge that no legal action can be taken against him.

Reid's assault also inspired liberal activists and candidates to new levels of coordination. There was the Boonstra assault. Protestors grew at the biannual retreats the Kochs hold for Freedom Partners. Every Democrat facing a tough reelection began running ads claiming that every attack ad against them came from the "dark money" Kochs. The Democratic Congressional Campaign Committee demanded that the IRS investigate the tax status of AFP. The usual names—the Center for American Progress, Media Matters, Citizens for Responsibility in Washington—lambasted the Kochs, and filed complaints with the FEC and IRS. Environmental groups accused the Kochs of buying elections. This was particularly amusing given that one of the largest players in the 2014 election was Tom Steyer, a billionaire environmentalist who opposes the Keystone pipeline, and who spent $74 million trying to reelect Democrats.

"It was all about making it costly for us, delegitimizing us," says Holden. "And I can see why. Groups like AFP, who spread the word about freedom, are a threat to the entire power structure of the Democratic Party. The left's power is based on central control. We are the very opposite of that—limited central government, power to the people. And we are effective. So they'll do anything to shut that up."

And that means anything. And those attacks have had grave consequences. The Kochs these days routinely get death threats. They get phone death threats. Internet death threats. Death threats sent through the mail. And the threats aren't just directed at the brothers. Activists have threatened to blow up Koch facilities, to kill Koch employees. The Anonymous computer-hacking collective attempted to shut down the Koch Internet system. Tim Phillips, the head of Americans for Prosperity, the Koch affiliate, also told me those stories of bomb threats and bricks in the mail. Disclosure has consequences.

That's why Phillips and Holden and the rest are pushing back so hard against the Kamala Harris disclosure ruse in California. "Here's the question about this new push for disclosure laws, not just in Washington, but also in the states," says Holden. "Just look at the history, the groups, the motives, the attacks. Knowing all that, can anyone with a straight face claim that this push is about more transparency for the average person? Please. The real end goal is to get that average person's name. Because they don't make distinctions. They are coming after Charles and David right now, because they are easy targets. But they will go after anyone who disagrees with their view on government."

They already have.

CHAPTER 23

Prop Hate

THE CALIFORNIA SUPREME COURT in May 2008 legalized same-sex marriage, overturning a state ballot ban on the practice. In the ensuing months, opponents of gay marriage collected enough signatures to stand up a new ballot initiative banning same-sex marriage, this time as Proposition 8, an amendment to the state constitution. They poured money into the campaign, and on November 4, 2008, it passed with 52 percent of the vote. Gay marriage was again illegal in California.

Gay and lesbian groups were angry. And they knew who to direct their anger at. California had listed on its government disclosure website every person who had donated as little as $100 to the pro–Prop 8 campaign. More than a dozen activist websites started listing the names, "outing" supporters of the initiative, posting contact information for the "haters." (These are some of the same people who claim, justly, that it is offensive to "out" gays.) The information was soon viral. Some of the sites cross-referenced the names with employment information.

More chilling, anonymous activists created something called Eightmaps.com. The site combined the public disclosure information with a Google map. Users could zoom in to their neighborhood, get the names and addresses of every person who had supported the ballot initiative, and target them, house by house.

∿

Jim Bopp was sitting in his office in Terre Haute, Indiana, in December 2008 when he got a call from some folks he knew at the Alliance Defense Fund. The fund is a group of Christian attorneys who defend the rights of people to live out their faith. Bopp's contacts explained that some very nasty things were happening to some very ordinary people. Would he look at the details and give his opinion on whether he thought there was a legal case?

Bopp's the lawyer who worked with David Bossie to bring the *Citizens United* case, but that suit was only the more recent of his free-speech cases. He's made a career out of forcing courts to uphold the First Amendment. And he's seen a lot. But the information he was seeing here appalled him.

Activists were staging raucous rallies, pickets, and boycotts outside of small businesses. Ballot supporters had lost their jobs. Activists were defacing their houses and vandalizing their cars. People were getting e-mail threats and ugly phone calls. And all because they'd donated to a cause they believed in.

Bopp has litigated every kind of campaign finance case imaginable over thirty-five years, but he's had a particular interest in disclosure. He didn't take long to think about whether to take the Prop 8 case. He was in.

∿

James Bopp Jr. is sixty-five years old. He's tall, with blue eyes and a somewhat unkempt head of white hair. He talks like a midwesterner, because that's what he is. National Public Radio once described him as a "country lawyer," since he has lived and worked his whole life in Terre Haute, where he and his wife grew up. He's nonetheless perhaps the most influential country lawyer in modern America. He and his team of ten lawyers have been at the forefront of cases that have for thirty years reshaped the speech landscape. He doesn't come to Washington more than he has to, but the legal rulings he's brought about today define pretty much every political campaign the city produces.

Bopp's a big-time social conservative, and he got his start in speech issues in the 1980 election. National Right to Life had engaged in a massive distribution of voter guides that played a role in the defeat of about a dozen pro-choice congressional Democrats. This provoked the FEC to initiate a new rule that would have effectively banned such literature, on the grounds that it helps certain candidates. Bopp filed suit and ultimately got it thrown out. He'd soon thereafter end up defending Ralph Reed's Christian Coalition against the FEC investigation conducted by Lois Lerner, discussed earlier, as well as against the agency's subsequent claim that the coalition had illegally coordinated with Republican candidates. Bopp won on all counts.

"Those two cases, they really put me on the path to this," he tells me. "At first it just became a major part of my practice. But then it became a cause to me. It's an issue that I believe is essential for preservation of our democracy—a most rigorous enforcement of the First Amendment. It perhaps matters more than anything else."

Since those two cases, Bopp litigation has overturned state limits for candidates and judicial elections; helped strike down part of McCain-Feingold; and got rid of contributions limits for advocacy groups. Bopp has represented the whole conservative universe—National Organization for Marriage, National Right to Life, the Club for Growth, the Republican Governors Association, the National Federation of Independent Business, the Republican National Committee, and dozens more. He founded the James Madison Center for Free Speech.

One of his more notable Supreme Court cases was *Doe v. Reed*, which went directly to the question of disclosure and harassment. In 2009, Protect Marriage Washington, a pro–traditional marriage group in Washington State, gathered enough petition signatures to put on the ballot a challenge to a new state law expanding domestic partnership benefits. Gay-rights groups then demanded to see copies of the petitions, under the state's public records act. Bopp sued to keep the petitions under wraps, and the case went all the way to the high court.

He lost. Bopp's problem was that the question in front of the Court was whether petition disclosure in general violated the First Amendment. It ruled it did not. The Court nonetheless noted that if it had been asked to look at whether specific signers, in a specific instance, might potentially be subject to threats and harassment, the outcome might be different. The ruling was 8–1, with only Justice Clarence Thomas making the argument that no petition signer ought to ever have his name divulged, given the potential for retribution. A particularly unfortunate part of the ruling came via Justice Antonin Scalia, who went out of his way to write a concurrence complaining again about the *McIntyre* ruling and going on about "civic courage."

The bottom line is that *Doe v. Reed* was too broad to test the Court's support of disclosure in *Buckley*. The Court never had reconciled its embrace of disclosure with its prior holdings about the rights to anonymity. It instead dodged the question by claiming in *Buckley* that anyone who might be subject to threats or harassment or reprisals could just come back to the Court for relief.

Bopp thought he might have better luck with Prop 8, because there was nothing theoretical about the threats, harassment, and reprisal going on in that situation. His legal team, along with Alliance Defense Fund attorneys, embarked on a herculean campaign to track down and get signed affidavits from those who'd been attacked.

The news media documented some of the bigger horror stories. The director of the Los Angeles Film Festival, Richard Raddon, gave $1,500 in support of the ballot initiative. When his name came out, his critics threatened to boycott the festival.

He stepped down. The artistic director of Sacramento's California Musical Theatre, Scott Eckern, had to resign when the news broke that he'd given $1,000 to the campaign. To further atone for the sin of having political beliefs, he promised to write a check for $1,000 to Human Rights Campaign, the LGBT group.

Margie Christoffersen was a manager of the popular El Coyote restaurant in Los Angeles. Her ninety-two-year-old mother owns it. Christoffersen, a Mormon, gave all of $100 for Prop 8. Activists whipped up a boycott over the Internet; they crowded on restaurant review sites to trash the joint. A mob showed up outside its doors, shouting "Shame on you" at customers. The police had to shut the mob down. The restaurant lost so much business that it had to close parts of the facility and cut workers' hours. Many of those workers were gay. Christoffersen later sat for an interview with the *Los Angeles Times*; she burst into tears a few minutes in. "I've almost had a nervous breakdown. It's been the worst thing that's ever happened me," she told the writer.

Perhaps the most famous case of retribution was that of Mozilla CEO Brendan Eich. Eich had worked for years as the company's chief technology officer, and in 2008 gave $1,000 for Prop 8. Nobody said boo. Only when Eich was made CEO five years later in March 2014 did the left seize on the donation and cause a firestorm at the company, ginning up an "online shaming" campaign and threatening a boycott of Mozilla products. Eich lasted eleven days in his new job before he stepped down.

Activist groups also launched boycotts of the Sundance Film Festival, angry that it is based in Utah, the source of lots of Prop 8 dollars; the Manchester Grand Hyatt hotel in San Diego, to punish its owner's donation; and the A-1 Self Storage Company, whose founder, Terry Caster, had donated to Prop 8.

The activists wanted attention and aimed their biggest campaigns at high-profile and public figures. They ruined lives. And as awful as these stories are, it's almost more painful reading the affidavits Bopp submitted to court from nonpublic figures—normal, average, everyday Americans who lived for months under harassment and reprisals, and who to this day fear it will continue to happen.

A number of the Bopp affidavits feature small but nonetheless intrusive instances of harm. Citizens would wake up in the morning to find that intruders had come onto their property to steal or deface their yard signs or bumper stickers. This might not sound so awful. But take a minute to imagine people creeping around your property at night, taking your things.

Many instances were more severe. One donor to Prop 8 explained that he owned some grocery stores. Liberal activists came and put flyers on the cars in the parking lot of one store, maligning him for his donation. They set up three groups on Facebook urging boycotts of his business. Someone paid for a site urging a boycott and then paid for it to be a sponsored link on Google, so that anyone who looked up his store got directed there. They swarmed Yelp to write ugly reviews. Protestors came and occupied the entrance to the store to hand out flyers and to tell people not to shop there. They showed up again and demanded that customers sign a petition. One activist went into the store, loaded a cart with groceries, made the cashier ring them up, and then refused to pay. Random people came in to complain about the Prop 8 donation, hassling employees. The phone kept ringing with harassing calls. The owner had to install sixteen additional security cameras, for fear the activists might come in and tamper with products. "These experiences will hinder me from donating to a cause similar to Proposition 8 in the future," reads the affidavit.

One lawyer's office started receiving hate e-mails: "hello propogators [sic] & litigators burn in hell"; "I AM BOYCOTTING YOUR ORGANIZATION AS A RESULT OF YOUR SUPPORT OF PROP 8"; "your contribution to Prop 8 has caused great harm to society and proves that your store and your owners are homophobic sick individuals who would suppress a significant portion of our society. I will tell all my friends not to use your business."

An artist in New York made her living with paintings of drag queens and gay parades, yet she donated to the pro–traditional marriage cause. She came home one day to find two reporters waiting outside her house, which unnerved her; her husband had just had a heart attack and she worried that unannounced people could aggravate his situation. She received more than sixty ugly e-mails: "your work is garbage and should be defaced!"; "you better not ever show your face again at any gay gathering"; "I for one was really never that impressed with your 'work.' I will bang some heads together to get these queens to boycott anything you have a hand in." Lots of Prop 8 donors received e-mails that promised efforts to have them fired or their place of business shunned. One woman was told that activists intended to call all the parents in the school at which she worked.

Another donor recalled how activists distributed a flyer that contained a picture of the donor in his/her neighborhood, the headline "BIGOT," and information about the individual's relationship with a local church. An activist wrapped a heavy object, likely a rock, in a "Yes on 8" sign and destroyed a Lutheran church's window. One man had a book sent anonymously to him via Amazon containing the greatest gay love stories of all time. The night of the election, someone defaced the statue of Mary outside his church. Some people showed up to work to find offensive voice messages: "Hey, it's really disheartening to know that one of my neighbors supported Proposition 8 so heavily. What a scum-fuck." Some found voice messages waiting at home: "I certainly hope that someday somebody takes something away from you and then you'll realize what a fucking bitch you are." This woman also received harassment over her Facebook and MySpace accounts, including a threatened assault. She had to coordinate with her security department at work to ensure she remained safe.

One donor, a senior citizen, had their back car window bashed in. Another donor had their car keyed. Yet another had their car keyed and the air let out of the tires. That same person came out-side to their balcony a week after the election to find urine all down the steps and a puddle of it at the bottom. Yet a different donor had their house egged night after night. Activists poured honey on this person's cars—repeatedly (honey destroys the fin-ish). The same person's temple was vandalized with graffiti.

One person simply told the very sad story of how his sister-in-law would no longer speak to him.

There's plenty more, all of it bad. Even Ted Olson, former solicitor general, who successfully represented the anti–Prop 8 community in its Supreme Court battle, was worried by the tac-tics. "I hate to see this from the LGBT community; they are overdoing and hurting their own cause. When you see those kind of abuses out there, it really does make you think about the cases going way back, *NAACP* and the like."

Bopp and the team collected the details and filed a lawsuit in early January 2009, asking a federal court to stop the release of personal names and information. The suit challenged part of California's campaign finance laws that required disclosure to ini-tiatives. Bopp's suit, like all campaign finance litigation, delved into highly complex questions of constitutional and state law—the kind that makes your brain hurt. Far more notable were some of the bigger points that the case highlighted.

One of them got to a most basic question: What is disclosure for? Good-government types and the courts argue that it is neces-sary to inform voters, to act as a "disinfectant" against corruption. But the original idea was to inform voters about who was funding specific candidates. The Prop 8 measure didn't involve candi-dates; there was no potential for a quid pro quo. So what benefit was served by releasing the donations? How did this result in "cleaner" elections?

The question wasn't really ever whether opponents of the ini-tiative had the right to organize peaceful protests or boycotts. Of course they do. This, too, is part of democracy. The question is whether the government should be playing a role in providing them targets, via enforced disclosure.

Bopp: "This wasn't about opening up the system or even helping with debate. It was about retribution. It was about revenge. This was about a faction that was perfectly prepared to do anything—illegal things, too—to punish those who disagreed with them. Is that what we want these laws for?"

But the case also highlighted the absurdity, in today's world, of the *Buckley* holding on anonymity. The Supreme Court message was essentially this: If you think you might be harassed, just come back to us and we'll make an exception to the disclosure rules. It clearly had the *NAACP* case on its mind. But *NAACP* was an entirely different situation, and in a different age. An attorney general was demanding a list that only the NAACP held. It refused to hand it over, and it obtained Court backing to keep it secret.

Today's modern disclosure system makes personal details a requirement of contributions. You can barely donate anything without first providing your name, address, and sometimes other details. From the moment you press send, that information is in someone else's hands—the government's. In most cases, it is then near-instantly put into a public database that is searchable by all and sundry. Or it is subject to sunshine laws. "Years ago we would never have been able to get a blacklist that fast and quickly," bragged Candace Nichols of the Las Vegas Gay and Lesbian Community Center during the Prop 8 harassment. So when exactly is the moment at which a citizen can request a court to shield them from potential threats or abuse?

Bopp's request was that the court force the state to expunge the existing records, and to prevent this sort of information from going out in future elections. He'd proven the harm, which is what is supposedly required under *Buckley*.

And, yet again, he lost. A lower court came up with a bunch of excuses as to why Prop 8 supporters weren't entitled to protection. The decision of the Ninth Circuit Court of Appeals took a

totally different tack, and in doing so provided the final bit of absurdity to *Buckley*'s disclosure regime. The Ninth Circuit declared
the whole issue moot. It explained that there really was no point
to taking any action; the names had already been out there for five
years. What was done was done. And the Supreme Court, in the
spring of 2015, refused to hear Bopp's appeal—allowing that ruling to stand.

So what protection is there, ever, for a citizen, against threats
and reprisals? Go to the courts prior to it happening and be told
that you have no proof it will happen. Go to the courts after
and be told that it's too late, it already happened. *Buckley* and
subsequent campaign finance laws eviscerated anonymity, and the
courts have grown more callous since then to the threat.

One of Bopp's frustrations is that he in fact doesn't believe the
judiciary really understands how pernicious simple intimidation is.
"There was a case we cited in *Doe v. Reed*, and it had to do with
the Ku Klux Klan," he remembers. "And what the Court realized
in that case was that intimidation is as grave a threat to the health
of democracy as anything else. Sure, the Ku Klux Klan did things
like lynch people; they committed crimes. But the vast majority of
their activities were aimed at simple intimidation—burning a cross
in a yard, showing up in those hoods. So you put people's names out
there, and you couple it with the new willingness on the left to intimidate people who disagree with their political strategy, and you
drive average folk out of the system. It's a grave threat."

There's little question that the Prop 8 campaign was primarily
about intimidation. Fred Karger launched Californians Against
Hate, one of the main websites that outed larger Prop 8 donors—
listing names, addresses, telephone numbers, and website addresses. He told the *Washington Times* in 2009, "One of my goals
was to make it socially unacceptable to make these mega-
donations that take away people's rights. I want them to think
twice before writing that check."

CHAPTER 24

On the Side of Might

THE PROP 8 retribution campaign was nasty, and it earned the left-wing activist community criticism even from some on its own side. That required it to come up with justifications, most of which were flimsy. It argued that the public had a right to know, and that Prop 8 supporters had violated the civil rights of gay Americans and so had forfeited their own.

The excuses nonetheless all boiled down to one argument: The left was fighting the "good" and "moral" fight, and any voice that opposed that fight needed to be eliminated. In the years since Prop 8 that argument has come to frame endless campaigns against ordinary Americans who dare to oppose the left's goals.

That includes any scientist who doesn't sign up for the left's view on global warming. Democrats tried for years to pass comprehensive global warming legislation, but the public didn't like the idea. And these days, the party has grown more wary of trying to push through such a bill. In 2009, liberal Democrats squeaked the Waxman-Markey cap-and-trade bill through the House. Yet former majority leader Harry Reid wouldn't bring it up in the Senate because, by most estimates, it didn't even have forty votes. President Obama so understood the legislative reality that he didn't try passing the bill again. He instead imposed his own modified version of the legislation on the country by executive fiat, via regulations at the EPA.

Democrats want an even more robust system regulation, but that will involve persuading far more Americans that the threat is real. For some, like Democratic presidential aspirant Bernie Sanders, this is an overriding priority. The Vermont socialist declared in a 2015 debate that global warming was the biggest national security threat the country faced—bigger than ISIS, terrorists, or a nuclear Iran. Which gives you a sense of the left's need to shut down any scientists who throw doubt on their theories.

A group of scientists in February 2015 received such a blast, from the office of Arizona representative Raúl Grijalva, the ranking Democrat on the House Committee on Natural Resources. The global warming purist had read an article in the *New York Times* about Willie Soon, a Harvard astrophysicist who for many years has argued that the Earth's climate is significantly tied to solar variability. The *Times* piece wrote that Mr. Soon had received some funding over the years from the fossil-fuel industry. This wasn't news; it had been released years ago. But the *Times* took issue with the fact that Soon hadn't noted the funding in recent work he'd done.

It was a small and silly topic, but it was the left's opening to go after researchers. Grijalva instantly launched his own pressure-disclosure attack. His office sent letters to universities asking about seven climate scientists, all chosen solely for the fact that they had at one time or another objected to climate change hysteria. They included David Legates (University of Delaware), John Christy (University of Alabama), Judith Curry (Georgia Institute of Technology), Robert Balling (Arizona State University), Roger Pielke Jr. (University of Colorado), Steven Hayward (a respected author and scholar), and Richard Lindzen (recently retired from MIT).

The letters demanded that the universities cough up any details about the seven scientists' funding. Anything—speaking fees, consulting fees, travel expenses, honoraria, consulting fees, salaries, compensation. They also demanded any communications with anybody about that compensation. No, Grijalva admitted, he had no evidence that these seven had done anything wrong. But in light of the Soon information, he explained, it was important that he root out any conflicts of interest.

The Grijalva campaign was in perfect keeping with the other recent congressional Democratic intimidation campaigns, like those against ALEC and the Chamber of Commerce. Only the Arizonan wasn't going after groups—he was going after private individuals who were producing facts that were inconvenient to the left. As one of the targeted scientists, Richard Lindzen, wrote on the *Wall Street Journal* editorial page, "Mr. Grijalva's letters convey an unstated but perfectly clear threat: Research disputing alarm over the climate should cease lest universities that employ such individuals incur massive inconvenience and expense."

Lindzen pointed out in the piece just how militant Grijalva and his climate cronies were about enforcing the liberal party line. Among those targeted was Pielke, who happens to believe in climate change and supports reductions in carbon emissions. Pielke had nonetheless dared to claim that he could find no basis for the global warming community's increasingly alarmist claims that climate is associated with extreme weather. That would not do, Lindzen noted, because it "contradicts the assertions of John Holdren, President Obama's science czar." So Pielke got teed up too. "I know with complete certainty that this investigation is a politically motivated 'witch hunt' designed to intimidate me (and others) and to smear my name," he wrote on his blog.

A trio of three Democratic senators—California's Barbara Boxer, Massachusetts's Ed Markey, and Rhode Island's Sheldon Whitehouse—backstopped the Grijalva effort with their own letter campaign. The senators sent a missive to 107 different companies, think tanks, independent organizations, and trade associations, demanding information about anybody in the climate arena to whom they had given funding. Among those getting the letters were plenty of groups that had already come under congressional attack. ALEC got one, and Lisa Nelson remembers it with frustration: "The answer was zero dollars. It was pure harassment," she says. Koch Industries got one. Holden wrote back to the senators in reply, "To the extent that your letter touches on matters that implicate the First Amendment, I am sure you recognize Koch's right to participate in the debate of important public policy issues and its right of free association." Holden refused to provide the senators with the information.

Pretty much everyone did. The episode quickly took on the feel of the pushback to the Durbin letter about ALEC. The American Meteorological Society was downright offended: "Publicly singling out specific researchers based on perspectives they have expressed and implying a failure to appropriately disclose funding sources—and thereby questioning their scientific integrity— sends a chilling message to all academic researchers," wrote the institution in a letter back to Grijalva. The American Geophysical Union declared that "singling out" scientists "based solely on their interpretations of scientific research" was a threat to free inquiry.

Think tanks were practically unhinged in their own response. They could barely believe this was happening again, and this time they were ready with choice words. "It surprises nobody that you disagree with CATO's views on climate change—among a host of issues—but that doesn't give you license to use the awesome power of the federal government to cow us or anybody else," wrote Cato Institute president John Allison in a letter to the three senators. Heartland Institute president Joseph Bast excoriated the senators for "attempting to silence public debate," scathingly inviting the Democrats to inspect the nonprofit's public tax returns. All eleven Republicans on the Senate Environment and Public Works Committee slammed the ploy. By March, Mr. Grijalva had somewhat backed off, acknowledging that perhaps his demand for financial information was "overreach," though still insisting that the basis of his inquiry was legit.

. The three senators never did express any contrition. They were, rather, among the dozen Senate Democrats who in the fall of 2015 sent that letter to every member of the Chamber of Commerce's board demanding to know whether they supported the chamber's climate "denial."

∿

Congressional Democrats' decision to refocus their intimidation tactics on individuals—climate scientists—was new in Washington. But they didn't come up with this campus-assault idea on their own. For years, the usual crew of left-wing organizations, unions, and environmentalists have been using "disclosure" to sully the names of conservative professors and attempt to shut down their programs. Any scholar who challenges the liberal ideology has come in for a professional takedown.

Their hook for these silencing campaigns are endowments—namely any provided by conservative-leaning individuals or philanthropies. Not that giving money to universities and earmarking it for specific purposes is usually controversial. The left is particularly good at it. Billionaire environmentalist Tom Steyer and his wife several years ago pledged $40 million to Stanford to start the TomKat Center for Sustainable Energy. The Morningside Foundation, established by the family of the late T. H. Chan, last year gave Harvard $350 million to fund work on, among other things, gun violence and tobacco use. The Helmsley Charitable Trust has given money to several schools to advance the Common Core.

Nobody in the liberal ecosphere has any problem with money like this, or the strings that are attached to such endowments—strings, say, that focus on a particular liberal idea. Is "sustainable energy" a good idea, economically or even environmentally? Such academic questions aren't the focus of Steyer's TomKat Center. Sustainable energy is assumed to be awesome, and the center's only job is to produce work documenting all that awesomeness.

The only kind of earmarking or strings that are not allowed are any that might "undermine . . . environmental protection, worker's rights, healthcare expansion, and quality public education," according to an organization known as UnKoch My Campus. Stopping such research is the mission of this group, which is spearheaded by Greenpeace, Forecast the Facts (a green outfit focused on climate change), and the American Federation of Teachers. And, unsurprisingly, these groups are focused on the Kochs. Various Koch foundations do give money to universities to fund and support all types of programs—in the arts, literature, and, yes, also in free-market ideals. Environmentalists, unions, activists—the same old universe—have mobilized against this.

UnKoch My Campus got its start a few years back, and is already proliferating around the country. The group's website directs student activists to a list of universities to which Koch foundations have given money, and provides a "campus organization guide" with instructions for how to "expose and undermine" any college thought that works against "progressive values."

The instructions are incredibly detailed. Students are first directed to recruit "trusted allies and informants" (including liberal faculty, students and alumni) and then are given a step-by-step guide on hounding universities and targeted professors with demands for records. The American Federation of Teachers and the National Education Association devoted nearly a full day at a conference in the spring of 2015 to training students on the "necessary skills to investigate and expose" any "influence" the Kochs have at universities.

In March 2015, Michigan State University released documents to student activists who had targeted political-theory professor Ross Emmett, director of the Michigan Center for Innovation and Economic Prosperity. His offense? Using Koch grant money to fund a reading group, called the Koch Scholars, which brings together students to discuss competing political economy ideas. The first two weeks were devoted to Marx, though the activists apparently couldn't tolerate an equal discussion of capitalism.

A far more disturbing example concerned Art Hall, who runs the Center for Applied Economics at the University of Kansas School of Business. He was forced in 2014 to file a lawsuit to try to stop a state records request from student activists demanding his private e-mail correspondence for the past ten years. Mr. Hall was targeted because his center got a seed grant from the Fred and Mary Koch Foundation, which provided a lot of money overall to Kansas educational facilities. In 2003, Hall had left Koch Industries to work for Kansas Democratic governor Kathleen Sebelius. He then entered academia and became a respected teacher at Kansas. His ties to Koch were never hidden and always publicly disclosed.

What really torqued the student activists was that Hall had gone to the state capitol and exercised his free-speech rights by offering testimony about Kansas's bad idea for green energy quotas. These are mandates that require utilities to produce a certain amount of their electricity from renewable sources. Those quotas tend to drive up consumer electricity bills, and Mr. Hall testified to some of those economic realities. The complaints against Hall are in line with the left's new standard for what counts as a climate "denier." Anyone who opposes any green energy initiative, even on the basis of sound economics and consumer protection, is a climate heretic, even if they acknowledge that climate change might be a problem.

The UnKoch activists have meanwhile been aided from within and without. Liberal professors dominate campuses, but many nonetheless can't bear to hear an opposing argument. Activists dish dirt on the rare conservative university professor. And professional academic organizations have proven just as feckless, at least when it comes to free-market scholars. Several years ago, the American Association of University Professors went to the

mat to defend climate scientist Michael Mann against a conservative group's demands for his records. But when Hall came under
assault, the Kansas chapter of AAUP helped fund the students'
demand for his correspondence.

These UnKoch tactics have also spread beyond just student
activists to more professional left-wing agitator groups. In February 2015, Right to Know, a California nonprofit opposed to
genetically modified food, filed Freedom of Information Act requests at four universities, demanding correspondence between
a dozen academics and outside agriculture companies and trade
organizations. Or there is the Kentucky Center for Investigative
Reporting, a left-leaning organization, which recently forced the
University of Louisville to release information about the founding
of a new Free Enterprise Center, partly funded by Koch money.

In mid-April 2015, Mississippi State University approved a
plan to create an Institute for Market Studies, and explained
that the Charles Koch Foundation intended to give more than
$350,000 over the next two years to support it. The school's
leadership made a point of saying that academic freedom was its
core value and that the new institute would be "faculty led" and
with "complete freedom" over its research.

Within a week, American Bridge, the "progressive research"
organization founded by David Brock (who also runs Media Matters and other Hillary Clinton–promoting organizations) had filed
an open-records request with the school. The request offers a remarkable insight into the harassing, threatening nature of such demands. It wanted all e-mail correspondence between the Charles
Koch Foundation and the university president; the provost; the
general counsel; the vice president for budget and planning; the
vice president for research and economic development; the vice
president for development and alumni; the vice president for
student affairs; an assistant professor of economics; and an associate dean of economics. It wanted all these documents going
back nearly eighteen months. And it also wanted any documents,

proposed or finalized, budget or otherwise, pertaining to the new institute. It made clear that "correspondence" included mail, faxes, memos, and e-mails.

Activists obtain these documents so that they can comb through them for anything they think might be explosive—especially if taken out of context. One goal is to make an association with the Kochs so difficult that no university will want to attempt it. Another is to name specific professors and scholars who are associated with such efforts, or who give testimony on conservative issues, and to let them know they are being watched.

It's all fundamentally aimed at shutting down debate. The media has focused some attention on this, with regard to the recent and growing trend of colleges disinviting conservative speakers when their liberal students protest. But the mainstream press is largely failing to cover the drumming out of conservative thought and scholarship at university campuses. Which is—again—being accomplished under the auspices of disclosure.

And you don't have to be just some yahoo conservative professor to get the treatment. Anybody who gets out of liberal line is fair game.

∿

Ask Elizabeth Warren. The Massachusetts liberal was among the Dirty Dozen of Democratic senators who sent that climate letter to the chamber. But that was just a warm-up for a more personal vendetta.

Warren has been among the most aggressive enemies of the financial sector, blaming companies for all the country's economic woes and advocating for piles of new regulations. Prior to her election to the Senate in 2012, Warren was a Harvard law professor and passionate advocate for a new government agency to "protect" consumers. That entity came into being in the Dodd-Frank law of 2010, as the Consumer Financial Protection Bureau.

Among the first to endorse Ms. Warren's proposal was a Democratic scholar and economist at the Brookings Institution named
Robert Litan.

Litan spent forty years at Brookings and is well respected. He
is a liberal, but an honest one. His scholarship is based in that
old-fashioned notion that liberals really are supposed to make
things better, not worse. In that vein, Litan in July testified to the
Senate about a controversial Labor Department proposal called
the "fiduciary rule" that would force financial advisers to put their
clients' interests ahead of their own. That sounds pleasant, but in
reality the rule makes it harder for investors to get advice from
professionals. Litan got into this in his testimony, noting that his
own research showed that "the benefits of the rule do not out-
weigh its costs. In fact, during a future market downturn, we
estimate the rule could cost investors as much as $80 billion."

Litan, as noted, is a good liberal, and so added this important
caveat: "The notion that all retirement investment advisers should
be held to a best interest of client standard is not controversial.
It's the way the Department proposes to implement it, which
because of its costs and risks, will lead to many clients going
without an adviser, or if they are able to retain one, only at sub-
stantially higher costs."

This was hardly intellectual treason, but it was too much for
Warren, who has been among the biggest proponents of the new
rule. She tried for a bit to rebut the Litan analysis, but when she
got nowhere, she chose instead to engage in character assassination.
She wrote a letter to Brookings president Strobe Talbott accusing
the scholar of "vague" disclosure about the funding of his research.

Which was more than a little weird, given that the following
appeared on the first page of his prepared testimony to Congress:
"The study was supported by the Capital Group, one of the
largest mutual fund asset managers in the United States." You can
argue with whether Litan may have been biased by the funding,
but you can't argue that nobody knew about it.

Brookings folded like a cheap suit. The think tank (by contrast to Cato or Heartland, when attacked by Democrats) meekly noted that Litan had in fact apparently violated a rule when he'd testified before the Senate. He wasn't supposed to identify himself as a Brookings scholar. The *Wall Street Journal* reported that the rule was a recent creation, and that Litan realized he had erred after the testimony and had apologized. Brookings had thought nothing of it until Warren commenced her attack.

Yet once she did attack, the institution threw him overboard. Litan was forced to resign after decades at Brookings. Warren had successfully muzzled independent research, and sent the message that other scholars who oppose her passions on the Hill will be in for the same treatment. Warren's other message: It doesn't matter what side of the political aisle you are on.

∿

If you've made it this far in this book, you might be thinking yourself lucky. You might be feeling grateful that you never went to a Tea Party meeting, you never wrote a climate research paper, you never donated to Prop 8, you never supported Scott Walker, you never donated any money to ALEC, you never ran a company subject to shareholder proxies, you never volunteered for Americans for Prosperity. You have never had your speech rights assaulted.

Only you'd be wrong. You have. Every person in the United States of America did on September 11, 2014. That day goes down in constitutional infamy.

In some ways, it shouldn't have come as a surprise. The left started its intimidation campaign by trying to silence a nonprofit here, a company there, a big donor here, a trade association there. But along the way it wrapped in small donors, and scholars, and scientists, and petition signers, and shareholders, and free-market professors, and grassroots groups. It was only a matter of time before it came to the obvious conclusion: Everybody has too much speech.

And so on September 11, 2014, fifty-four members of the Senate Democratic caucus voted to do something that had never been attempted in the history of this glorious country: They voted to alter the First Amendment. Henceforth, "Congress and the states may regulate and set reasonable limits on the raising and spending of money by candidates and others to influence elections," and may outright "prohibit" corporations and non-profits from spending any money "to influence elections." The amendment gave incumbent legislators and state officials near-total power to suppress undesirable political speech.

Why were Democrats proposing a change to the Constitution, rather than just legislation? Because such legislation *is unconstitutional*. Money funds speech. If you ban certain forms of money, you ban certain forms of speech. The Supreme Court has held so. And so the problem, in Democrats' minds, is the First Amendment itself. It is just too damn free.

George Will, in one of the most skewering and insightful columns he has ever written, lambasted the Democratic majority for thinking it might "improve" on James Madison. He also pointed out that Floyd Abrams, "among the First Amendment's most distinguished defenders," had noted that Democrats were proposing to limit only political money that funds speech. Will wrote that Abrams had said that "this would leave political speech less protected than pornography, political protests at funerals, and Nazi parades. That, by aiming to equalize the political influence of people and groups, it would reverse the 1976 *Buckley* decision, joined by such champions of free expression as Justices William Brennan, Thurgood Marshall and Potter Stewart. That one reason President Harry Truman vetoed the 1947 Taft-Hartley Act was that he considered its ban on corporations and unions making independent expenditures to affect federal elections a 'dangerous intrusion on free speech.' And that no Fortune 100 corporation 'appears to have contributed even a cent to any of the 10 highest-grossing super PACs in either the 2010, 2012 or 2014 election cycles.'" Will was so appalled by the exercise that he devoted space in his column to listing, by name, every one of the Democrats who had chosen to mark their name down for such "extremism."

The scary thing is, they don't see it as extreme. In April 2015, Hillary Clinton, a Democratic candidate for the presidency, called for a similar constitutional amendment. She named it one of her four priorities were she to obtain the White House. The Democratic Party as a whole is now adopting this proposal to overthrow the First Amendment. It won't happen anytime soon—passing an amendment to the Constitution is hard. But the fact that Democrats are trying to marks a radical shift in the political culture. The left is done with debate.

David Rivkin, the D.C. lawyer who fought on behalf of O'Keefe, finds the idea not just horrifying, but shortsighted. "What they've done up to now—it's about screwing people at the retail level," he says. "The Bauer stuff, the Walker stuff. It's manageable. You ride the tiger, you dismount at some point, and you hope the other side doesn't use the same tactics on you. You can manage it. But when you get to the constitutional level, all bets are off. Let's say they actually got this change. What happens when all the barriers are gone, and the devil turns on you? What happens when there is a Republican administration, and they use this to totally shut *you* down? That's such a big risk."

Rivkin is one of the savviest people I know. And he makes an important point. Then again, there's a good case to be made the left isn't planning on there ever being another moment when the other side is in power. Their intention is to make sure they forever own the debate.

That's the point of shutting down speech. That's the point of the intimidation game.

CONCLUSION

THE INTIMIDATION GAME is real, and it is now a defining feature of today's political environment. Americans tend to worry about Washington gridlock and political dysfunction and rampant partisanship. Their greater worry ought to be the steady erosion of their own rights.

The left has a term it likes to employ whenever it wants to sow fear about political money and free speech. That term is "special interests." They whip out the supposed threat of shady and powerful actors as their excuse for their tactics, and for shutting groups out of debate. They have largely been successful in frightening Americans into forgetting the purpose of the First Amendment.

The Founders had their own word for special interests: "factions." They knew that factions—different strains of society, with different views about the country's future—were a basic reality of a nation. Their answer to this tension wasn't to crack down on one group or another, to have government balance the equation. Their answer was to set "faction against faction" to inspire an explosion of debate. Each faction would have its opportunity to convince others of the rightness of its cause. And the citizens would decide, armed with more and better information.

The United States in the past hundred years, and in particular since Watergate, has gone down a very different path. In the name of "clean and transparent" elections, it has layered ever more restrictions on political spending, and by extension on speech. It has instituted a vast new disclosure regime, ostensibly to better inform voters about political actors and the workings of government. This disclosure has instead empowered the intimidators to silence those who question them.

Ronald Reagan once quipped that "the nine most terrifying words in the English language are 'I'm from the government, and I'm here to help.'" Nobody should ever forget who dreamed up campaign finance and disclosure laws. It was the politicians. A corrupt Washington told the nation that these laws would stop Washington from being corrupt again. The American people bought it, and in fairness, they were desperate for anything that might make their government better toe the line.

Yet decades on, it's incumbent on every thinking person to step back and evaluate these laws on the merits. They certainly sound good on their face. They were supposed to lead to cleaner elections, less "special interest" influence, more accountable politicians, a better-informed electorate. Only none of that has really happened. Instead, the laws that were designed to keep the political class in check are being used to keep the American people in check.

Consider disclosure. Justice Louis Brandeis famously said that "sunshine is the best disinfectant." He meant for that sunlight to apply to government. The idea was to shine the light on the rat-filled corners of the state, to flush out the dirty deeds of politicians and bureaucrats.

And how is all that sunshine working out? Obama came to office promising to oversee the most transparent administration in history. Instead, his government may go down as the most secretive in the modern era.

Since 1950 Washington has operated under the Federal Records Act, which requires the government to preserve documents about its actions and decisions. And since the 1960s the government has been subject to the Freedom of Information Act, which gives citizens the right to view those records.

Yet in the spring of 2015, Americans found out that Democratic presidential aspirant Hillary Clinton had conducted all of her business while secretary of state on a private e-mail server. This news only came to light when a House committee began investigating the 2012 Benghazi attack and was unable to locate key Clinton records. When caught, Clinton made the unilateral decision to go through her e-mails and delete any that she felt were "personal." She then handed over the rest to the federal government and asked the country to trust that she had given a complete record. Clinton later claimed that she used her private e-mail for "convenience," an absurd assertion. She maintained a private e-mail account so that she could keep control over what the public could see of her government work.

She isn't alone. We have found out that Secretary of Defense Ash Carter also used private e-mail. Former EPA administrator Lisa Jackson used private e-mail. She and Agriculture Secretary Tom Vilsack also used e-mail aliases for their government accounts, making it harder for watchdog groups to FOIA their correspondence. Former Health and Human Services secretary Kathleen Sebelius used private e-mail. As did a onetime Obama acting head of the Labor Department. Lois Lerner had two private accounts. Lerner also used an instant-messaging system that wasn't archived, in order to shield her conversations from the public. Watchdog groups have discovered that many midlevel officials and federal bureaucrats used these off-grid accounts to work secretly with outside liberal organizations to craft sweeping regulations.

In the summer of 2015, the Council of the Inspectors General on Integrity and Efficiency, which represents the offices of more than six dozen inspectors general across the government, had to ask Congress to intervene after the Obama administration put up bars to their investigations. The administration had recently informed those watchdog inspectors that from here on out they would need to get permission from the very agencies they were investigating to look at crucial documents.

The administration these days outright refuses to comply with subpoenas from Congress. Years into their investigations, Republicans still don't have all the IRS documents. They still don't have the Benghazi documents. They still don't have the Fast and Furious documents. Outside watchdog groups have fared better, but they too face unprecedented roadblocks. Agencies have actively discouraged outside groups from FOIA requests by attempting to charge them huge fees. Departments sit on records, trickle them out, drag along proceedings in court. Their newest excuse for noncompliance is that they don't even have the records. Why? Because their employees have been using private e-mail accounts.

The entire concept of disclosure has in fact been flipped on its head. The American people know almost nothing about the working of government. Instead, disclosure is trained on the electorate, allowing the government to know everything about the political activities of Americans.

One beautiful example: The *Huffington Post* until recently maintained a dedicated website that conveniently dumped Federal Election Commission data straight into Google Maps. Any visitor could pull up a street map of any corner of America and identify every political donor. Each one was conveniently represented by either a blue or red dot, to indicate to which party they donated. Click on the dot and you got names, addresses, amounts of contributions, and the organization that received the dollars. Anyone could look at this information: your boss, your neighbor, your landlord, your kids' teachers and coaches.

At the height of Senator Dick Durbin's attack on ALEC, liberal organizations made the argument that groups like ALEC and its donors needed to be held "accountable" to the public. That shows the degree to which disclosure has been hijacked. Since when does government get to decide what is "accountable" political behavior? The First Amendment was crafted to protect citizens from their government. Yet we have entered a realm where citizens, if they want to donate to a political cause, must first register their details with the very government they seek to criticize.

And so the politicians know who is doing the criticizing, and with whom to settle scores. Former Senator John Kerry made sure that Sam Fox never got his ambassadorship to Belgium. Fox was disciplined for having donated to Swift Boat Veterans for Truth. The government subjected Frank VanderSloot and Catherine Engelbrecht to multiple audits as punishment for their conservative work. The IRS segregated out Tea Party applications and put them on hold as a penalty for opposing Barack Obama.

Meanwhile, the forced disclosure of information from independent political actors serves only one purpose—to tee them up for intimidation. It certainly doesn't enlighten the public, which is supposed to be the goal of disclosure. The best example of this failing is the Clinton Foundation. The foundation likes to crow that it discloses all its donations and spending. Yet that information meant little to the public until Hillary Clinton was forced to reveal some of her e-mails from her time as secretary of state. Only then did the nation discover the degree to which Clinton had used her position as secretary of state to funnel money from governments across the world to her family charity, which also operates as a quasi–super PAC for the presidential candidate. And the nation still doesn't know half the story. Because Clinton deleted her e-mails.

Campaign finance laws, too, have been turned against the Americans they were supposed to protect. Take Wisconsin, where prosecutors and the Government Accountability Board used a poorly and loosely written state statute to concoct a new definition of what counted as "illegal coordination" and to spend years persecuting independent organizations that supported Scott Walker. While Walker was certainly looked at as part of that probe, the politician was never the prosecutors' main quarry. They were going after average Americans who had dared to engage in elections.

The Obama administration is now attempting something similar. In March 2015, the Justice Department announced that it was gearing up to prosecute its own definition of "illegal coordination" under federal law. Justice put out a statement explaining that it intended to "aggressively pursue coordination offenses at every appropriate opportunity." Questions of improper coordination are normally left to the bipartisan Federal Election Commission, which handles civil complaints. The Obama Justice Department was making it clear that it didn't intend to wait for the FEC, and moreover would skip directly to criminal prosecution. The warning was meant for Republican candidates and the super PACs that support them. And no one needs to tell those players that the federal government can subpoena their documents, their e-mail, their computers, and their bank records in any political fishing expedition it chooses. These threats are made in the name of democracy.

Yet the coordination question gets to the heart of the Constitution. One man's coordination is another man's freedom of association. If the National Rifle Association believes in gun rights, and Politician A believes in gun rights, why shouldn't they confer? What is nefarious about like-minded Americans working to advance an agenda? This is what the Constitution was designed to protect—it safeguards both speech and association. Yet we have traveled so far down the complex campaign finance road that basic constitutional rights have been made to look suspicious. And that has provided an opening for government prosecutors to go after political rivals.

∿

And so it's time for a rethink.

It's time to rethink disclosure laws. Those rules were put in place to hold politicians and parties accountable for the money they received and spent. It's time to remove those disclosure requirements from independent political actors—such as Tea Party organizations, or environmental outfits, or free-market advocacy groups like the Wisconsin Club for Growth. The requirement that these groups disclose their political spending serves no purpose other than to arm politicians and rivals. How does it enlighten the public to require an advocacy group to detail the spending of an independent ad campaign? All it does is strip independent political actors of the freedom to speak freely and without fear of retribution.

It's likewise time to remove the requirement that these groups report their donors to the IRS and other government agencies. True, nonprofits are shielded from having to release that information to the public. But they do have to submit details about their larger donors to the IRS. Those forms are supposed to be confidential, but they are hardly safe. The IRS was caught leaking donor information to the press. There is good reason to believe the service used donor reports to single out and audit Republican contributors. And state attorneys general are moving to change state law to require that these IRS forms be made public. The government has no right to this information.

If the government believes that such a group or a donor has violated the law or engaged in fraud, it can go to court and make the case that it has a right to subpoena financial information. But the burden ought to be on government to make that case. Private actors should not be required to automatically provide all the details and make it easier for the government to conjure up supposed crimes and to exact retribution.

It's time to rethink how disclosure is applied to the political class as well. Some conservatives in recent years have proposed that disclosure should be limited to contributions to (though not spending by) candidates and political parties. The argument is that Americans arguably might benefit in knowing who is donating to elected politicians.

Maybe so. Then again, even this type of disclosure gives the government—in particular incumbents—extraordinary power.

In 2010, a professor, James Huffman, ran for a Senate seat in Oregon. He lost. The next year, he ran a piece in the *Wall Street Journal* describing his experience with disclosure.

"Here's how it works. A challenger seeks a contribution from a person known to support candidates of the challenger's party. The potential supporter responds: 'I'm glad you're running. I agree with you on almost everything. But I can't support you because I cannot risk getting my business crosswise with the incumbent who is likely to be re-elected.'

"Sometimes he adds that he has matters pending before a federal agency. Or that she has been working with the incumbent on legislation that will benefit their company. Or that he has a government grant pending.

"I heard these responses literally dozens of times in my campaign in Oregon. Sometimes I was told that someone on my opponent's staff had called with a reminder that supporting me was not a good idea."

At the very least, it's time to rethink the levels at which citizens are required to disclose contributions. They need to be dramatically raised. If the left's argument is that democracy is at risk from "powerful" players, then it can have nothing to fear from the donor who gives $5,000 or $10,000 or even $20,000 to a candidate or party. That is peanuts compared to the more than $70 million that billionaire environmental activist Tom Steyer spent in the 2014 elections to (unsuccessfully) retain a Democratic Senate. It's a simple fact that in today's big-money political arena, no politician can be "bought" with a mere $10,000.

The current disclosure requirement of $200 is primarily designed to ensure that every citizen's political activity is known to the federal government. It is driving average Americans out of the political arena, surrendering the space to the very "powerful" players that the left claims to worry about. Those billionaires have a right to speech, too. But they deserve to be challenged by smaller players.

It's time to rethink transparency requirements on government. The Republican Congress included in its spending bill at the end of 2015 a provision barring IRS employees from using private e-mail for work. That bar ought to be imposed on every employee of the federal government. Modern technology makes this very "convenient"—to use Clinton's words. Any smartphone gives users the ability to seamlessly switch from one e-mail account to another. There should never be any excuse for using private e-mail.

It's difficult to think of any federal employee's excuse for sacrificing their obligation to transparency. They serve the American people, and have a basic duty is to preserve a record of their work. That's why it is also time to rethink the Federal Records Act and the Freedom of Information Act. Both need to be overhauled, to include provisions that ease and streamline the ability of outside groups to obtain records, and to impose severe penalties on agencies and federal employees who fail to comply.

It's also time to strip federal agencies and employees of the ability to harass citizens and political actors. An easy first step is the aforementioned proposals to deny government the financial records of independent political actors and smaller donors in the first place.

That 2015 year-end spending bill also included a provision barring the SEC from moving ahead with its corporate disclosure rule. But Congress might consider legislation that formally prohibits federal agencies from willy-nilly ginning up their own political disclosure requirements. The power to force citizens to provide records of their political activity to their government is an awesome one and should never be in the hands of unaccountable federal bureaucrats. Disclosure is a policy for Congress to debate, in the open and under the scrutiny of voters.

Agencies need more enforcement manuals, of the type Don McGahn tried to get at the Federal Election Commission. Those manuals need to spell out in exacting detail the rules that government employees must follow when dealing with questions of political speech. The onus needs to be on the government to justify its investigations, rather than on Americans to justify their speech.

It's time to rethink the oversight of speech and to put it back into the hands of the bipartisan federal body that was created to oversee elections and spending: the FEC. The IRS is a tax agency. Its only duty should be to collect tax information and verify that Americans are correctly filling out their tax forms. The agency never had any business judging the political motivations and actions of nonprofits. Congress needs to clarify the rules of engagement. If the IRS believes, on the basis of a tax report, that a nonprofit has violated a rule, its job should be to refer that nonprofit to the FEC commissioners who specialize in campaign law. Those commissioners have the added benefit of having been appointed by the president and confirmed by the Senate. They are accountable. Lois Lerner was not.

It's time to rethink campaign finance laws, at both the federal and state level. This was what Wisconsin did in the wake of the John Doe scandal, and the resulting law is now one of the better ones on the books. These revamps need to provide better protections for political actors, and to strip away the ability of prosecutors and regulators to subjectively apply the law.

It's time for Americans, and conservatives in particular, to rethink their views on corporate speech. It's easy to buy into Obama's populism, to join the rabble that accuses corporations of harming the country. In fact, free enterprise is a foundation of American democracy. It is what has made the country great. Corporate actors have an enormous stake in the political debates that shape regulations and the tax system and trade policy. They have a right to speak.

It's time for corporate America to help Americans do that, by earning their trust. They cannot expect other Americans to stand up for their free-speech rights when they lack the courage to stand up themselves. And they can't expect Americans to respect corporate speech when such speech is aimed at garnering crony government handouts and special favors.

It's time for the left to reevaluate its history and wonder what went wrong. The left was once the party of Vietnam War protests, and bra burning, and Woodstock. It railed against the establishment, and defended the right of everyone else to do so, too. The Democratic Party opened itself up to competing voices. The party that made Nancy Pelosi the first woman Speaker of the House in 2006 was as diverse and big-tent as at any time in its recent history. It encompassed southern Blue Dog Democrats, and West Virginia coal miners, and blue-collar and green-collar unions, and Northeast liberals, and Alaskan libertarians. But as Obama imposed his agenda, and as the public turned against that agenda, the Democratic Party and its allies turned inward, circled the wagons. First they drummed out dissent from within their ranks. (There is today not a single white southern Democrat in the House.) They are now attempting to shut down debate across the country.

It's time for the right to guard against doing the same. This book related instances where Republicans sought to use speech laws against their political opponents—the Bush IRS's pursuit of a liberal California church; the conservative pressure on FEC commissioners to shut down liberal 527 groups. True, over the years the conservative movement has by and large come to recognize the tyranny of campaign finance and disclosure laws. It has had to. It has been on the receiving end.

Even so, the temptation by Republicans to use those laws for their own purposes remains. At the end of 2015, Senate majority leader Mitch McConnell and free-speech advocates like Brad Smith moved to include in the year-end spending bill a provision that would have lifted the limits on how much political parties could spend in coordination with their candidates. It would have been an enormous free-speech victory.

Instead, self-styled House conservatives objected. They complained that such a provision would empower the "establishment." Their only interest was in preserving a system that they calculated would better benefit them politically. Instead of celebrating an expansion of free speech, they made a crass political decision. If conservatives ever hope to live up to their limited-government and liberty principles, they will have to find it in them to stand up for the First Amendment all the time—not just when it suits.

It's time for the courts to wake up—and to recognize Clarence Thomas's prescient observations about where today's disclosure and speech law regime has left the country. It's time for the courts to recognize that we are once again in an environment in which average citizens are afraid to speak. It's time for those free-speech legal scholars to think hard about the cases that they bring to the courts, and to craft ones that require the judiciary to confront today's speech and disclosure realities and to recognize the degree to which the campaign finance regime has been aimed at citizens.

Mostly, it's time for Americans to speak up. The intimidation game only works if its targets let it. When citizens blow the whistle on abuse and stand up to it, they are by definition rejecting intimidation. They inspire others to come to their defense and to speak out themselves.

The Constitution guarantees certain liberties, but those promises are only as good as the society that they seek to protect. Every American has an obligation to demand those rights, to exercise them, and in doing so, to strengthen them.

Only then do the intimidators go away.

ACKNOWLEDGMENTS

Things I learned while writing a book:

I've learned that book editors are wonderful; that some are more wonderful than others; and that mine, Sean Desmond at Twelve, is perhaps the most wonderful of all. I can't thank him enough for his boundless guidance, encouragement, and patience. (Dana, thank you for the introduction!) I'm grateful to Deb Futter, Brian McLendon, Paul Samuelson—and all the team at Twelve—for their belief in this project and for all the hard work.

I've learned why people hire book agents. Jay Mandel was there at every right time, saving me from mistakes I didn't even know I was making. And doing it with such grace that I only much later realized I'd been saved. I'd have been at sea without his knowledge and support, and I can't thank him enough.

I've learned that the most successful writing happens when surrounded by the best and the brightest—which includes the amazing crew at the *Wall Street Journal* editorial page. Most of this book is based on events I covered for the page, and all that coverage was made better by the daily insights and creativity of my colleagues. A special thanks to Paul Gigot, who just let me get on with this book—despite the looming prospect of election-year coverage.

The *WSJ*'s Collin Levy blazed her own trail on many of these free-speech themes, and I owe her endless gratitude for laying the foundation upon which I rested key parts of this book. Brilliant writer aside, she's also my best friend, and she has helped me these past eighteen months in ways that can't be described in words. Love you, dear.

I've learned deeper appreciation for the people and institutions that drive and support freedom. That includes men like Thomas W. Smith, whose foundation is an extraordinary force for liberty. My thanks to Steve Moore for the introduction, and to Tom himself for proving such a champion. My big thanks, too, to Larry Mone and the Manhattan Institute for all the support.

I've learned that everything we are really does come from our beginnings. I'd have never had the ability or the endurance for this project were it not for a mother who devoted so many nights reading to me as a child, and a father who always showed us that we must work for what we want. It was also a comfort all along to know my three sisters would have my back even if this book proved a monumental failure—beer, and homemade wine, to hand. The Strassel Girls.

I've learned just how much community is a source of strength. I love my Hillsboro crew, and I send a huge shout-out to Nez and Steve Morgart, Amy and Jonathan Ressler, and Kim and Henry Stribling. I'd never have survived the writing of this thing without dog-watch-sharing, emergency washing-machine use, and late-night firepit wine breaks. There are also the PTA goddesses, Karen Burbage and Tauvas Johnson; the yoga queen, Carol Lenhart (just breathe); and dozens of teachers and coaches and sports parents and charter-school heroes who showed endless support and encouragement.

I've learned that nothing wipes away book worries faster than a child's laugh. At the same time, I've learned that few things motivate book completion more than a ten-year-old who gets up every morning and counts down, on the dry-erase board, how many more days until your book deadline. Or an eight-year-old who, every time she walks by the dining-room work center, exclaims: "Geez, Mom, aren't you done *yet*? How hard can it *be*?" Or a four-year-old who grumps: "I *hate* this book-writing thing!" A particularly heartfelt and special thanks goes to Matthew, who always told me I could do this, and who spent many hours helping me figure out the initial direction and many boring hours more watching me work. He never stopped encouraging me, even through the roughest times.

I've learned the unexpected joy of new friends and places. One day you are just going along, and an old family friend named Gene Braukman calls and suggests you go salmon fishing with him in Alaska. You do, and the boat breaks, and you end up at the shop of one Nick Van Dyke, where you are introduced to tepee fires and bar trailers and extraordinary mountains and a lot of fun Wasilla moose hunters. You get a chance to slow down, breathe, and you remember you always wanted to write a book. Thank you, Nick and Gene and Nancy. And thanks, too, to Bill Waibel, and Dan and Brett and Deena and Audrey and Larry.

Finally, I've learned that America really is full of unsung heroes. This book started as an account of political intimidation. Along the way, I realized it also had become a tribute to the many extraordinary men and women who fought against that intimidation, who refused to go quietly, and who daily defend that brilliant thing we call the First Amendment. Their day jobs aside, they spent hours with me on the phone and in person—telling me their stories, helping me with facts, explaining law or history. And for the dozens of people who were openly quoted in this book, there were dozens more who offered me time and guidance behind the scenes.

I thank every one of them.

INDEX

ABOUT THE AUTHOR

Kimberley Strassel is a member of the editorial board for the *Wall Street Journal*. She writes editorials, as well as the weekly "Potomac Watch" political column, from Washington, D.C. Ms. Strassel joined Dow Jones & Company in 1994, working with the *Wall Street Journal Europe* in Brussels. She moved to London in 1996 as a reporter covering technology and in 1999 transferred to New York to cover commercial real estate. Soon thereafter she joined the *Journal*'s editorial page, and assumed her current position in 2005. She is a 2014 Bradley Prize recipient and a regular contributor to the Sunday political shows. An Oregon native, she attended Princeton University and lives in Virginia with her three children.

ABOUT TWELVE
MISSION STATEMENT

TWELVE was established in August 2005 with the objective of publishing no more than one book per month. We strive to publish the singular book, by authors who have a unique perspective and compelling authority. Works that explain our culture; that illuminate, inspire, provoke, and entertain. We seek to establish communities of conversation surrounding our books. Talented authors deserve attention not only from publishers but from readers as well. To sell the book is only the beginning of our mission. To build avid audiences of readers who are enriched by these works—that is our ultimate purpose.

For more information about forthcoming TWELVE books, you can visit us at www.twelvebooks.com.